THROUGH THE CODES DARKLY

Slave Law AND *Civil Law* IN *Louisiana*

VERNON VALENTINE PALMER

THROUGH THE CODES DARKLY

Slave Law and *Civil Law* in *Louisiana*

VERNON VALENTINE PALMER

THE LAWBOOK EXCHANGE, LTD.
Clark, NJ

ISBN 9781616193119 (hardcover)
ISBN 9781616193263 (paperback)

The Lawbook Exchange, Ltd.
33 Terminal Avenue
Clark, New Jersey 07066-1321

Please see our website for a selection of our other publications and fine facsimile reprints of classic works of legal history:
www.lawbookexchange.com

Library of Congress Cataloging-in-Publication Data

Palmer, Vernon V.
Through the codes darkly : slave law and civil law in Louisiana / by Vernon Valentine Palmer.
p. cm.
Includes bibliographical references and index.
ISBN 978-1-61619-311-9 (hardcover : alk. paper) -- ISBN 1-61619-311-5 (hardcover : alk. paper) -- ISBN 978-1-61619-326-3 (pbk. : alk. paper) -- ISBN 1-61619-326-3 (pbk. : alk. paper)
1. Slavery--Law and legislation--Louisiana--History. 2. Slaves--Legal status, laws, etc.--Louisiana--History. 3. Civil law--Louisiana--History. 4. Law--Louisiana--Codification. I. Title.
KFL401.6.S55P35 2012
342.76308'7--dc23

2012040465

Printed in the United States of America on acid-free paper

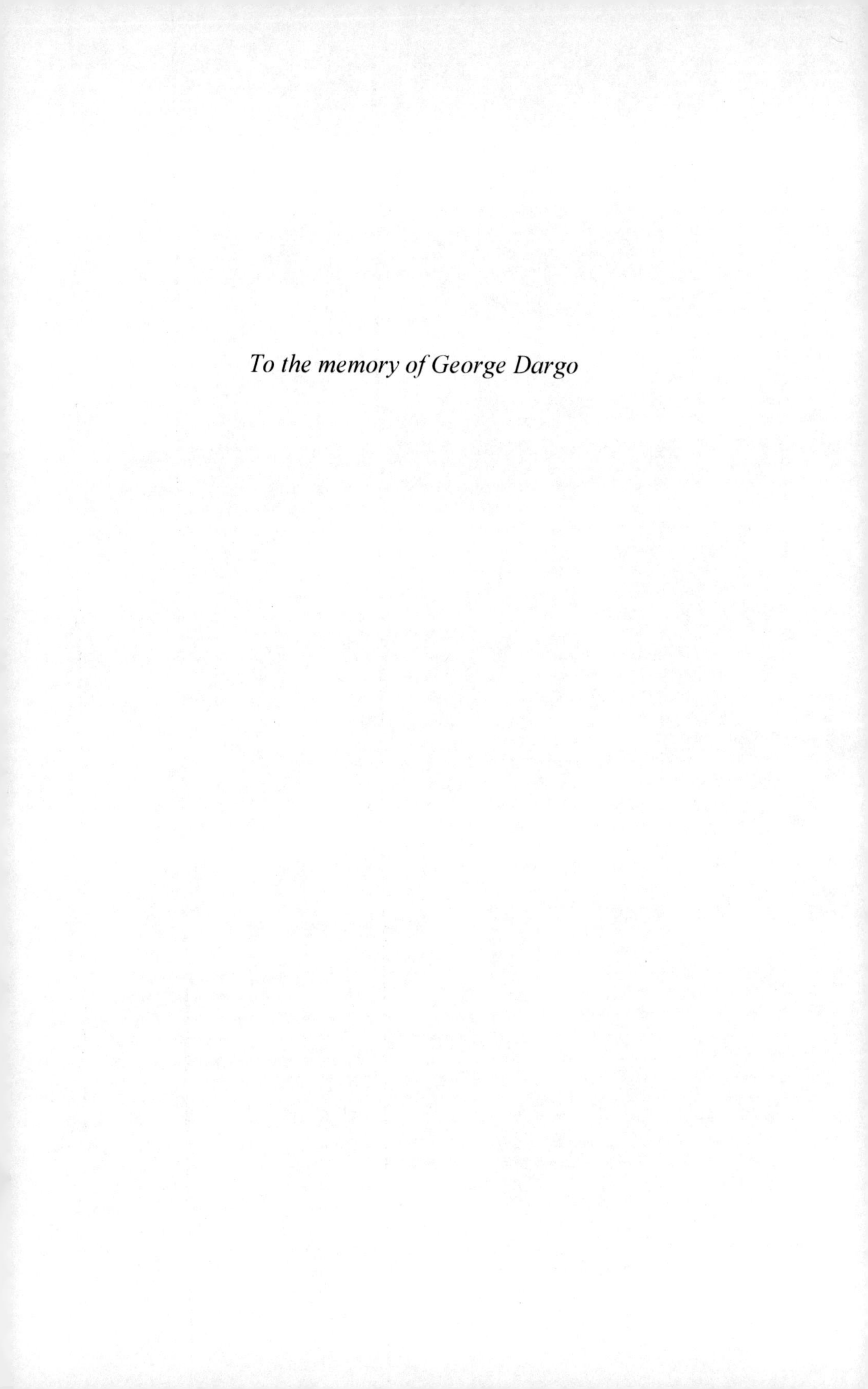

To the memory of George Dargo

Contents

Key Dates of Louisiana Slavery

1685	*Code Noir* decreed by Louis XIV for the French isles *sous le vent.*
1719	First slave ships arrive in Louisiana.
1724	Code Noir introduced in Louisiana.
1762	France cedes Louisiana to Spain.
1768–1769	Spain takes possession of Louisiana. Gov. O'Reilly introduces Spanish slave law.
1770	Governor Unzaga decrees slaves are immovables and all slave transactions must be recorded.
1778	Cabildo drafts a new slave code (Reggio/Ducros draft) attempting a return to France's Code Noir.
1791–1793	Beginnings of slave revolt in Haiti—French Civil Commissioners abolish slavery.
1795	Governor Carondelet issues new slave regulations.
1803	The Louisiana Purchase. De Laussat attempts to exhume the Code Noir, but the decree is ignored.
1806	New Black Code showing significant American influence enacted by first Territorial Legislature.
1807	Black Code restricts emancipation to those 30 years or older, coupled with proof of "honest conduct" during preceding 4 years.

1808	Digest of 1808 enacted. Only codification to integrate slavery into the civil law.
1809	Influx of Haitian refugees into Louisiana, including 2,000 free people of color.
1811	Great slave uprising near New Orleans—ruthlessly suppressed.
1812	Louisiana enters the Union. State Constitution denies political & civil right to free people of color. Only "free white citizens of U.S." are electors.
1816	Jurisprudence recognizes *statuliberi* as legal category.
1817	Decision in *Cottin v. Cottin* exposes the uncertainty of the Digest of 1808.
1819	*Las Siete Partidas* translated into English by Moreau Lislet and Carleton.
1825	New Civil Code enacted. Authored by Livingston, Moreau Lislet, and Derbigny.
1828	Sweeping repeal of the Spanish and Roman law.
1830	Legislature orders all persons of color, manumitted after 1825, to leave the state. Number of *gens de couleur libres* reaches 16,000.
1852	Legislature orders all manumittees to be sent to Liberia, owner to pay passage.
1855	End of deportations to Liberia. Manumission to be decided by jury trial, and jury to determine whether freed person must leave the state.

1857	All emancipations prohibited.
1861	Louisiana secedes from Union.
1870	All slavery articles deleted from Louisiana Civil Code.

PREFACE

Louisiana's legal history has been aptly called, to use John Cairns' expression, the history of Europe in one state. Originally a French colony, then ceded to Spain and later sold to the United States, Louisiana was a far-flung outpost of the European *ius commune.* Legally speaking, it was destined to become America's most foreign state. It seems less well-known, however, that these same historical forces also produced a unique law of slavery that was distinctive from the slave law in the rest of the United States. At various stages it had French-Caribbean roots, Spanish-Roman rules, and an assortment of American borrowings. This law evolved over a period of nearly two hundred years, stretching from the codification of the *Code Noir* in 1685 all the way down to the abolition of slavery in the mid-nineteenth century. My book is focused squarely upon the questions surrounding this law—its origins and authors, its transformations, its codification and Romanization, and its importance to the civilian experience and the legal history of Louisiana.

This can be of course only a selective exploration of a broad subject. I do not pretend to cover the whole law or the whole period in detail. The reader will not find a systematic history of events (although I believe most important events are in fact discussed at some point), but rather an interpretative history of law and legal change. The work is entitled "Through the Codes Darkly" because I have used the slave codes and the statutory laws as the general framework of analysis, but at the same time I am conscious we must go well beyond them, as far beyond as our research can furnish new light. The positive laws, read in isolation, would be a deceptive prism through to see the law of slavery clearly. Indeed in my opinion a purely positive law portrayal, which took no account of the contradictory realities of the times, would probably be the most misleading portrait imaginable. As St. Paul wrote to the Corinthians, we see ourselves with limited knowledge and comprehension, as through a glass darkly. So it is with the phenomena of legal history. At a remove of three centuries the legal historian should be conscious of the uncertainty and possible distortions in his own looking glass. What passes for historical truth is often an argument from incomplete data which later research may correct, clarify or contest. As we see in Chapter One, the historical controversy over the authors and origins of the *Code Noir* is a case in point.

Chapter One seeks to identify and unmask the actual authors, the sources, and the aims of Louis XIV's infamous *Code Noir* of 1685. My conclusions, which are based upon archival research and close attention to primary documents, fundamentally revise the earlier view that "Roman law was the inevitable model" of the *Code Noir*. Indeed the evidence shows that Roman slave law was no more than marginally involved. The actual sources of this law were developed in the islands of the French Caribbean, namely in the existing local decrees, the advice of leading citizens, and in the experience of the on-the-scene drafters, who were not lawyers but rather the King's two top administrators of the islands. This finding is important to understanding all subsequent phases of Louisiana's slave history. Louisiana's own *Code Noir* of 1724 must be seen as both an appendage and a continuation of the Caribbean experience. In terms of its first slave law, Louisiana was the heir of Martinique and St. Domingue rather than of Rome. Romanization finally occurred, but it was at a subsequent stage in history, and *via* the laws of Spain.

Chapter Two entitled "The Customs of Slavery" introduces almost a new subject in the history of slavery. It involves reconstructing the actual economic and cultural practices of masters and slaves and then comparing these practices to the positive commands of the codes or statutes. This comparison allows us to see to what extent the slave law "in action" was different than the law "on the books." The study of the customs thus functions as a different set of lenses—as an essential corrective to misleading impressions gained by reading the *Code Noir* or other statutes in isolation. My findings suggest that the customs often subverted and effectively rewrote the black letter law on a large scale. Thus the provisions governing the required food rations of slaves, their hours of work and free time, the celebration of slave marriages, the exemption from work on the Sabbath, the operation of the provision ground system, and even the allowable avenues of manumission were all regulated considerably differently than the letter of the law indicated. And these findings reveal a hidden truth about slavery, which is that theoretically "rightless" individuals in totalitarian conditions somehow managed to obtain from their masters a certain number of personal rights and property rights which improved their lives.

Chapter Three deals with the first effort in modern history to integrate slavery into a European-style civil code. This was the Digest of Orleans of 1808. This chapter is called "The Strange Science of Codifying Slavery," because there were formidable technical problems in the way of confecting an integrated *slave-and-civil* code and there was no model for this prodigious effort. I have tried to bring the reader behind the scene to see the process in action. The chapter explores why this integration was attempted, how it was accomplished and what difference it made to the Louisiana legal system in the long run.

Finally Chapter Four analyses the jurisprudence of slavery under the Civil Codes from 1808–1860. One of the most interesting aspects of this jurisprudence was the progressive Romanization and systematization of the law of slavery in the antebellum period. The Supreme Court decided about one thousand two hundred slave cases, an unparalleled output which in effect created a specialist court. There were obstacles and difficulties, but it remains one of the most remarkable displays of classical learning by any court in the United States. I have attempted to show it was facilitated by the reigning "Digest Methodology," which exhumed and revived old Spanish-Roman rules for a new career in Lousiana.

The Appendix contains the authentic French edition of the *Code Noir* of 1724, as issued at Versailles. On the facing pages will be found my own original translation of this *urtext*. To my knowledge this is the most reliable English translation available. Indeed most previous translators skipped over a great number of provisions because of their technical legal difficulty, or worse, gave to them fanciful and misleading interpretations. The Appendix contains the first translation of all the provisions, and it is hoped that this may provide an important resource in the future.

It is also my hope that this book may in some way encourage Louisiana jurists to take greater interest in their own legal history. Slavery remains vitally important if we are to understand our contemporary society and our present legal system. The era of slavery has been extensively and often brilliantly researched by historians both within and without Louisiana. It is curious to observe, however, that very little of that research, has been conducted by those trained in Louisiana law. For unknown reasons Louisiana jurists have not been very interested. Unfortunately this neglect has effectively abandoned legal history to the legal judgments of historians specializing in slavery. In the long run that is not a healthy situation for the future of Louisiana legal history.

—

I would like to express my gratitude to a number of friends and colleagues for their comments and conversations during this research: John Cairns, Georgia Chadwick, Jim Gordley, Shael Herman, Larry Powell, Judith Schafer, Rebecca Scott, and Alan Watson. A great debt is owed to Caroline Busuttil Naudi who cheerfully read the entire manuscript and saved me from so many errors. I am also grateful to Greg Talbot and Valerie Horowitz at The Lawbook Exchange for their splendid support and assistance. I also thank the *American Journal of Legal History* and the *Louisiana Law Review* for permission to use previously published work, and my thanks as well to the organizers of the Edinburgh conference on Louisiana Legal History for allowing me to include in this volume the study I presented in May 2011. Finally, I must thank my own university, my faculty and Dean David Meyer for allowing me to take sabbatical leave in the fall of 2011, which allowed me to complete this book.

Vernon Valentine Palmer
July 2012
New Orleans

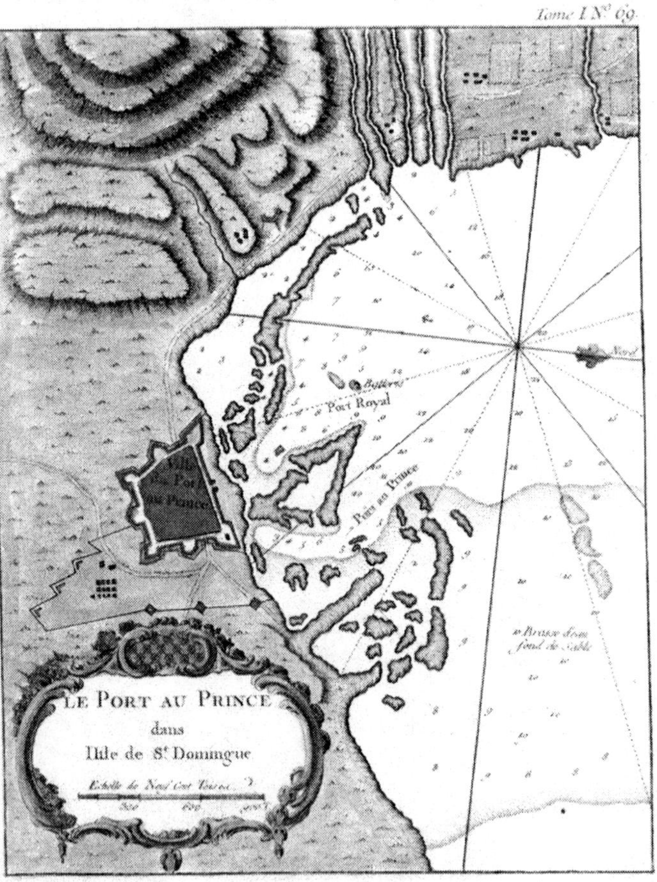

LE PORT AU PRINCE
dans
l'Isle de St. Domingue

Map of Le Port au Prince, Saint-Domingue

CHAPTER 1

The Authors and Origins of the *Code Noir*[*]

INTRODUCTION

The *Code Noir* marked France's historic rendezvous with slavery in the Americas. It was one of the most infamous and important codes in the history of French codes. First promulgated by Louis XIV in 1685 for his possessions in the Antilles, then introduced in Louisiana in 1724 with slight changes, this code was, unlike the Custom of Paris, the only comprehensive legislation which applied to the whole population, both black and white. In these colonies where slaves vastly outnumbered Europeans and slave labor was the engine of the economy as well as its greatest capital investment, the *Code* was a law affecting social, religious and property relationships between all classes.

The *Code* should be regarded as a sociological portrait, for no legislation better revealed the belief system of European society including its fears, values and moral blindspots. No legislation was more frequently amended and regularly adapted to adjust to France's evolving experience with slavery. Furthermore, almost no aspect of the *Code*—whether one refers to its motives and aims, compares it to other slave systems, or questions its enforcement—seems free of contemporary controversy.[1]

---

[*] This chapter was written for the colloquium entitled "The Romanist Tradition in Louisiana" which was held at the Tulane Law School under the auspices of the Eason-Weinmann Center for Comparative Law. All translations into English of manuscripts, articles and books in French and Spanish are my own.

[1] *See* Laura Foner & Eugene D. Genovese eds., *Slavery in the New World: A Reader in Comparative History* (Englewood Cliffs, N.J.: Prentice Hall 1969). *See also* Antoine Gisler, *L'Esclavage aux Antilles Françaises* (Paris: Editions Universitaires, 1965); Louis Sala-Molins, *Le Code Noir ou le calvaire de Canaan* (Paris: Presses Universitaires, 1987); Gabriel Tardieu, *Le destin des noirs aux Indes de Castille* (Paris: L'Harmattan, 1984); Thomas Ingersoll, "Slave Codes and

Among these controversies, none is more interesting than the *Code*'s actual antecedents and origins. Who were its authors and what sources did they use in drafting the *Code*? And what difference does it make? Some have claimed that the *Code Noir* derives from Roman law and that we have here an example of legislation from the civil law which contrasts with slave legislation in the English colonies. But to what extent is this conclusion justified? Indeed, the claims about Roman sources usually include the argument that slave laws like those of France and Spain were susceptible of being codified because the Roman reservoir of rules was available from the start, whereas English law developed *ad hoc* experientially, and could not be codified at the outset.[2] Some even argue that Rome's legal influence improved the quality of life of slaves in the New World. France's and Spain's laws, they argue, were relatively more "humane" or less dehumanizing than slavery rules developed by English colonies, and Spanish slavery regulation was milder than that of France because of the greater degree to which Spain absorbed Roman law into its law of slavery.

Scholars had no basis for these assertions other than by looking directly at the text of the *Code Noir*, by noting certain similarities to solutions arrived at by the Romans, and by then arguing that these similarities were unmistakable signs of Roman indebtedness. "Roman law," Alan Watson declares categorically, "was thus the inevitable model for the French law of slavery."[3] It is not without relevance that these scholars are usually specialists in Roman law.

The attribution of Roman origins to the slavery law of a country such as France has, initially, a plausible ring because we are well aware of France's romanist tradition. That tradition,

---

Judicial Practice in New Orleans," *Law and History Review* 13 (1995): 23.

[2] Thus, Leonard Oppenheim alluded to this alleged difference between civil-law and common-law slave systems by stating:

> Louisiana drew its law from civilian sources, but since the other slave states had no common law of slaves to turn to, they had to seek other channels, namely, statutes, jurisprudence built up within a particular state, analogies to existent common law doctrines and slight borrowings from the Roman law and other civilian sources.

Leonard Oppenheim, "The Law of Slaves–A Comparative Study of the Roman and Louisiana Systems," *Tulane Law Review* 14 (1940): 384, 395.

[3] Alan Watson, *Slave Law in the Americas* (Athens: University of Georgia Press, 1989), 85.

however, was stronger in the southern region of France *(les pays de droit écrit)* and less vigorous in the northern two-thirds of the country, which included Paris where custom was the primary source of law. At the time of the drafting of the *Code Noir*, moreover, France had no tradition of slavery and no laws on slavery had been in force in metropolitan France for centuries.[4] French custom was silent on the subject. The *Coutume de Paris*, the compilation of Parisian custom in statute form which was chosen by the King to govern his subjects in the New World, had no slavery provisions. Roman law in the northern parts of France was possibly a subsidiary system ready to fill gaps where customs and edicts were silent, yet it had never been called upon in the past to be a source of slavery regulation. If it was indeed used in the seventeenth century to fill a "need" faced by the *Ancien Régime*, we should examine the evidence carefully before yielding to the conclusion.

Professor Watson correctly notes that France acquired slaves in the American possessions before France possessed a law of slavery. In his view, the legal needs generated by the institution preceded formal legislation, and where else, he asks, would the French draftsman have turned to if not to Roman rules? As we shall see below, however, in the fifty year period preceding the *Code Noir* (1635–1685), the French developed slave law and usages in the Antilles almost as quickly as they imported slaves.[5] The claim that slavery preceded law in France's case may be chronologically correct but substantively quite misleading. Equally misleading is Watson's theory that France's alleged recourse to Roman rules was "artificial." According to this distinguished author, it was not law made "on the spot" in Louisiana or Hispaniola where local conditions and needs would have been of paramount interest to the legislator. Rather, he supposes that the *Code Noir* was made far away in the "very different circumstances of Paris."[6] On this

---

[4] Slavery was abolished in France by a series of edicts issued by French kings, beginning with the order of Louis le Gros emancipating the serfs in 1135.
[5] The French began to acquire slaves at St. Christophe and other islands as early as 1635. By 1654, there were about 12,000 slaves distributed in the islands. Alfred Martineau & Louis Philippe May, *Trois siécles d'histoire antillaise, Martinique et Guadeloupe* (Paris: Societé d'histoire des colonies françaises 1935), 23, 29.
[6] Watson, *supra* note 3, at 85.

assumption he presumes Paris adopted non-racist rules from an ancient society that held slaves of many nationalities,[7] and extended these rules overseas to a white supremacist society holding African slaves. Though social conditions in ancient Rome were not those in French America, this did not deter French lawyers trained in Roman law and accustomed to its use from adopting these artificial rules of slavery. Professor Watson primarily supports his conclusion by noting how closely the *Code Noir's* provisions on emancipation resemble the Roman law of emancipation, and he suggests that France's civil law roots made recourse to Roman texts inevitable. Indeed, if this account of the *Code Noir's* history were accurate, it would lend further support to the distinguished author's well-known theory that legal culture and legal tradition, in this case France's, aided by the indifference of monarchs with better things to do, can provide a sufficient explanation for the migration of legal ideas into different settings and distant lands.[8]

In addition to Watson, other writers have focused upon the legislative preferences and biases shown by the codifiers of the King's *Code*. The selection of Roman rules found in the *Code Noir*, it is argued, produced qualitatively different law than Spain's *Siete Partidas*, even though both rested upon Roman sources. In Professor Hans Baade's view:

> France had, as it were, codified those parts of the Roman law of slavery that were to the advantage of slaveholders. . . . Spanish law, on the other hand, had received, implemented and expanded the rules and notions of Roman slave law favoring the well-being and the ultimate freedom of slaves: peculium, self-purchase and judicial protection.[9]

---

[7] French *philosophes* seemed to contrast the Roman institution with their own. "The first Romans treated their slaves with more generosity than any other peoples. Masters regarded their own slaves as companions. They lived, worked and ate with them." M. le Chevalier de Jaucourt, *Esclavage*, *in Dictionnaire encyclopédique* (Denis Diderot ed., Paris: Brière, 1821), 492.

[8] Watson, *supra* note 3, at 1–4. The difficulty here may not be the general theory but the particular application. To think that Louis XIV was indifferent to the minutia of law reform, or to slave regulation in particular, is to ignore his genius for detail and to overlook entirely the commanding presence, relentless energy and meticulous oversight of Jean-Baptiste Colbert who produced (in the King's name) five great *ordonnances* prior to his death, as well as his posthumous creation, the *Code Noir*. *See infra* notes 34–36 and accompanying text.

[9] Hans W. Baade, *Law of Slavery in Spanish Luisiana, 1769–1803*, in *Louisiana's Legal Heritage* (Edward I. Haas ed., Florida: Perdido Press, 1983), 43, 53.

At this moment, it is not my purpose to pursue the argument about qualitative differences between Spanish and French slavery, but rather to note the similarity between the positions of Professors Watson and Baade. Both are manumission-centered in their appraisal of the *Code*'s provenance. Both have concluded that Roman law was the main source of the *Code Noir*, and to the extent that French or Spanish law seems on the whole more "humane" or less dehumanizing than English slave law, they share the view that this qualitative difference results from the reception and application of Roman ideas, not from genuine French or Spanish reactions to local conditions in their colonies. Yet neither author *appears* to have investigated the actual circumstances of the *Code*'s redaction.[10]

This study employs a different approach. In searching for the sources of the *Code Noir*, I shall discuss the authors, their instructions, their preliminary memoranda, the sources which they used and cited, and finally a comparison of these sources with the final product. What emerges from this analysis is an unfamiliar *Code Noir*, one which requires reappraisal and perhaps a different place in history. The *Code Noir* this research unveils is a code drafted in the Antilles by the highest officials in the islands: the Governor-General and the Intendant. These officials followed royal instructions which called for them to examine and incorporate previous ordinances and judgments rendered by the three Sovereign Councils on the islands (Martinique, Guadeloupe and St. Christophe),[11] to seek out the advice and sentiments of members of these governing Councils, as well as to incorporate their own views about the proper regulation of slavery.[12] The instructions *did not*

---

[10] I hasten to note that I am only basing this statement upon appearances and the type of research evidenced in their works.

[11] The Sovereign Councils (*Conseils Souverains*) were the dominant governing institutions in the French colonies. Their powers were roughly equivalent to those possessed by the provincial parlements of France. Their unusual mix of legislative and judicial powers is discussed *infra* notes in 24–26 and accompanying text.

[12] The King's instructions in this regard show a willingness to incorporate into the *Code Noir* the views of local slaveowners and administrative officials and this, more so than a biased selection of Roman rules, generally explains why the *Code Noir* often reflects planter interests. If the *Code* had been drafted in Paris based purely on Roman references, or imagined planter preferences, and without this local consultation, its provisions might have been more protective of slaves, but such provisions are notoriously difficult to interpret in terms of motivation. *See*

authorize recourse to Roman rules, and there was not one allusion to a Roman rule, text or term in any of these documents. The *Code* emerges in this study as law undergirded by firsthand experience and local contemporary sources. The grounding of the *Code* is fifty years of France's own experience with slavery in the New World, not its reliance on the ancient law of Rome. The consequences of this discovery cause the Rome-based thesis and its spiraling corollaries to fall to the ground. Why French slave law could seem milder than English law (if indeed it was) seems to have nothing to do with the different traditions of civil law and common law. Ancient tradition was not the French guide, and, therefore, was not the reason for the alleged qualitative differences. Moreover, why one type of rule instead of another attracted the French drafter had nothing to do with the legal culture and training of the redactors. Out-of-touch romanists sequestered in Paris did not author the *Code*. The authors were on-the-scene administrators, non-lawyers, who were surely not conditioned to think in Roman-law terms and categories. This may explain why they produced a profoundly racial document embodying the prejudices of their own white supremacist society,[13] but at the same time crafted a law adapted to Caribbean circumstances

infra notes 42, 108–109 and accompanying text.

[13] Certainly there was no editorial attempt to conceal the racial nature of this slavery. France called its law a "*Code Noir*," not a "Code de l'Esclavage." Indeed throughout the provisions the *Code Noir* uses the term "nègre" as a synonym for the word "slave", thus highlighting the imbedded characteristic of race. Furthermore, it contained exquisitely cruel provisions designed for "inferior" beings (by way of example, the punishment for running away was the cutting off of ears, the cutting off of cheeks, the branding of the face with the fleur de lys, and so forth). Beyond its many racial provisions, we must not overlook the highly localized provisions specifically designed for an island monoculture for which there is obviously no Roman counterpart. Such "localized" provisions would include prohibitions on giving *eau de vie de canne* to the slaves, rules detailing African musical instruments played by slaves, such as tambours, rules prescribing specific dietary regime composed of local foods, rules regulating the hours of plantation work and allotment of clothing, and rules specifically geared to sugar and indigo mills. Professor Watson has said Roman law would not have furnished rules of this kind because it followed the principle "Law keeps out," or because its position on the subject is simply unknown. His explanation for the absence of counterpart rules, however, is less important than the admission that Roman law was actually *not* the model for such a large portion of the *Code Noir*. In a reply to this essay he agrees that as many as five out of the seven titles of the *Code Noir* have no Roman counterpart. Alan Watson, "The Origins of the *Code Noir* Revisited," *Tulane Law Review* 71 (1997): 1041, 1051.

and specifically tailored to the exploitation of large labor-intense plantations. To achieve these ends, the distant, color-blind rules of Roman slavery lacked relevance and did not provide a model.

In writing this chapter I was able to secure from the colonial archives at Aix-en-Provence certain manuscripts and memoranda of the authors of the *Code Noir*. I propose to review (in chronological order) four documents which reveal the aims, sources and interior process of the drafting. For convenience, I will refer to these documents as The Instructions, The Rough Notes, The Preliminary Report, and the *Avant-Projet*.[14] These documents tell the essential story of the origins and authors of the *Code*.

THE INSTRUCTIONS

The first document is the King's *Mémoire* to his Intendant, dated April 30, 1681. This *Mémoire* is a statement of reasons or motifs why a slavery code is desired, and it contains a set of instructions for the preparation of an "*ordonnance*" in the Antilles. The King entrusted the task to Jean-Baptiste Patoulet and the Comte de Blénac, his two top officials in the Antilles.

The relevant terms of the *Mémoire* may be freely translated as follows:

> [S]ince His Majesty observes in [Patoulet's] dispatches and in those of de Blénac, certain articles dealing with the Blacks, and that there is no ordinance or custom [*ordonnance ou coustume*] in the Kingdom which speaks of slaves, He wishes that he [Patoulet] examine with care all the orders and regulations which have been decreed by the Sovereign Councils on this subject, that he, in coordination with de Blénac, the principals on the councils, and other inhabitants of the islands, examine all which is relevant to this subject, that he draw up precise memorandums on the subject in order that His Majesty may lay down the prohibitions, injunctions and everything touching the conservation policing and judging of these people, so as to create an ordinance [*ordonnance*] whereby this jurisprudence can be established on the basis of the authority of His Majesty. And since this subject is new and unknown in the

[14] These documents are referenced in the Archives d'Outre-Mer under Col F3/90.

> Kingdom, all the more ought he apply himself to penetrate it. He [Patoulet] will observe by His Majesty's letter to de Blénac the sequence which he must observe which will consist in always beginning by the subject of Religion and thereafter will come provisions dealing with Arms, Justice, Finance and Commerce.

To understand the importance of these Instructions one must first look to the persons appointed as draftsmen, then to Colbert's role and influence upon the Instructions and the Projet, and finally to the light which the Instructions shed upon the debate about the origins of the *Code Noir*.

What little we know about the redactors' lives and careers shows that they were hardly cut in the august mold of Tribonian or Portalis. History has, with some justice, largely forgotten them. The Comte de Blénac (1622–1696) (né Charles de Courbon) was Governor-General of the French islands from 1678 until his death.[15] His co-redactor, Patoulet, served as Intendant of the French islands for the years 1679–1682. Both owed their careers to the Marine and to the patronage of Colbert, who, as Louis XIV's Intendant and *Contrôleur Général,* incarnated the role of first minister of state.

De Blénac first served with distinction in the army before entering the Marine in 1669 or 1670.[16] He was a ship commander in the war against Holland and continued a career at sea until May, 1677 when he was nominated Governor and Lieutenant-General of the Antilles.[17]

Patoulet had been, prior to his appointment as Intendant, *contrôleur de marine* at Rochefort and *commissaire de marine* at Brest.[18] He was the first Intendant to be given jurisdiction over all the French islands. His official rank was second only to de Blénac's, but superior to that of the individual Governors of the islands. By virtue of their commands, both he and de Blénac were in a favorable position to understand the administrative and

---

[15] With the exception of the year 1690–1691.

[16] De Blénac's entry into the service of the Marine occurred at just about the time when the administration of the islands, formerly attached to the Ministry of Foreign Affairs, passed to the Ministry of the Marine.

[17] De Blénac's life and his career in the Antilles is fully treated in the biography by André Baudrit, *Charles de Courbon, Comte de Blénac*, in *Mémoires de la Société d'Histoire de la Martinique* (Fort de France: Societé d'Histoire, 1967), 2.

[18] In his later career, he was Intendant in Flanders. Patoulet died in 1695.

governmental problems of slavery. Patoulet's portfolios over police and justice brought him into daily contact with the public-order measures related to slaves, with judging trials and administering punishments and, in his role as presiding officer over the Sovereign Councils, with deliberations regarding necessary slave regulations. De Blénac's overall role in the execution of laws and in the affairs of the Sovereign Councils would have made him almost equally informed on slave matters.[19] Both would have known the leading citizens and planters and would have been familiar with their views about the treatment of slaves.

To understand de Blénac's and Patoulet's collaborative role more clearly, it is important to note the sources of slave law within the French colonial system. Slave law essentially emanated from four sources: edicts and *ordonnances* issued by the King, decrees of the Governor-General and Intendant of all the islands, local regulations (*arrêts*) issued by the Sovereign Councils within their insular competence (Martinique, Guadeloupe, St. Christophe), and customs and usages which arose out of practices on particular islands. The King's edicts or *ordonnances* about slavery were obviously of general application and took precedence over local regulations and customs. As the Instructions to the drafters acknowledge, there was no royal legislation about slavery prior to 1685. The *Code Noir* was the first and most conspicuous example of this type of legislation.

The three other sources of slave law were purely local, and produced a body of law which pre-existed the *Code*. Legislatively speaking, the Governor-General and the Intendant together shared competence over slave matters with the Sovereign Councils. The two executive officers jointly possessed[20] an island-wide police power which in addition to control over ports, coasts, roads, and public gatherings, included responsibility for slave crimes, revolts, and *marronage* or running away. Thus, a considerable number of slave regulations took the form of joint decrees issued solely in the

---

[19] There is historical evidence that de Blénac owned a certain number of slaves. In 1679 he sent two young slaves to his family in France and on another occasion he mentioned in a letter to Colbert that he had sold off four blacks. Baudrit, *supra* note 17, at 14, 46–47.

[20] Beginning with Patoulet's appointment in 1679, this police power was shared.

name of "*Messieurs les Général & Intendant*."[21] Nevertheless, the primary sphere of jurisdiction over slaves fell to the Sovereign Councils. The drafters' Instructions assumed, with good reason, that the *arrêts* of these Councils contained the bulk of the pertinent regulations, and these regulations derived from powers ancillary to the Council's judicial authority.

The *Conseils* of Martinique, Guadeloupe and St. Christophe (and St. Dominique after 1685) were primarily regarded as courts of law for deciding cases brought before them. By 1679 they were composed of six judges or *conseillers*[22] who were generally military men (*officiers d'épée*) or other leading citizens. Some council members were large slaveowners, such as Roy, the *doyen* of the Martinique Council, who reportedly owned several sugar plantations and a vast quantity of slaves. It is logical to assume that council members owned at least a few slaves since one of the privileges which the King granted to each *conseiller* was an exemption from capitation tax on twelve slaves.[23] They were not, however, legally trained judges. To the contrary, most had no education of any kind.[24] Nevertheless, these *Conseils* possessed roughly the same powers and prerogatives as the *Parlements* of France during the *Ancien Régime*, meaning that the *Conseils* were endowed with far more than judicial attributes.[25] Like the *Parlements*, the *Conseils* also possessed important legislative functions, including the prerogative of refusing or delaying registration of the King's ordinances,[26] the right of remonstrance,

---

[21] *See, e.g.*, Ordonnance of June 7, 1734 *sur le taxe des négres justiciés*; Ordonnance of October 4, 1749 *concernant les négres empoisonneurs*.

[22] Before 1679 the number had been ten.

[23] Cabuzel A. Banbuck, *Histoire politique économique et social de la Martinique sous l'ancien régime*, Chapter IX (Paris: M. Riviére, 1935).

[24] Thus, we are told that the *Conseil* at Petit-Goave (St. Domingue) included at various times a jail keeper, a filibusterer, the operator of a gambling house and *gens de metier*. Reportedly the president of the *Conseil* in 1692, M. Boisseu, could neither read nor write. Pierre de Vaissiére, *Saint-Domingue: la société et la vie créole sous l'ancien régime, 1629–1789* (Paris: Perrin, 1909), 83–87.

[25] *See* Banbuck, *supra* note 23, discussing the *Conseil's* evolution in Martinique.

[26] Thus, the Custom of Paris and other *ordonnances* on civil procedure and commerce had no force of law in Martinique until they were formally enrolled by the *Conseil Souverain* of that island on November 5, 1681. The *Code Noir* was similarly not deemed locally in force until formally registered in each *Conseil*. Banbuck, *supra* note 23, Chapter IX.

Memoire pour Le Roy sur la religion
La police la nourriture, et autres matieres
Concernant les Esclaves des Isles francoises
de l'Amerique concerté avec monsieur le
Comte de Blenac apres avoir pris les avis
des officiers des trois conseils souverains et
des principaux habitans de toutes les dites
Isles pour servir de projet d'une ordonnance
que les dits habitans supplient sa majesté
de leur accorder sur cette matiere.

1
De la Religion
que les Esclaves ne pourront faire profession
d'aucune autre religion que de la catholique, apostolique
et romaine a peine de punition exemplaire contre
les maistres
2.
que lors qu'il arrivera dans les isles des Negres qui
ne seront pas baptisés, les habitans qui les achetteront
seront obligez d'en avertir par escrit les prestres
ou missionnaires qui auront soin de leur quartier
afin qu'ils puissent travailler a les instruire
3
Si lesdits Esclaves tombent malades avant qu'ils
soient baptisés leurs patrons seront tenus d'avertir
lesdits prestres ou missionnaires de leur maladie

Mémoire pour Le Roy, 1682

and the power to make *arrêts de réglement*. The *Conseils* established wide-ranging slave regulations in the period before the *Code Noir* was promulgated,[27] as well as in the period afterwards by the use of this last power. In this capacity, the *conseillers* could make regulations having the force of law for the island in question

[27] For examples of *arrêts de réglements*. *See* the *arrêts* of 3 June 1680 and 12 January 1682 of the Sovereign Council of St. Christophe, which are discussed *infra* in the text accompanying note 46. *See also* examples *infra* note 61.

upon all points not settled by prior law, edict or *ordonnance*, provided the subject matter fell within their judicial competence and their regulatory intervention in that area was not forbidden by law. Since, as we have seen, slavery was an area previously unregulated by the King and only occasionally regulated by the joint decrees of the Governor-General and the Intendant, these Councils had a relatively free hand in enacting the earliest laws on the subject.

The Intendant served as first president on each of the Councils. Thus, as executive officer and chief judge in the islands, he had a preponderant voice in shaping the laws of slavery. Since it was the Intendant's responsibility to draft and sign the *arrêts* on slavery issued in the *Conseil*'s name, he was a logical choice to become an author of the *Code Noir*. Yet, if by office these officials were well-qualified to be redactors, their strained relationship with one another nearly disqualified them. Colbert knew all too well that the Comte de Blénac and Patoulet were bitter rivals and that he was entrusting the task of writing a slave code to estranged collaborators. Well before receiving this assignment, they had waged what de Blénac's biographer calls a "declared war" over the questions of power, authority, and protocol.[28] They had constantly complained in letters to Colbert of each other's conduct, and on more than one occasion Colbert had been forced to arbitrate or issue reprimands. One of Colbert's letters reproached de Blénac for meddling in the sphere of the Intendant's police power and for interfering with the *Conseil Souverain* by suspending execution of its *arrêts*. Colbert had told de Blénac, "(i)n a word I want you to let the Sovereign Councils act freely in all areas of police and justice."[29] In the same letter Colbert even established the order of precedence for their ceremonial processions so that they might avoid petty disputes over protocol.[30]

This history of personal tensions, as well as Colbert's role as referee between the protagonists, probably explain why the King's Instructions to Patoulet advise him that in the event of any disagreement on any subject, including the *Code Noir*, he should

---

[28] Baudrit, *supra* note 17, at 52.
[29] *Id.* at 50.
[30] *Id.*

defer entirely to the wishes of the Governor-General, his superior.[31] These tensions played no small part in Patoulet's subsequent personal downfall and explain why he was not allowed to finish the process of drafting the *Code Noir*. In 1682, de Blénac happily informed Colbert about the Intendant's misappropriations in office and this quickly led to his replacement.[32] In all these matters, Colbert's role was paramount. He was the ruling spirit behind the scenes. He was very likely the actual author of the royal Instructions set forth above.[33]

Colbert's presence behind the slave code's Instructions can be felt in a number of ways. His interest in developing a comprehensive slave ordinance was a natural extension of his mercantilist ideas.[34] The "sugar islands" of the Antilles had become the most-prized overseas possession held by any European power, but extracting the maximum profit from them demanded an efficient administration of slave labor through clear, uniform laws. The choice of redactors and the terms of their Instructions followed the classic pattern which Colbert had established in his other great law reform projects.[35] First, as in the previous projects which Colbert directed, the King once again selected a small team outside of the official world of courts, men with practical experience rather than legal training.[36] The King thus passed over his chief legal

---

[31] De Blénac had poor working relations not only with Patoulet but with the Governors of the islands and other officials as well. He was prone to outbursts of temper and early in his career was imprisoned at Rochefort for insulting an official of the Marine. Towards everyone except perhaps Colbert, he was known to be intemperate and somewhat intimidating. Nevertheless, de Blénac's long tenure as Governor-General may be explained by his military successes, his efficiency as an administrator, and his sycophantic relationship with Colbert. He was the father of eleven children who, it is said, had only two inclinations: all the sons went into the Marine and all the daughters went straight into the convent. *Id.* at 11.

[32] *See infra* note 54.

[33] A search through his collected letters and memoranda, however, failed to locate this document. *See* Jean-Baptiste Colbert, *Lettres, instructions et Mémoires de Colbert* (Pierre Clément ed., Paris: Imprimerie imperiale, 1863).

[34] On Colbert's mercantilism, *See* Andrew Trout, *Jean-Baptiste Colbert* (Boston: Twayne, 1978), 84–88.

[35] He is credited with five great *ordonnances*: Civil Procedure (1667); Waters and Forests (1669); Criminal Procedure (1670); Commerce (1673); and the Marine (1681).

[36] *See* Margueritte Boulet-Sautel, *Colbert et la législation,* in *Un nouveau Colbert* (Paris: CEDES-CDU, 1985), 119–132.

officials and institutions, the Chancellor and the courts, in favor of career marine officials who possessed a wealth of practical experience, yet almost no formal education.[37] Second, the Instructions follow the familiar two-step procedure of Colbertian reform: an on-the-scene investigation of the relevant facts and consultation with those knowledgeable in the field, followed by a period of study, reflection and redaction.[38] Thus, the selection process reveals much about the practical nature of the enterprise and virtually demolishes the view that lawyers in Paris, with a purely antiquated Romanistic knowledge of slave law, could have provided the material or the tools in the drafting of the *Code Noir*. Third, in contrast to the style of pre-Colbertian ordinances which simply compiled articles one after another in disconnected fashion, the Instructions required the systematic division of the subject into titles arranged in a certain sequence. The Instructions sought comprehensiveness of treatment ("examine all which is relevant to this subject") and clear logical arrangement ("beginning by the subject of Religion and thereafter provisions dealing with Arms, Justice, Finance and Commerce"). Colbert's great *ordonnances* were the predecessors of the codes enacted under Napoleon, and his Instructions envisaged an edict that would possess the technical characteristics one would expect to find in a modern code.

The Instructions also show that Roman law was not a primary source for the future slave code. Instructions calling for the study of local ordinances and regulations and for coordination with officials and citizens on the islands are simply not compatible with the

---

[37] De Blénac and Patoulet's lack of literary gifts made them somewhat ironic choices to author a code. De Blénac's letters reveal an author almost illiterate in grammar and spelling (his biographer calls his system of spelling "*fantaisiste*"). Patoulet's hieroglyphic hand made him almost impossible to read. Neither could have carried out the task without secretarial assistance.

[38] The method of drafting the *ordonnance* on Waters and Forests illustrates Colbert's empirical outlook:

> Since the forests were in danger, Colbert ordered an inquiry. His investigators went into the provinces to interview inhabitants, gather evidence of maladministration, and inspect the woodlands. They punished local officials for laxity and examined old regulations and proposed new ones. These recommendations were studied in preparation for the most comprehensive series of forest reforms hitherto known.

Trout, *supra* note 34, at 149.

notion that Roman law was the natural starting point. The Instructions refer to slave law as "new and unknown in the kingdom" and exhort Patoulet to "penetrate" it fully. They do not ask to accomplish this by considering what the Romans laid down. They are the opposite of a call to study ancient sources or to make comparisons with other European nations. They portray the King as wishing to use his authority to convert "this jurisprudence" found in the Antilles into a comprehensive ordinance. It would have made little sense to expect non-lawyers living in the Antilles (where books on Roman law must have been nearly unavailable) to conduct research so far beyond their means and abilities. However, they could have been expected (and were in fact instructed) to turn to local law, usages and advice in fulfilling their mission. In addition, the sequence of subjects to be treated had no relation to Roman ordering or to Roman categories. In short, the claim that Roman Law was the "inevitable model" for the *Code Noir* cannot rest upon the Instructions that the King gave to his draftsmen.

Instructions, of course, are one thing and execution in accordance with them is another. The redactors could have surreptitiously introduced Roman law rules at some later stage of their work. A review of the later documents, however, shows this was not the case. Let us now consider the fruits of the collaboration between Patoulet and de Blénac.

THE DRAFTERS' ROUGH NOTES

On December 3, 1681, de Blénac and Patoulet compiled what is essentially a set of notes comparing their views and seeking consensus on specific problems and topics relating to slavery. Two vertical columns divide each page. The right-hand column reads, "Advice of M. de Blénac on several issues in the Isles of America" and the left-hand column carries the heading "Response of Sieur Patoulet."[39] De Blénac took the initiative in the drafting, organizing

---

[39] Was this bifurcated format due to the usual shortages of paper or could it be a manifestation of their stormy relationship? Perhaps the latter, for de Blénac inserts an icy prefatory line just before the first article: "The King orders him by his letter of April 30 to confer with Sieur Patoulet in order to write in collaboration."

his thoughts into nine articles. Article one deals with convening sessions of the Sovereign Councils, article two with matters of taxation, article three with the problem of the diminishing number of Europeans on the islands, article four with criminal and civil trials, procedures and punishments of slaves, article five with questions arising out of racial mixing (status of offspring, marriage, customs in Martinique and Guadeloupe, and so forth), article six with the desirability of introducing feudal fiefs in the islands, article seven with establishing an inspectorate to monitor the treatment of slaves on each island, and article eight with police control (passes, runaways, etc.). Article nine contains a miscellany. De Blénac wrote these sections of the memorandum and then sent the papers on to Patoulet for his response or comments. Patoulet completed his "Response" three days later, and returned the entire document to de Blénac who then added a postscript stating that he would appear the following Monday at Patoulet's office to work further on the drafting.

De Blénac's procedure in this memorandum was to pose a general problem at the beginning of each paragraph within an article and then to list possible solutions by shorthand annotation. Patoulet's responses either approved, disapproved, or supplemented these solutions. These agreements and disagreements formed the basis of their subsequent working session.

These notes allow glimpses into the formative stage of the redaction. They also illuminate aspects of the personalities of the authors and the sources at their disposition. The notes first reveal that the authors took quite seriously the obligation to collaborate with the three Sovereign Councils. De Blénac outlined a procedure, in article one, whereby the Councils of all the islands were to meet every two months and to remain in continuous session where matters required it. The authors apparently interpreted their instructions as permitting some parts of the slave code to arise out of the deliberations of these assemblies. This was a sensible interpretation. Since the Intendant served as First President of these Councils with responsibility to take the votes, draw up and sign and promulgate the regulations, and since the Governor-General had full rights of audience and was expected to attend,[40] these sessions

[40] Their respective roles within the Sovereign Council were described by Colbert's letter (1682) reproduced by Baudrit, *supra* note 17, at 50–51.

would have been the most convenient means by which the authors might comply with their duty to seek consensus and collaboration. Yet this shows that they built the *Code* not merely out of previously established laws and customs, but from on-going legislative activity during the redaction period itself.[41] Thus, to Patoulet and de Blénac "collaboration" did not exclude the passage of new legislation by the local representative institutions which they led. This was the antithesis of an "artificial" process of discovering rules by the light of Roman sources in faraway Paris.

Second, the notes give hints as to the personalities and motives of the codifiers. De Blénac appears the more humanitarian and racially tolerant of the two. He called for inspectors to be placed on each island to monitor the treatment of slaves, and he wanted to outlaw the use of cruel punishments like "*la brimballe*" and "*le hamac*." Patoulet, however, did not find these practices "too rude" to be employed. Patoulet believed in strict separation of the races. He was scandalized by concubinage between Europeans and Africans, whereas de Blénac considered miscegenation a normal, even inevitable, phenomenon in the colonial context.[42]

Though the drafters may have had somewhat differing outlooks, we should guard against the tendency to confuse their motives with our own views. Judging by these notes, some allegedly "protective" rules may have had a completely different motive than that of protecting the slaves. For example, de Blénac and Patoulet reached the conclusion that the law should require owners to provide their slaves with minimum food and clothing allotments, and this rule passed into the *Code Noir*.[43] They did not originally discuss this measure as a matter of decency or humanity

---

[41] This simultaneous activity was shown when they included in their first report of May 1682 to the King new regulations passed only four months earlier by the Council of St. Christophe. Patoulet expressly noted that "The Sovereign Councils of Martinique and of Guadeloupe rendered different *arrêts* and regulations on the same subject [as that of the St. Christophe *arrêt*] but since they all tend in the same direction and they have no other intentions than the two set forth above, Patoulet did not esteem it necessary to have them transcribed."

[42] "Foreigners," he wrote in Article 5 of the notes, "did not establish themselves abroad except by this means." He also reported, without alarm, that the majority of the French officers at St. Christophe have married mulatresses. He thought the mulattoes will "ally themselves" with the whites and adopt their morals and religion.

[43] *Code Noir* Art. 22 (1685).

toward slaves (as might be supposed), but as a means of halting the diminishing white population in the islands. The drafters' notes argued that when slaves were not properly fed, they had a tendency to run away in search of food and to steal from the *petit blancs*, causing these whites to sell their lands and leave the islands. Readers of the *Code* may search for higher motives behind the rations provision, but the *Mémoire* provides evidence that cold-eyed efficiency primed every other consideration.

Finally, the drafters' notes contain important references to the existence of customs and usages about slavery which had already taken root in the Caribbean islands. These practices were a vital part of the dynamic by which indigenous slave law developed. De Blénac tells us, for example, that there was a usage on the isle of Martinique regarding the emancipation of mulattoes: the men are freed automatically when they become twenty years old, the women when they reach fifteen years. The father of a mulatto child was obliged to pay a fine to the Church as a penalty, and if he claimed the child for himself from the owner of the mother he had to pay the owner a similar sum. On Guadeloupe and St. Christophe, however, de Blénac outlines the development of other laws and customs. De Blénac takes all of these rules and practices into account in stating his position to Patoulet. As mentioned earlier, the presence of these diverse legal elements and sources shows that the picture of French slave law drawn by Professor Watson is quite misleading. Professor Watson assumed that France would have turned inevitably to Roman sources because there was a legal vacuum existing with respect to local law and custom. This took no account, however, of the speed and diversity with which law and custom incubated on small islands isolated by great distances.[44] None of this development could have been visible from Paris, nor would it have depended upon Rome.

---

[44] Elsa Goveia is one of the few commentators who notes that, "before the *Code Noir* was instituted, the French colonies already possessed a fairly comprehensive series of slave laws and . . . the *Code Noir* really may be regarded as an extended codification of these laws." Elsa V. Goveia, *The West Indian Slave Laws of the Eighteenth Century*, in Foner & Genovese, *supra* note 1, at 128.

THE PRELIMINARY REPORT

The work of Patoulet and de Blénac reached an intermediate stage in 1682. As seen above, by then the Governor-General and the Intendant had conferred and compared views. They had also gathered together pertinent *arrêts* of the three Councils and sounded out those Councils on other proposed provisions for the *Code*. At this point they prepared a preliminary report, a ten-page *Mémoire* to the King, dated May 20, 1682. It covers only four of the eventual seven subject areas of the *Code Noir* and omits entirely the subjects of religion, the civil status of slaves, and emancipation. Only Patoulet signed it, but a marginal note affirms de Blénac's collaboration in stating, "(t)his *Mémoire* has been communicated to Monsieur de Blénac who has found nothing to change." The preamble then paraphrases the King's original instructions.[45]

The *Mémoire* affords two new perspectives on the drafting process. First, it presents many rules in their earliest formulation, thus establishing a baseline for tracing the integration of the provisions into the *Code Noir*. Second, and more importantly, the *Mémoire* discloses sources and origins and, thereby, permits us to test the validity of the Roman-law thesis.

The sources cited in the *Mémoire* are of two kinds. The first are the *arrêts* of the Sovereign Councils, which are quoted at length and cited by date in the body of the text. The second are the "*sentiments*" or the advice (*avis*) of the three Councils which are presumably mingled with Patoulet's and de Blénac's own advice. Rules resting upon *sentiments* and *avis* are always signaled by a notation in the margin in Patoulet's own hand.

The title "*La Police*" illustrates his extensive use of the *arrêts*. In the *Mémoire*, Patoulet transcribed at length two *arrêts* of the Council of St. Christophe and requested simply that the King confirm the rules in these regulations so that they could be assimilated into the *Code Noir*. He set forth an *arrêt* of June 3, 1680, which contained a variety of police measures, including the

---

[45] The preamble reads, "*Mémoire* to the King regarding the conservation, police, judgment and punishment of the slaves of his subjects in America, which Patoulet gives to his Majesty after having taken the advice of the Sovereign Councils and to which he has conformed his own."

interdiction of all slave assemblies by night or day (weddings included), the placing of two inspectors at the market to halt traffic in stolen commodities, the authorization for whites to fire upon illegal assemblies and to apprehend slaves, the necessity of a letter of permission to be carried by any slave away from his master's home, and the authorization to fire upon and kill "*sans scrupul*" any slave not carrying such a letter, etc. He also transcribed for the King an *arrêt* of January 12, 1682, enacted only four months earlier, that dealt with the same police questions. Patoulet noted that since all the Sovereign Councils had passed similar measures, the *arrêts* from St. Christophe could serve as prototypes and it was unnecessary to include the others in the Report.

These regulations were later received into the *Code Noir* and, therefore, the King did confirm them as Patoulet requested. In some cases the *Code* took them over bodily, including their turn of phrase.[46] In many other instances, the *arrêts* simply furnished the substance of later provisions. For instance, the proposition that no mutilation or torture of slaves would be allowed except by the authority of justice was accepted as a restraint upon private owner violence and became Article 42 of the *Code*. Similarly based upon the *arrêts* was the rule that if a slave has stolen goods or caused injury, the master must pay the damage, "unless he would prefer to abandon the slave to the injured person," ("*s'il n'estime mieux abandonner l'esclave*"). Incidentally, this rule of optional liability, which later became Article 37 of the *Code*, affords another interesting example of the dangers of freely associating Roman legal rules. The distinguished French scholar Pierre Jaubert, who has made many imaginative connections between Roman law and the *Code Noir* (about forty by his count), points to this provision as an allusion to noxal surrender.[47] Neither the *Mémoire*, the later *Avant-Projet*, nor the *Code Noir*, however, used Roman terminology. To this writer, the source of the provision is plainly indigenous and it would be strange history to maintain that the Romans held an intellectual monopoly on such a simple conception as abandonment

---

[46] *See, e.g.*, the near verbatim incorporation of these regulations in *Code Noir* Arts. 16, 19, 20 (1685).

[47] Pierre Jaubert, *Le Code Noir et le droit romain* in *Histoire du droit social– Mélanges en hommage à Jean Imbert*, Jean Louis Harouel (ed.) (Paris: PUF, 1989), 321, 328; *See also* Watson, *supra* note 3, at 86.

of an offending object in lieu of damages. This concept existed at English law (the deodand and the bane)[48] and can be found in many primitive systems which had no connection to Rome.[49]

As already indicated, the Intendant also proposed regulations bearing the notation "*avis*" or "*sentiments*" of the Sovereign Councils. Here the lineage of rules seems to have been more informal, perhaps a local usage in one of the islands or an original idea proposed by the drafters which had received approval by the council members. Patoulet listed about a dozen articles in the text with various inscriptions in the margin stating, for example, "(t)hese advice (*avis*) are in conformity with that of the Sovereign Councils," and "(a)ll these articles [here he placed brackets around eight articles in text] are drawn from the *sentiments* of the three Sovereign Councils which also gave them and which were followed by Patoulet's advice." Some of these rules provided that all property acquired by slaves belonged to their owners; slaves should be judged by the ordinary judges according to the same process as free persons; they should not be mutilated or tortured except by authority of law, etc. Without exception every rule based upon these *avis* later passed into the *Code Noir*. One interesting idea or usage of this kind was a scheme of mutual insurance, whereby owners whose slaves the justice system condemned to death would be reimbursed for their market value. Patoulet noted that

---

[48] Professor Watson has rejected my argument about the deodand by stating: "English deodand has little in common with Roman noxal surrender or the rule in the *Code Noir*. English deodand did not apply when the injurer was a slave, son, or other subordinate person, but only when the injury was caused by a thing or a personal chattel. It did not apply in theft or minor personal injuries, but only when a person was killed." "The Origins of the *Code Noir* Revisited," *Tulane Law Review* 71 (1997): 1041, 1048. While I had never meant to deny or ignore the existence of these differences, the relevance of the comparison lies simply in the fact that the English had thought of the idea of noxal surrender, and so had the Romans, apparently independently of each other. It is hardly important that the two actions were different in scope or application.

[49] Sir Frederick Pollock & Frederic W. Maitland, *The History of English Law* Vol. 2 (Cambridge: Cambridge University Press, 1968), 472–474. To indicate how tenuous this practice of free association becomes, Jaubert also claims that Article 31 (which allows a master to sue for damages against one who injures his slave) is an "incontestable" reference to the *Lex Aquilia*. Jaubert, *supra* note 47, at 326. By this logic, however, we could easily conclude that the common law derived the action of trespass from the *Lex Aquilia*.

reimbursement was essential to the detection of crime because experience showed that masters would otherwise carefully hide the crimes of their slaves out of fear of losing them to capital punishment. This unique system, which was funded by a slaveowner tax levied upon the head of each slave, also passed into the *Code Noir*.[50] Another proposition emanating from the "*avis*" of the Council is that a child born of a slave mother shall be a slave ("*toute personne née de mére esclave sera esclave*"). This is the direct source for the *Code Noir*'s rule that the child follows the condition of its mother, not that of its father.[51] Pierre Jaubert's speculation that this principle of descent has a Roman provenance[52] can be based only upon coincidence. Since there are only two rules of descent available and the rule based upon paternity is impracticable, it is little wonder that the French, working independently of the Romans, would choose the practical rule.[53]

In conclusion, the *Mémoire* of 1682 has a direct bearing upon the debate over origins and authors. More clearly than any other document, the *Mémoire* reveals that the actual sources the codifiers used were twofold—the *arrêts* and the *avis* gathered together by Patoulet and de Blénac. Within the notion of *avis* and *sentiments* may be understood usage, custom and consensus as to what constituted traditional and proper slave regulation. While the *Mémoire* did not cover every subject of the future *Code Noir*, it demonstrates that the redactors followed their Instructions and did not bookishly resort to Roman law sources. This brings us to the *Avant-Projet* of 1683, the last and most important document that they produced.

---

[50] *Code Noir* Art. 40 (1685). The 1683 *Avant-Projet* proposed a modified funding formula (i.e., an imposition would be placed on the sale of the next one hundred slaves). The *Code Noir* returned to the formula proposed in Patoulet's *Mémoire*.

[51] Consequently, in marriage between slaves the children belong to the owner of the mother, not that of the father, where the husband and wife have different owners. *Code Noir* Art. 12 (1685). If the mother was a free woman of color, the child is born free though the father was a slave. *Code Noir* Art. 13 (1685).

[52] Jaubert, *supra* note 47, at 323 (citing G. Inst. 82, ("*ex libera et servo liber nascitur*").

[53] A rule of paternal descent (the child follows the father's condition) would have called for unverifiable proofs of paternity, whereas proof of maternity was easily established. Additionally, female slaves were not as numerous as male slaves in the Caribbean, and childbearing was regarded as one of the chief economic benefits of the woman's owner.

THE *AVANT-PROJET*

The events of 1682–1683 were crucial to the preparation of the *Code Noir*. In July 1682, the King abruptly replaced Patoulet as Intendant barely three months after he had submitted the Preliminary Report discussed in the previous section, apparently because Colbert discovered through de Blénac that he had been operating an illegal importation scheme.[54] It may be that all work on the *Code* ceased in the three month interim until Patoulet's successor, Michel Bégon, arrived in the islands in September or October, 1682.[55]

Bégon's letters of appointment instruct him to collaborate with the Governor-General to bring the slave ordinance to completion. One suspects that the work must have been near completion at the time of his appointment, for in February 1683, barely four months after his arrival in Martinique, Bégon and de Blénac submitted a carefully written *Avant-Projet* to the King. The *Avant-Projet* consisted of fifty-two articles arranged into seven titles.[56]

The preamble recited that its authors had taken advice from the three Sovereign Councils and other leading citizens, and declared

---

[54] The incident is recounted by Baudrit, *supra* note 17, at 141. According to de Blénac, "he (Patoulet) had brought in watches, clocks, mirrors, barrels of beef, etc." all of which violated rules prohibiting royal officials from engaging in commerce. It is interesting that Versailles would discover in 1694 that de Blénac too was engaged in illegal trade, *id.* at 141–142, but it is not clear whether any sanction was applied.

[55] Michel Bégon (1638–1710), a cultivated civil servant better known as a collector of engravings than a redactor of laws, became the third author of the *Code Noir*. He had entered the service of the Marine under Colbert in 1677 and would remain Intendant of the French Isles for two years. He left in 1684 to become *Intendant des Galéres* (i.e. officer in charge of ships propelled by oars and rowed by convicted criminals) and subsequently became Intendant of Marseilles (1685–1688) then Intendant of Rochefort (1689–1710).

[56] The titles of the *Avant-Projet* were as follows:

Religion (eleven articles)
Nourishment and Clothing (six articles)
Police (six articles)
Crimes and Punishments (sixteen articles)
Witnesses, Donations, Successions and Actions (three articles)
Legal Seizures, Slaves as Movable Property (six articles)
Grant of Liberty (four articles).

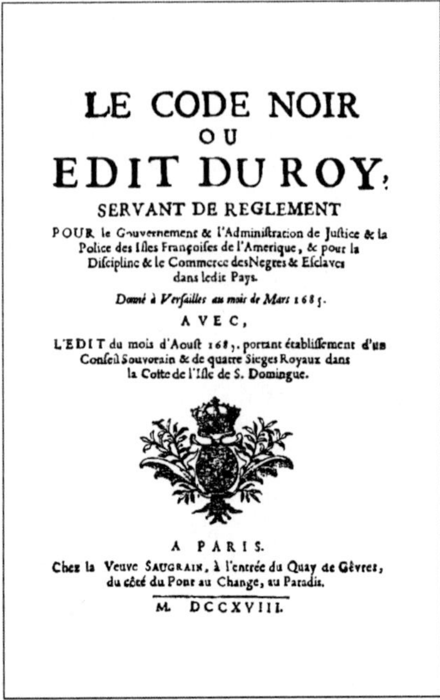

LE CODE NOIR
OU
EDIT DU ROY,
SERVANT DE REGLEMENT
POUR le Gouvernement & l'Administration de Justice & la Police des Isles Françoises de l'Amerique, & pour la Discipline & le Commerce des Negres & Esclaves dans ledit Pays.
Donné à Versailles au mois de Mars 1685.
AVEC,
L'EDIT du mois d'Aoust 1685, portant établissement d'un Conseil Souverain & de quatre Sieges Royaux dans la Coste de l'Isle de S. Domingue.

A PARIS.
Chez la Veuve SAUGRAIN, à l'entrée du Quay de Gêvres, du côté du Pont au Change, au Paradis.
M. DCCXVIII.

Le Code Noir ou Edit du Roy, Mars 1685

that the *Mémoire* was to serve as a *projet* for an ordinance on slavery ("*pour servir de projet d'une ordonnance*"). We know, of course, that the final version of the *Code Noir* took shape thereafter in Paris, and it is also clear that some transformation of the *Avant-Projet* was made in Paris. The number of articles, to penetrate no further, increased from fifty-two to sixty. The question arises, therefore, to what extent Bégon and de Blénac's *Avant-Projet* actually served as the model for the finished *Code*. Did this *projet* written in the Antilles become the core of the future *Code* or was it perhaps cast aside by the Paris drafters in favor of a return to Roman sources? These questions require me not only to discuss the *Avant-Projet* itself, however summarily, but also to measure its role and influence upon the promulgated *Code Noir*.

To answer these questions with article by article comparisons would, I fear, exhaust the patience of the reader and unreasonably expand the scope of this study. Nevertheless, the results of such a comparison may be shortly stated. About ninety to ninety-five percent of the substance of the *Avant-Projet* passed directly into the

Code Noir, much of it in verbatim form. It appears that the *Projet* carried with it a presumption of *substantive* validity. Unfortunately, the actual instructions to the Paris revisers are not available, nor in fact is their identity known,[57] but it may be deduced from the nature of their interventions that they were essentially instructed not to change substance and policy, but only to improve whenever possible the clarity, cohesiveness and effectiveness of the rules. Accordingly, there are a number of stylistic changes. A few articles were transferred or reassigned from one title to another title where they were thought to be better placed or have greater effect.[58] Paris also did not hesitate to rearrange the sequencing of provisions within titles, and ultimately it suppressed the title headings themselves and instituted continuous numbering. Nonetheless, the inner structure of the original seven titles remained distinct even after the provisions had been transposed and rearranged into the continuous numbering scheme.

These changes were therefore for the most part stylistic. A more significant type of revision was those which modified rules in the *Avant-Projet* that produced an ambiguous result or stated no sanction at all in case of violation. Such changes accomplished a major goal of Colbertian codification, which was to use limpid language requiring no interpretation by judges and to obtain clear results from every rule.[59]

---

[57] They were perhaps appointed by Colbert before his death in September, 1683.

[58] An example of one of these changes was that the *Avant-Projet* treated racial concubinage between a married master and his slave as a criminal offense. *Avant-Projet* Title IV, 12–13 (1683). Paris transferred this rule to the articles on religious matters, *Code Noir* Art. 9 (1685), as if to subscribe to the view that adultery with slaves was not so much a question of public order as a serious religious dereliction.

[59] *See* Boulet-Sautel, *supra* note 36, at 123. The redesign of a police provision, *Avant-Projet* Title III, I (1682), intended to reduce crime and to suppress traffic in stolen goods may serve as an illustration. The provision forbade slaves from selling goods at public market unless they carried a letter of permission from the slave's owner specifying what goods could be sold in his name. The provision did not indicate, however, what would happen if stolen goods were bought from a slave without such a letter. To remedy this defect, Paris created in *Code Noir* Art. 19 (1685) a buyer-beware sanction: the true owner of the stolen goods could revendicate them from the purchaser without restitution of the purchase price, and the purchaser was also subjected to a fine. *See also Avant-Projet* Title III, 4 (1683), as revised by *Code Noir* Art. 26 (1685). In this instance, instead of

Yet while the revisers in Paris sometimes altered enforcement procedures, rarely did they change the substance of an original prohibition or imperative rule.[60] As previously indicated, the revision did not attempt substantive reform of Caribbean policies. As to the existence or extent of Roman law influence upon the revision process, the influence was almost non-existent. There are, in this writer's opinion, perhaps only two instances—those dealing with the slave's *peculium* and the modalities of his manumission—where Paris seems to have made unambiguous use of or allusion to Roman law rules.[61] The modest scope of this Roman contribution will be discussed below.

With these general observations in view, let me now address in a more systematic way the relationship between the *Avant-Projet* and the final version of the *Code*.

Title One

All eleven provisions, save one, in the *Avant-Projet*'s title on Religion became the foundation of *Code Noir* articles 1–14. The close correspondence between the two sets of articles is due to direct quotes and borrowed phraseology. These rules in their ensemble, such as that of the Roman Catholic church being the sole church, that slaves must become Roman Catholics and must be baptized, married and buried within the Church, that there should not be slave labor on Sunday ("from midnight to midnight") and so

---

imposing fines upon owners who failed to furnish slaves with rations and clothing, as the provision in the *Avant-Projet* proposed, Paris placed enforcement in the hands of the *Procureur-Général*, granting slaves standing to lodge complaints directly and calling such deprivations "barbarous and inhumane." As Peytraud noted, the remedy was purely illusory and there were no prosecutions. Lucien Peytraud, *L'Esclavage aux antilles françaises avant 1789*, at 23 (1897). The reference to inhumanity, the sole reference to this word in the *Code Noir*, was window-dressing invented in Paris which disguised the underlying practical reason for the provision. *See supra* note 43 and accompanying text. *See also Code Noir* Art. 47 (1685), in which a special penalty for breaking up slave families through separate sales was added to the provisions of the *Avant-Projet*.

[60] One instance was the crime of striking the master. Originally a slight blow of any kind was a capital offense. *Avant Projet* Title IV, 4 (1683). The revision provided that death was warranted only where the blow was to the head or at least caused contusion or blood to flow. *Code Noir* Art. 33 (1685).

[61] *See infra* discussion of Titles Five and Six of the *Avant-Projet*.

forth,—all had church and local antecedents without Roman connotations.[62]

The opening article of the *Code*, calling upon French officials to chase the Jews out of the French isles, deserves special mention, for it has no counterpart in the *Avant-Projet*. The *Avant-Projet* was written in 1683, prior to the King's definitive decision (September 1683) to banish Jews from the islands and prior to the revocation of the Edict of Nantes (1685). It was apparently not foreseen that the King would alter his position on the Jewish question.[63]

Why the King placed this anti-Semitic provision in the *Code Noir* has been a source of astonishment for some and a source of speculation for others. The nineteenth-century Louisiana historian Charles Gayarré could find no reason to include a ban on Jews within a code ostensibly regulating slavery.[64] However, Bertram Korn and Alan Watson in modern times seem to suggest that the French monarch may have been thinking of old Roman strictures, dating from the era of Constantine, which forbade Jews from owning Christian slaves.[65] Korn suggests that the "double-edged" denial of the right of Jews to settle, as well as the right to indoctrinate slaves in any faith other than Roman Catholicism, would therefore serve to guarantee the proper Catholicization of the slaves.[66]

---

[62] The *Avant-Projet's* rules on baptism of slaves, Sunday rest, and marriage are undoubtedly church regulations, but they had been the subject of local laws in the islands since the 1650's. *See arrêts* in Martinique of 7 October 1652 (slaves cannot be worked on Sundays and holidays) and 19 June 1665 §§3, 6 (masters prohibited from preventing blacks and *engagés* from going to mass on Sundays and holidays; masters must baptize slaves and have them married in church).

[63] Rather the *Avant-Projet* apparently envisaged that Jews would own slaves in the islands. It, therefore, simply ordered Jews as well as Protestants to permit their slaves freely to exercise the Roman Catholic religion and to observe all the religious duties applicable to slaves. *See Avant-Projet* Title I, 8 (1683).

[64] "By what concatenation of causes or of ideas these provisions concerning the supremacy of the Roman Catholic religion and the expulsion of the Jews came to be inserted into the Black Code, it is difficult to imagine." Charles Gayarré, *History of Louisiana*, Vol. 1, (New Orleans: Gresham, 1879), 362–363.

[65] Bertram Korn, *The Early Jews in New Orleans* (Waltham, Mass: Amer. Jewish Soc, 1969), 4; Alan Watson, *Slave Law in the Americas* (Athens, Ga: University of Georgia Press, 1989), 34. For Constantine's decree in 339 A.D., *see* C.1.1.0.1. For Justinian's decree on the subject, *see* C.1.10.2; 1.3.54 (56) 8 (3).

[66] Korn, *supra*, at 4. Watson argues that Louis XIV's slave code rotely followed in the Roman traces, but with one difference. Since the *Code Noir* said there could be

Professor Watson pointed out that since Jews themselves were banned, this preempted the need for a rule forbidding Jews to have Christian slaves.[67]

The rules repressing Jews, however, do not represent a vestigial Roman-law legacy within the *Code Noir*. They represent, rather, the resolution of a long-smoldering controversy surrounding their slaves, their commercial activities, and their freedom of conscience in the Antilles. Jewish immigration to the French isles had begun in the early seventeenth century, but it had always provoked controversy and ambivalence. By an order of the Council of February 4, 1658, Jews were forbidden to engage in commerce on the isle of Martinique, yet this order was later rescinded on September 2, 1658.[68] Colbert instructed Governor-General de Baas in 1671 that Jews must be permitted to enjoy complete liberty of conscience and should be accorded the same privileges as other persons on the islands since they have made "considerable expenditures" to cultivate their lands.[69] Nevertheless, ten years later Governor-General de Blénac's note in the *Mémoire* of December 3, 1681, indicated that the policy was far from settled: "To learn if the King wishes to permit the Jews to practice their religion."[70] On the eve of the *Avant-Projet*'s completion in 1682, the Jesuits prepared a memorandum summarizing the reasons why both Jews and Huguenots should be excluded from the islands and prevented from holding slaves.[71] Colbert, who had defended toleration of Jews only

---

no Jewish colonists, there was no need for a provision corresponding to Roman and Spanish law forbidding Jews to own Christian slaves. Watson, *supra* note 3, at 90.

[67] In my original essay I inadvertently distorted Alan Watson's views, by claiming he thought the French monarch was "rotely reiterating old Roman strictures." I have deleted that phrase in the above paragraph. As Professor Watson subsequently pointed out, he merely contended that the ban had a pre-emptive effect on the need for the Roman rule. *See* Watson, "The Origins of the *Code Noir* Revisited," 71 *Tulane Law Review* 1041 (1997): 1044–1045.

[68] 1 Moreau de St. Méry, *Loix et constitutions des colonies françaises de l'amérique sous le vent* (1784) 83.

[69] Arthur Hertzberg, *The French Enlightenment and the Jews* (New York: Columbia University Press, 1968), 24. According to Hertzberg, in making this statement Colbert was stating his own policy when the growing Christian orthodoxy of Louis XIV was not yet so powerful. Colbert had been informed that the Jews in Martinique and other French-American islands were contributing in an important way to agriculture. *Id.* at 24.

[70] "Scavoir si le Roy entend que l'on permette les Juifs de professer leur relligion."

[71] "They (the Jews) have in their homes a great number of slaves whom they instruct in Judaism, or at least whom they divert away from Christianity; they

insofar as they contributed to the economic life of France, found himself fighting a losing battle in the last decade of his life.[72] The King's definitive order expelling the Jews came in September 1683, only days after Colbert's death, and well after the *Avant-Projet* had been submitted. This order then became the opening salvo of the *Code*: Jews should be driven out of the islands, while Protestants may remain on condition that they refrain from practicing their religion publicly.[73] Here then is an example of an alleged Roman-law influence, or preempted influence, that has been made in disregard of the *Code*'s immediate history.

Unfortunately this tendency to misconceive the Code's origins continues unabated into the next titles we will consider.

Title Two

Paris received the *Avant-Projet*'s title on sustenance and clothing practically *en bloc* into the *Code*.[74] The two texts prescribed the same minimum food rations and clothing allotments which masters must furnish. Both prohibited dispensing alcoholic beverages (*eau de vie* or *guildive*) as a means of discharging this

---

prevent them from having instruction, and they destroy all religious faith that the missionaries can inspire." Lucien Peytraud, *L'Esclavage aux Antilles françaises avant 1789* (Paris: Hachette, 1897), 174.

[72] Hertzberg, *supra* note 69, at 24.

[73] These official pronouncements were compromised by their less-than-complete enforcement. Both Jews and Protestants continued to live and to be admitted to the islands long thereafter. A similar practice developed in Louisiana, where both Protestants and Jews lived, but Protestantism and Judaism officially did not exist. Despite the ban, a few Jews settled in Louisiana during the French domination. Isaac Monsanto was the most prominent in New Orleans, and his sudden expulsion, along with that of Mets and Brito, by General O'Reilly in 1769 was said to be pursuant to the *Code Noir*'s ban. O'Reilly said that "all three are undesirable on account of *the nature of their business* and the religion they profess." Korn, *supra*, at 32. The Spanish general appeared to enforce French law more diligently than the French, but he was under a kind of double mandate. Spanish law also restrained Jews, even converted Jews, from settling in the Indies. Book VII, Title V, Ley 29 *Recopilacíon de las Indias* (Madrid: 1681). (Jews to be expelled from the Indies); Book IX, Title XXXVI, Ley 15 *Recopilacíon de las Indias* (Jewish converts not to enter Indies without express permission of the King).

[74] *See Code Noir* Arts. 22–27 (1685).

duty, and both forbade giving slaves a day off to farm foodstuffs on their own in lieu of dispensing rations.[75] Here one might note that the *Avant-Projet* and *Code* provisions stating that slaves who become infirm by old age or disease cannot be abandoned came from the pen of de Blénac and Patoulet, and not from an edict of the Emperor Claudius, as Jaubert hints.[76] The desire of slaveowners to abandon slaves when they became unprofitable may have been common to both societies, but their experiences and solutions were different. The Romans granted freedom to the mistreated slave, while French law turned the slave's care over to the hospital and charged the owner for his subsistence.

Title Three

As we have seen earlier,[77] the sources of the security measures which the third title "La Police" contains may be traced to the local laws of the islands. The main purposes of the provisions were to control the theft of commodities and to prevent slave assemblies and violent revolts. These rules passed directly into the *Code Noir* with few modifications.[78] Thus, the *Avant-Projet* provisions declaring that slaves cannot sell goods at market without carrying a letter of permission,[79] that goods in the hands of slaves without

---

[75] Peytraud, *supra* note 59, at 219, explains that this injunction was designed to counteract a practice in Guadeloupe and Martinique of giving slaves Saturday off and a plot of land to cultivate ("*à la façon du Brésil*") in lieu of furnishing food and clothing. The practical problem was that in a sugar monoculture there was too little effort to produce foodstuffs to feed the slaves. However, the experiment of turning over the task of raising foodstuffs to the slaves themselves had been tried and failed. It had only led to increased theft rather than actual farming. This experience was the basis for forbidding the practice, both in the *Avant-Projet*, Title II, 3, and in the *Code Noir*, Arts. 22, 24. The only significant difference between the *Avant-Projet* and *Code Noir* provisions lay in the enforcement. The former stipulated a fine for each violation while the latter placed enforcement of these alimentary duties in the hands of the *Procureur-Général* and vainly expected powerless illiterates to petition him with their grievances.

[76] Jaubert, *supra* note 47, at 324, argues that this provision originated in an edict declaring that abandoned, old and sick slaves would be given the right of the city.

[77] *See supra* note 45 and accompanying text.

[78] *See Code Noir* Art s. 15–21 (1685).

[79] *Avant-Projet* Title III, 1 (1683).

such permission may be seized by any citizen[80] and that officers are to be placed in the markets to enforce these requirements,[81] became Articles 19, 20 and 21 of the *Code*. Likewise, provisions forbidding slaves to carry large sticks or weapons,[82] or to assemble[83] and declaring owners who tolerate such assemblies liable for all damages,[84] furnished the language for Articles 15, 16 and 17 of the *Code*.

Title Four

"Crimes and Punishments" formed the longest title of the *Avant-Projet*. These articles became the basis of Articles 32–43 of the *Code Noir*. The Paris revisers rearranged and consolidated some provisions and in one case created a new offense.[85] In other respects, however, the provisions passed unscathed. These provisions made two underlying assumptions about slave crimes.

The *Avant-Projet* assumed that while slaves were incapable of civil acts, they were responsible moral agents for criminal law purposes. They were capable of discerning right from wrong and thus should be judged by the same criminal process which applied to free persons. Nevertheless, the province of crime in a slave code was distinctive and limited. Both the *Avant-Projet* and the *Code* dealt only with crimes unique to the status of slave and slaveowner. Neither dealt with general crimes which anyone might commit such as murder, rape, arson, burglary, and so forth. Instead, the slave crimes of striking the master,[86] insolent or violent behavior toward free persons,[87] and running away (*marronage*)[88] were criminal acts which no free person could commit. To these, however, the *Avant-Projet* and *Code* apparently added two offenses that slaves typically

---

[80] *Avant-Projet* Title III, 3 (1683).
[81] *Avant-Projet* Title III, 2 (1683).
[82] *Avant-Projet* Title IV, 4 (1683).
[83] *Avant-Projet* Title III, 4 (1683).
[84] *Avant-Projet* Title III, 5 (1683).
[85] *See Code Noir* Art. 34 (1685).
[86] *Avant-Projet* Title IV, 4 (1683); *Code Noir* Art. 33 (1685).
[87] *Code Noir* Art. 34 (1685). There was no antecedent in the *Avant-Projet*.
[88] *Avant-Projet* Title IV, 8 (1683); *Code Noir* Art. 38 (1685).

committed: the theft of livestock[89] and the theft of commodities.[90] They did not treat murder or homicide except to specify that it was a crime for a master or overseer to kill a slave.[91] Crimes perpetrated by one slave upon another slave, moreover, were not dealt with at all, perhaps because the society considered injuries to slaves as damage to private property and thus the subject of private punishment and/or compensation and, therefore, not a concern of the state.

The second underlying assumption was that slaves might receive both private and public punishment for their offenses. The slave served two masters and was subject to a kind of double jeopardy for the same acts. The main distinction was that private punishment could encompass whippings with cords or branches, but could not include death, physical mutilation or the use of torture.[92] Public punishments by authority of law, however, were designed for maximum deterrence and in certain cases expressly called for physical mutilation, such as the cutting off of ears or the severing of hamstrings.[93] In cases of capital punishment, the *Code* adopted the mutual insurance scheme proposed in the *Avant-Projet*.[94] Its premise was not that capital punishment of a slave constituted a "taking" of private property for a public purpose, but rather that an uncompensated owner would hide crime rather than lose his slave.[95]

Title Five

The *Avant-Projet's* treatment of civil incapacity was short and skeletal and the revisers supplemented it substantially. The original articles fully disqualified slaves as testimonial witnesses in civil

---

[89] *Avant-Projet* Title IV, 5 (1683); *Code Noir* Art. 35 (1685).
[90] *Avant-Projet* Title IV, 6 (1683); *Code Noir* Art. 36 (1685).
[91] *Avant-Projet* Title IV, 6 (1683); *Code Noir* Art. 43 (1685).
[92] *Avant-Projet* Title IV, 1–3 (1683); *Code Noir* Art. 42 (1685).
[93] *See Code Noir* Art. 38 (1685). *See also Code Noir* Art. 35 (1685) which allowed for unspecified "*peines inflictives*."
[94] *Avant-Projet* Title III, 11 (1683); *Code Noir* Art. 40 (1685). *See supra* note 48 and accompanying text.
[95] This crime-detection rationale is expressly stated in the *Avant-Projet*, but it was edited out of the *Code Noir*.

and criminal proceedings,[96] denied them all testamentary, contractual and donative capacity to dispose of, acquire or to receive property,[97] and rendered slaves incapable of being sued or pursued in civil proceedings.[98] These three articles achieved the *capitis deminutio* of slaves as witnesses, litigants, and authors of juridical acts, without elaborating the consequences. Paris enlarged these incapacities in several ways. Article 28 denied slaves the capacity to acquire any patrimonial rights,[99] conceiving of them as mere instruments of acquisition for their masters and declaring all their promises and obligations to be null. It also took away the possibility of all public functions, such as those of agent, arbitrator or expert. In a most interesting intervention, however, the revision provided that the master was civilly obligated for the commercial acts of his slave executed pursuant to his command or (assuming there was no command) if those acts turned to his profit. If there was no profit to the master, the *peculium* of the slave might be invaded to satisfy creditors.[100]

Romanist scholars have pointed to these references to the slave's *peculium* and to the master's commercial liability based upon command or profit as evidence of a Roman borrowing.[101] In this case, their view is plausible and the reason is not without importance. The rules appear to be more than a parallel to Roman law. They had no source in local legislation, nor did previous memoranda or the *Avant-Projet* discuss them. It is evident that Paris supplied the reference to *peculium* and other Romanesque features of the provision. Nevertheless, it may be observed that the *Avant-Projet* had already settled the essential policy regarding the incapacity of slaves. The additions were modest borrowings, not new statements of policy.

---

[96] *Avant-Projet* Title V, 1 (1683).

[97] *Avant-Projet* Title V, 2 (1683).

[98] *Avant-Projet* Title V, 3 (1683).

[99] "We declare slaves can own nothing which is not their master's." *Code Noir* Art. 28 (1685). While not in the *Avant-Projet*, this rule comes from the Preliminary Report and rests upon *avis* of the Councils. *See supra* note 47 and accompanying text.

[100] *Code Noir* Art. 29 (1685).

[101] Watson, *supra* note 3, at 89 (citing similarities to the *actiones adiecticiae qualitatis*, *actio quod iussu*, *actio institoria*, and *actio de peculio et in rem verso*).

Title Six

The sixth title of the *Avant-Projet*, "Of the Seizure of Slaves and Their Status as Movables," became the underpinnings of Articles 44–54 of the *Code Noir*. Taking its lead from the *Projet*, the *Code Noir* declared that slaves were to be classified as movable property,[102] that husbands, wives and small children could not be seized and sold separately,[103] and that slaves laboring on plantations could not be seized and sold for debts (other than for the debts of their own purchase) unless the land itself were seized (*saisie réelle*).[104]

These rules originated in the French isles. There had been considerable controversy over the status of slaves as movable or immovable property, and the *arrêts* of the Councils had fluctuated back and forth in a confused effort to adjudicate the question.[105] Any attempt to treat slaves one way in one context had caused inconvenience in another.[106] In a long note set forth in the margin of the *Avant-Projet,* Bégon alluded to this confusion, explaining that decisions of the three Sovereign Councils had recently changed the jurisprudence by treating slaves as immovables. This, he said, had given rise to "an infinity of ridiculous questions," *viz*. whether slaves *en terre féodale* were to be treated as fiefs, or whether the *droit d'ainesse, rétrait lignager* and mortgages applied to slaves. The Paris redactors used this marginal note as the keynote for drafting a wholly new provision.[107] This provision carefully spelled

---

[102] *Avant-Projet* Title VI, 4 (1683); *Code Noir* Art. 44 (1685).
[103] *Avant-Projet* Title I, 6 (1683); *Code Noir* Art. 47 (1685).
[104] *Avant-Projet* Title V, 1–2 (1683); *Code Noir* Art. 48 (1685).
[105] For details, *see* Peytraud, *supra* note 59, at 247 *ff.* As early as 1658 Guadeloupe's Council ruled that slaves were immovables by destination.
[106] The vacillation of these local bodies was in reality the search for a way to satisfy different goals. On the one hand was the desire to bind the labor force to the land and, in the event of seizure by creditors, to prevent the breakup of plantations and slave families. This argued for treating slaves as part and parcel of the immovable property. On the other hand was the desire that this form of wealth should pass through the community of *acquêts* and that gains between husband and wife be shared equally by co-heirs within families. This argued for designation as movables. The solution finally reached by the redactors was to declare slaves to be movables as a general rule and for most purposes, but to create special rules designed to hold plantations and slave families intact.
[107] *Code Noir* Art. 44 (1685).

out clear answers to the "ridiculous questions" which Bégon said had arisen in the islands. There was no reflexive resort to Roman tradition, even though the distinction between movables and immovables was originally Roman.

Title Seven

We come to the final title of the *Avant-Projet* on the liberation of slaves. I have already mentioned the tendency of certain writers to be manumission-centered, an emphasis that has tinged their views about the origins of the *Code Noir*. In view of the importance attached to it, let me examine manumission as a closing subject.

The final title of the *Avant-Projet* contains a key provision on the manumission of slaves. Freely translated, it says the following:

> Masters can bestow liberty upon their slaves by will or acts *inter vivos*, which shall render them capable of receiving legacies or gifts which are made to them by the same acts declaring them free—and they will enjoy the privileges of other inhabitants without being obliged to obtain letters of naturalization, even though they were born in foreign lands.[108]

Here the island officials took a remarkably liberal position on manumission. An owner could free his slaves by a unilateral act without seeking permission of the government, without special formalities, for whatever reasons the owner may have, whether mercenary or affectionate.[109] An owner could create a citizen. They did not exclude the purchase of freedom, although it would have to be a *voluntary* system of freedom purchase.

This provision captured the essence of manumission without Roman overtones in its language. The provision flows from Caribbean sources through the pen of Bégon and de Blénac. It would be presumptuous to argue that the very concept of

---

[108] Avant Projet Title VII, 1 (1683).

[109] That the owner need not state reasons for the enfranchisement is implicit in the text, but the point was explicitly added for sake of clarity in the final version. *Code Noir* Art. 55 (1685).

manumission has to be exclusively Roman or that they would not have thought of it except by reference to Roman law. Manumission (a word they did not employ) simply means liberation. Liberty is a generic concept freely occurring to all peoples at all times.[110] Furthermore, we must not be quick to assume that such a provision would have been Roman-inspired simply because it seems "protective" and liberal toward slaves. The widest freedom of manumission is also completely consistent with the interests of planters since the maximum power of disposition over their slaves, including the power to liberate them, increases the value of their property. Thus, the original instructions to consult the views of the Sovereign Councils and the leading citizens may have easily yielded a property-oriented rule which can be read as "protective" in one sense and yet, in another more basic sense, may have only reflected the freedom of property which slaveholders eagerly sought.

As stated earlier, this initial provision in the *Avant-Projet* captured the essence of manumission. When the *Avant-Projet* was sent to Paris, however, some additions and deletions were made. The remarkable part was that the additions and deletions widened the scope of manumission *to make it more unfettered.* Paris introduced a lower age cut-off for manumitting owners (twenty years) which was more liberal than the twenty-five-year age that the *Avant-Projet* provision had silently presupposed. Paris also drafted a new article to recognize tacit emancipation, as the Romans had done.[111] The Parisian editors also dropped a provision of the

---

[110] It is interesting to observe that when Spain's *Codigo Negro* was being prepared and the planter views were consulted by the author of that code, Agustín Ignacio Emparán, he discovered that the untutored planters of Santo Domingo had notions of manumission comparable to those held by the Romans. "One aspect meriting comment is manumission. It is curious to note—if only because the majority of informants had no legal training and had no knowledge of the norms of Roman law on manumission—that the replies that were given coincide in principle and in some cases in their fundamentals with the rules governing the granting of liberty in the period of the Principate in Rome." Javier Malagón Barceló, *Codigo Negro Carolino 1784* (Santo Domingo: Ediciones de Taller, 1974), XLVI.

[111] *Code Noir* Art. 56 (1685). Thus, slaves declared universal legatees under their master's will were deemed free; and any slave who was made executor or tutor to the master's children was likewise deemed free. The logic of the provision was apparently that for a slave to function as executor or as tutor, he must have full capacity to represent the estate or his ward, and the grant of this office was consistent only with the intent to create a free person.

Avant-Projet by which a manumitted slave would be reenslaved if he committed theft. They introduced another article directing freed slaves to bear a singular respect toward their former masters.[112]

These additions look Roman, but they are only Roman touch-ups to the strong manumission policy quoted earlier. The question becomes, then, which came first, and which is secondary? This writer's argument is that an initial policy of free manumission came from the Caribbean, and the Roman flourishes are a secondary dimension, refining that policy. Indeed, the substantive and formal conditions that the *Avant-Projet* and the *Code Noir* imposed on owners were decidedly more liberal toward manumission than comparable Roman rules.[113]

Of course, even this original manumission policy would change in the light of later *experience*, and in time the Caribbean experience would serve as proxy for Louisiana. This retrenchment in the islands controlled Louisiana's destiny even before Louisiana had slaves or a slave code. By 1713, the laxity of the position taken in 1685 was deemed an existential threat to the system itself. Too many slaves were being freed and for the wrong reasons.[114] The royal Ordinance of October 24, 1713, now decreed that slaves could be freed only with the written permission of the Governor-General and the Intendant.[115] The Ministry soon attached the same requirement to the *Code Noir* for Louisiana,[116] and raised the age of majority for Louisiana manumitters to twenty-five years. The second code also completely repudiated the liberal policy of the first *Code Noir* with respect to making donations to slaves. The new donative ban even extended to ex-slaves and free-born blacks. Acts of manumission could no longer contain valid donations to the erstwhile slave.[117]

---

[112] *Code Noir* Art. 58 (1685).

[113] Jaubert noted this difference between the two laws. *See supra* note 47, at 328–329.

[114] The first reaction was a local decree of the Governor-General and Intendant on 15 August 1711 prohibiting manumission without formal authorization; it came in response to alleged abuses. "Blacks steal and negresses prostitute themselves in order to obtain money to purchase their freedom." Peytraud, *supra* note 59, at 403.

[115] *Id.*

[116] *Code Noir* Art. 50 (1724).

[117] "We declare, however, that all manumitted slaves and all free-born negroes, are incapable of receiving donations, either by testamentary dispositions or by acts

The reasons for these changes lie in contemporary reaction and adjustment to demographic insecurity. The number of *gens de couleur* simply grew too rapidly, suggesting to authorities that the *Code* was defectively liberal.[118] The suggestion that the memory of an old tradition in French *coutumes* connected to releasing serfs may have something to do with the sudden *volte-face* by the crown[119] is simply disingenuous and trivializes the historical experience of the French.[120] The truth is that once it was perceived that there were too many enfranchised slaves, a whole series of derogations to the manumission policy of the *Code* were made in the eighteenth century.[121] Rome's laws had little to do with the original policy of the *Code* and certainly nothing to do with its reversal.

Conclusion

The word *experience* plays a very important role in evaluating the origins of France's *Code Noir*. For fifty years before the *Code Noir* emerged, French colonists and administrators were developing new laws and customs to regulate slavery, and Colbert's concept of codification largely ensured that they would build upon these antecedents. It is a myth to think that codification succeeded in

---

inter vivos from the whites. Said donations shall be null and void and the objects so donated shall be applied to the benefit of the nearest hospital." *Code Noir* Art. 52 (1724).

[118] According to Peytraud, there were no emancipated blacks in St. Dominigue in 1665, but by 1715, there were already 1500, by 1770, 6,000, by 1789, 28,000. Peytraud *supra* note 59, at 414 (quoting the census of Moreau de St. Méry for St. Domingue).

[119] Watson, *supra* note 3, at 87.

[120] In a letter written in 1723 on the eve of the *Code*'s introduction in Louisiana, Governor-General de Feuquières sounded the alarm against France's manumission policies: "If we do not restrain the hand of those freeing slaves, there will be four times as many freed slaves as there are now, because here there is great familiarity and liberty between masters and negresses who are '*bien faites*,' which produces a great quantity of mulattoes, and the ordinary reward of their acquiescing in the wishes of the master is a promise of liberty." Peytraud, *supra* note 59, at 409.

[121] These included placing many new burdens on manumitters and slaves, such as heavy taxation on enfranchisement and a prohibition on freeing a slave who had no profession or means of livelihood. These measures are discussed by Maurice Satineau, *Histoire de la Guadeloupe sous l'ancién régime 1635–1789*, (Paris: Payot, 1928), 317–323.

the Antilles only because the Romans prepared the path. It is a myth to think that all roads lead to Rome or that every parallel is a provenance.

In Alan Watson's book *Slave Law in the Americas* the distinguished writer calls the French approach "artificial" and believes that they based their slave law upon the borrowed experience of the Romans. This story of origins and authors, however, shows not only that the experience was their own, but that the *Code Noir* was the embodiment of that very experience. This account of the *Code Noir* also has significant consequences for understanding Louisiana slave history in its proper light. Our *Code* was both an appendage and a continuation of the Caribbean experience. Where slave law was concerned, Louisiana was more the heir of Martinique and St. Domingue than of Rome.

"Market Boat, New Orleans" by Alfred Waud
(*Courtesy of the Historic New Orleans Collection*)

CHAPTER 2

War Without Arms

The Customs of Slavery

INTRODUCTION

Slave law was characteristically volatile. It was always an unfinished project, a growth industry through and through. Philip Schwarz aptly observes: "The most important characteristic of the law of bondage . . . was change. . . . A supposedly pure law of slavery would be absolute and immutable. The actual law was flexible and changed constantly. . . ."[1] The statute books convey a rough idea of this volatility. Over the period 1689–1865 Virginia enacted more than one hundred and thirty slave statutes among which were seven major slave codes, with some containing more than fifty provisions. Within a shorter time frame, Louisiana enacted or drafted as many as five slave codes, beginning with the *Code Noir* of 1724 which contained fifty nine provisions. The Black Code of 1806 contained thirty nine articles, to which was annexed a slave criminal code of twenty two more articles. It was followed by the Digest of 1808 and the Civil Code of 1825, where the subject of slavery was given extensive treatment in all relevant books and chapters on persons, property and transactions. Beyond the codes there was, of course, more legislation on the books. The Louisiana Legislature added special statutes on a yearly basis. On the eve of the Civil War the ordinances for the City of New Orleans contained one hundred provisions dealing with slavery issues. The

---

[1] Philip J. Schwarz, *Slave Laws in Virginia* (Athens: University of Georgia Press, 1996), 2.

same point could be made about practically every jurisdiction where slavery existed, irrespective of location and legal tradition.[2]

Yet, as prolific as slave law tended to be, it would be a serious mistake to judge its true scope merely by statutes alone. Statutes were not the most dynamic vehicle of change and actually they contained only a fraction of the 'law.' Custom was at least a co-equal form of lawmaking throughout the era of slavery, and of course judicial decisions played a creative role as well. Custom was particularly important to explain the beginnings of slavery. Historians have shown that the initial basis for slavery in the New World rested mainly upon 'public opinion' and the force of practice, so that the earliest laws on the subject were in effect giving legal sanction to established usage.[3] There is evidence of customs regulating slavery in the Caribbean islands well before the emergence of the slave codes of the 17th century.[4] According to Alexander Johnston, slavery in the British colonies of North America was not originally established by law, but rested wholly upon custom.[5] The first settlers and administrators in Louisiana thought it natural to seize and enslave the Indians and expected their *faits accomplis* to ripen into property rights.

Whether customs had historical priority, however, is not a central claim of this chapter. More important to my purpose is the role of custom as a factor of legal development, as a continuous

---

[2] The 1784 slave code for Santo Domingo drafted by Agustín Ignacio Emparán y Orbe is one of the lengthiest I have found. It contains one hundred and eighty one laws, distributed over thirty seven chapters, the overall text constituting seventy nine printed pages.

[3] *See* Theodore Wilson, *The Black Codes of the South* (Tuscaloosa: Alabama Press, 1965): "Slavery came about by the force of practice; the earliest laws merely gave legal sanction to established usage." *See also* E.V. Goveia, *The West Indian Slave Laws of the 18th Century* (Barbados: Caribbean University Press, 1970). "Law is not the original basis of slavery in the West Indian colonies. . . . Before the slave laws could be made, it was necessary for the opinion to be accepted that persons could be made slaves and held as slaves."

Other scholars, however, argue that the slave laws of the New World were inspired by or borrowed from earlier precedents within the legal tradition. *See* Bradley Nicholson, "Legal Borrowing and the Origins of Slave Law in the British Colonies," *American Journal of Legal History* (1994): 38; Alan Watson, *Slave Law in the Americas* (Athens: Georgia University Press, 1989).

[4] *See infra*, Section I.

[5] Alexander Johnston, "Slavery" in *Cyclopaedia of Political Science* (New York: Maynard, Merrill, 1899).

outgrowth of the master-slave relationship, as a competing norm of behavior which exerted pressure on lawmakers, and as a reservoir of norms from which statutes drew. As Lon Fuller observed, we are forced to deal with the role of custom even in codified systems of law that purport to be wholly enacted.[6] History can show that there was a continuous dialectical interaction between slave legislation and slave customary law. Indeed very typically customs sprang up round almost any activity or aspect of slave life, even if already the subject of statutory regulation. Important institutions, like the operation of public markets by slaves on Sundays, often rested upon nothing but custom and usage. Custom can be seen regulating (or after legislation, *re*regulating) the food rations of slaves, the intervals of work and free time, the celebration of slave marriages, the exemption from work on the Sabbath, and scores of other matters. Legislation was not infrequently a direct response to the effects of custom and at the same time a fresh basis for more custom. When legislators incorporated a custom into positive law, they both dignified and recognized it and highlighted the interplay of statute and custom.[7] Legislative recognitions were obviously not bound by technical criteria requiring the immemorial existence or the universality of the usage, as judges might require. Customs, including practices lying somewhere below custom, were more easily recognized by legislators not only because the rules of recognition were not formal but because many lawmakers were slaveholders and were knowledgeable witnesses or participants in the formation of the practices. Their efforts to suppress custom were a form of negative recognition. These are also of interest because they supply valuable evidence of custom's existence and

---

[6] Lon Fuller, *The Morality of Law* (New Haven: Yale University Press, 1969), 234.
[7] Spain's *Codigo Negro* (1789) cross-referenced frequently to "la costumbre del Pais." *See e.g.* Cap. I, Christian schooling of slaves ordinarily held on festival days, but not where custom recognizes an exception at harvest time; Cap II, quantity and quality of clothes or food furnished to slaves must be conform to "la costumbre del Pais." The provisions of the 1789 *Codigo* are set forth in Annex III (270) in Javier Malagon Barcelo, *Codigo Negro Carolino* (Santo Domingo: Ediciones Taller, 1974). Cross-referencing to custom is equally found in Louisiana's Black Code of 1806, *e.g.* sec 7: "That as for the hours of work and of rest, which are to be assigned to slaves in summer and winter, the old usages of the territory shall be adhered, to wit: [. . .]" Acts of Louisiana, 1806.

effectiveness.[8] Repeatedly issued but ineffective bans suggest the persistency and strength of custom and the correlation between the vigor of customary development and the general volatility of slave laws. Thus the study of law and custom can yield new insights and corrected assessments of the reality of slavery as a legal phenomenon.[9] One difficulty, however, is that the inquiry takes us along unexplored and unfamiliar paths where the historical sources are less documented and reliable. I have found very little treatment of slave customs in the vast literature on slavery.

This chapter investigates one of the neglected topics of slavery, namely the role of slaves, owners, overseers and certain officials in creating customary slave norms. To keep the subject within manageable limits, I have chosen to focus upon three or four selected customs that arose in the Caribbean, spread to Louisiana in the 18th century, and persisted into the 19th century. These concern the slave's use of his free time, his right to work for himself on the Sabbath, the right to cultivate grounds and gardens for his own use and sustenance, and the right to keep and dispose of property and wealth arising from his own industry. Individually these customs have distinctive characteristics but in an economic sense they are integrally related. They have in common a tendency to improve the material condition of slaves. They posed a direct challenge to the legal disabilities of slaves under the law.

Through an historical and comparative approach, I hope to demonstrate four points of general interest about the customs. The first, which has already been alluded to, is that a dialectical relationship existed between the different sources of law. This conclusion emerges from the historical overview in the first part of the chapter where we follow these customs from Caribbean beginnings to subsequent Louisiana development under French, Spanish and American rule. Here we visit briefly the major

---

[8] Thus when the Cabildo sought to revise Louisiana slave law in 1778, the draft took aim at what Louisiana planters perceived to be a number of objectionable customs, such as the right of slaves of different plantations to marry each other, the practice of hiring out and the Spanish institution of *coartación*. *See infra* Sec. I.

[9] Schwarz, *supra* note 1 at 5, ("The customary law of slavery is useful as the basis for constructing a model of the interrelationship between masters' and slaves' behavior and the changing law of slavery.")

legislative landmarks in Louisiana slave history and document the constant dialogue between the two forms of law.

The second point is that the customs serve as an essential corrective to the impressions gained by reading slave statutes in isolation. As many historians have pointed out, the statutes or Black Codes,[10] are frequently illusory and misleading portraits of normative reality. To accept them at face value without the offset of their accompanying customs, not to mention the related issue of their enforcement, is likely to create a distorted and unreliable picture.[11] In my view the modern reader has a vulnerability and should be particularly skeptical in this regard. Those steeped in today's positivist legal outlook tend to give credence to law's commands and would tend to assume that slave laws were obeyed and enforced as written. As I attempt to show in the second part of the chapter, recognizing the effect of custom can shed light on how statutory law was at times in stark contrast to the reality it regulated.

The point may be briefly illustrated. The *Code Noir* declared that slaves had no legal capacity to enter into contracts or to sell their labor or goods, yet it was an everyday experience, supported by custom, for slaves to hire out their services to their master or to third parties, and also to trade their own goods for profit in the markets. In so doing slaves freely entered transactions that were at odds with their alleged disabilities and slowly acquired rights

---

[10] This expression is not used here in a technical way. In the literature on slavery this expression has been applied to almost every New World slave regulation shaped by French, Spanish and American influences, undoubtedly because this slavery was always equated with black enslavement. Actually relatively few enactments employ the expression in their official title. (An exceptional example is the 1806 legislation in Louisiana, discussed *infra* Sec. I.) The term "code" is used quite loosely, only connoting a legislative act of some sort and no guarantee of comprehensive treatment. In reality this is a popular expression applied to any laws regulating African slavery.

[11] Robert Shaw states in his Preface: ". . . the laws of slavery frequently did not reflect accurately the realities of that institution. On relatively isolated plantations, and with slaves denied any access to the courts or the right to testify, "justice" was usually a private matter. . . . And it is also clear that many enactments were seldom enforced and, indeed, remained as almost dead letters in the statutes. This applies to laws both for the control and punishment of slaves and those for their protection." *A Legal History of Slavery* (Potsdam, N.Y.: Northern Press, 1991).

unrecognized by the Code. That law further declared that slaves could not own property of any kind. It declared that everything they might acquire or possess belonged to their owner. Nevertheless by custom certain wages belonged securely to the slaves and could not be taken away. Slaves regularly raised pigs, horses, chickens, and fowl and grew crops for their own consumption and for sale to others. They operated public markets as retail outlets where they bought and sold goods and retained the proceeds for themselves. Through barter, sale and exchange they generated wealth, however modest, and improved their diet, health, attire and quality of life. Their savings became the means of financing self-purchase and the freedom of others. To pass this property to their descendants and relations after death, slaves developed mechanisms equivalent to succession representatives. One of my aims, then, is to point to the sizable gap between the law on the books and the law on the ground—and to consider its relation to the question of law enforcement.

Obviously many historians are well aware of this reality gap, but they usually ascribe it to the fact that the law in question was simply under-enforced or not enforced at all, and leave the matter at that. No doubt non-enforcement was a reality, but I suggest that the explanation is too general to explain these discrepancies and may be even causally unrelated to some of them. In such cases, I will argue, the law would seem to be unenforced because it was superseded by a growth of custom which was relatively incompatible with it. It seems to be the case that the constant "push" of custom has often been mistaken for the non-enforcement of slave regulations. At first glance a new custom superseding law is practically indistinguishable from the perception that the law is not enforced. To this subject we will return at a later point.

My third general point is that comparable customs and practices existed in other slave societies and arose for basically the same reasons. The point is that the "gap" to which I refer was not basically unusual or peculiar to Louisiana. In a comparative excursus covering certain parts of the American South and some British and French Caribbean colonies, I rely upon the works of regional specialists to show this common pattern.

The fourth part of this study introduces a theory about the underlying basis of the slave customs. Building upon the theories of Lon Fuller and Bruce Benson on the origins of moral duties, I argue that the customs arise from the need to introduce incentives into a system of involuntary labor. Incentives were necessary because owners could not obtain the levels of productivity they desired through sanctions and intimidation alone, and slaves could not obtain degrees of autonomy through resistance alone. Incentives introduced reciprocity into the master-slave relationship and created tacit commitments between them. The theory also suggests that slaves were conscious participants in the creation and used their awareness of the law to advance their own interests.

We now turn to an historical overview of the dialectic of slave law and custom.[12]

LOUISIANA SLAVE LAW UNDER FRANCE, SPAIN AND THE UNITED STATES

Caribbean Beginnings

The French began to acquire slaves in their Caribbean islands as early as 1635.[13] In the first fifty years of French slavery, there was no general legislation on the subject. We have somewhat scanty knowledge of the various customs that were incubating in the islands during this period, but two or three customs were already sufficiently mature as to be recognized under Louis XIV's 1685 *ordonnance*. This *ordonnance* or 'Caribbean' *Code Noir* was the work of local administrative officials under instructions from Minister Colbert. The principal redactors were the Governor-

---

[12] I should signal that there is an important complication to this historical account. As we move from French slave law to Spanish law, or from Spanish law to laws passed in the American period, it is never stated that the former law is abrogated in its entirety. As a matter of principle, there would be "implied repeals" in places of substantive incompatibility between two laws, but where the laws *or the customs* were not incompatible, there may have been a kind of legal accretion. Unfortunately we cannot be sure that the legal actors were of this opinion, at least not until the American period when the judiciary clearly adopted the principle.

[13] By 1654 there were already twelve thousand slaves distributed in the islands of St. Christophe, Martinique and Guadeloupe. Alfred Martineau & Louis Philippe May, *Trois siécles d'histoire antillaise, Martinique et Guadeloupe* (Paris: Societé d'Histoire des Colonies Françaises, 1935), 23, 29.

General and the Intendant of the islands and their instructions called for them to work in consultation with the Sovereign Councils of Martinique, Guadeloupe and St. Christophe. [14] The Code they devised was primarily designed to meet the needs of the situation at hand—it was a plantation code for an economy based on the cultivation of sugar. It had little in common with the regulation of urban and domestic slavery.[15]

The codifiers recognized that an important customary practice had already taken hold in Guadeloupe, Martinique and St. Christophe. In these islands the owners, in lieu of furnishing necessary food and clothing, had sought to solve the problem of slave sustenance by giving them a plot of land to cultivate and a release from plantation work on Saturdays.[16] This practice had migrated from the sugar estates of Brazil, and French officials in the islands referred to this form of provisioning as "*à la façon du Brésil.*" The rapid spread of the method was due to the incentives it offered both sides of the master-slave relationship. In a sugar monoculture such as in the French Antilles, the owners had insufficient economic incentive to produce foodstuffs for slave consumption. To maximize profits, they preferred to devote their best land to the production of sugar and to have slaves provision themselves by farming fringe lands in their free time, which saved the owners from the expense of importing costly foodstuffs. [17] From a slave perspective the system was also advantageous. An allotment of land and the time to work it permitted them to plant gardens and grow healthier crops that varied or supplemented their otherwise monotonous diet, and it also produced surplus goods that could be sold on the plantation or at the Sunday market. The practice

---

[14] For details *see* Chapter One. *See also*, Louis Sala-Molins, *Le Code Noir ou le calvaire de Canaan* (Paris: Presses Universitaires, 1987); Gabriel Tardieu, *Le destin des noirs aux Indes de Castille* (Paris: L'Harmattan, 1984).

[15] For example, under Art. 30 the crime of slave theft was limited to stealing farm animals and farm produce. Under Art. 6, rest on Sunday meant freedom from "the cultivation of the land and the manufacture of sugar." Only exceptionally does the Code depart from its rural immediacy. *See* Art. 29.

[16] The custom is mentioned in an *arrêt* of the Sovereign Council of St. Christophe, dated 13 Jan. 1682, which the Code drafters quoted in their *Mémoire au Roy* de 20 mai 1682.

[17] *See* Lucien Peytraud, *L'Esclavage aux antilles françaises avant 1789* (Paris: Hachette, 1897), 23.

undoubtedly gave the slaves a taste of embryonic property rights since, albeit in a limited sphere, they were able to enjoy and retain the proceeds of their own labor.

The codifiers and the Sovereign Councils, however, decided that this custom should be banned. They felt that slaves would find it easier to steal their food in their time off rather than perform additional labor in the field. From an administrative and policing standpoint it was better for slaves to be completely dependent upon their owner for their food, clothing and housing. The master's obligation should be unavoidable and non-delegable. Accordingly the Code stipulated the exact food rations to be furnished, the length of breakfast and dinner hours in the field, the summer and winter clothing to be provided, all in accordance with this conscious policy of dependency. The minimum food rations or *l'ordinaire* consisted of exact measures of corn, meat or fish, which by one estimate corresponded to around 2,150–2,300 calories a day.[18] The Code also forbade masters to allow slaves to work one day of the week for their own account, or even to discharge their obligation by giving slaves "*eau de vie*" or "*guildive*" in lieu of furnishing food.[19] All other means for slaves to cultivate their own food for personal consumption or for marketing to others were deliberately cut off. The slave was not to work on Sundays or holidays, even for himself, and slave markets on these days were to be closed.[20] This initial ban on slave self-provisioning, however, was actually the beginning of a long capitulation that did not finally occur until a century later. The fundamental economic appeal of the practice of self-provisioning by slaves made it almost impossible to eliminate, and it continued to be practiced *contra legem* in the French Caribbean and then in Louisiana. Over the next century it constantly undermined the Code, until it finally prevailed and was recognized in the laws.

One other custom was specifically mentioned in the drafters' preparatory papers. Governor de Blénac and his co-author reported that "the usage of Martinique is that Mulattoes are freed at 20 years and Mulatresses at fifteen years." Judging by the rules they

---

[18] *See* http://perso.wanadoo.fr/yekrik.yekrak/.

[19] Arts. 23, 24 (1685).

[20] Arts. 6, 7.

eventually fashioned on manumission, the authors clearly suppressed this customary development. The Code would recognize no automatic emancipations by age nor did it provide any special rules for the manumission of slaves of mixed parentage. On the contrary, the Code condemned miscegenation by drastic penalties. It provided that if a master had a child by a slave, both slave and child were to be forfeited to the hospital and would never be eligible to be manumitted.[21] These draconian penalties reflect the vision that civil society would consist of two castes, one enslaved, the other free, without an intermediate status for former slaves. The redactors failed to anticipate the scale of racial mixing, and therefore failed to foresee the resulting flood of emancipations that would create a third caste.

Continuation in Louisiana

When the *Code Noir* was re-promulgated at New Orleans in 1724, its Caribbean assumptions arrived with it. The new law was not the product of the fledgling colony's independent experience and obviously it had no foundation in local custom. Prior to 1719, while there had been enslavement of Indians,[22] there were few or no black slaves. The first black slaves arrived from Africa aboard two ships in 1719, and from 1719–1743, twenty two more shiploads arrived, or a total of 5,951 slaves imported from Africa under French rule.[23] At that point Louisiana's agricultural focus was somewhat unsettled; it was not yet characterized by the widespread cultivation of sugar and cotton. The imported 'Caribbean' law was somewhat like a mirror of distant conditions which administrators supposed or hoped would obtain in Louisiana.

This *Code* was nearly a verbatim reissuance of its 1685 predecessor. It covered eight regulatory subjects: religious practice, marriage and cohabitation, police control, care and maintenance, civil disqualifications, crimes and offenses, property-law classifications, and manumission, though it contained five fewer

---

[21] Art. 9.

[22] Robert Shaw, *supra,* 7.

[23] *See* Gwendolyn Midlo Hall, *Africans in Colonial Louisiana* (Baton Rouge: Louisiana State University Press, 1992), 60 (Table 2).

articles. It also contained several interesting policy changes, however, that were based upon events that had occurred in the interim period 1685–1724. It now displayed a stiffening racial reaction to manumission.[24] The code could no longer be described as a comparatively liberal regime in which an owner could free his slave for any or no reason at all ("*sans qu'ils soient tenus de rendre raison de leur affranchissement*") but instead one in which an owner must first obtain permission from the *Conseil Supérieur* to ensure that his motives were "legitimate."[25] New restrictions were placed on intermarriage, concubinage and miscegenation with slaves. Free whites could no longer marry a slave and thereby emancipate her and her children,[26] and no freed person was capable of receiving a donation from a white, whether by act *inter vivos* or *mortis causa*.[27]

There was also a changing deference toward owners on the question of provisioning slaves and slave economic freedoms. The 1724 Code gave no specifics about the food and clothing to be furnished to the slaves. The question was postponed until the advice of the local *Conseil Supérieur* could be received .[28] Also the provision of the 1685 Code prohibiting the vending of slave goods at public markets on Sundays and religious holidays was deleted

---

[24] In an *ordonnance* of 1713 the liberal powers of manumission under the *Code Noir* were cut back in the French islands and the change was incorporated in the 1724 code issued at New Orleans. Under the *ordonnance* an owner would require written permission from the Governor-General and Intendant to free his slave, thus requiring the necessity of stating a good reason for the emancipation, not merely natural feelings caused by blood connection. According to a legislative *Mèmoire* written in Guadeloupe, "Out of 100 enfranchisements 5 at most have a praiseworthy motive. The 95 others were given to favorite concubines and some of their children." Maurice Satineau, *Histoire de la Guadeloupe sous l'ancien regime* 315 (Paris: Payot, 1928). The Governor-General was prompted to write, "If we do not hold the line ... there will be four times the number of enfranchisements, because there is here great familiarity and freedom between masters and negresses 'qui sont bien faites.'" (my translation) Of course this was to be Louisiana's destiny as well. "In reality antebellum Louisiana was a three-tiered society." Judith Schafer, *Slavery, The Civil Law and the Supreme Court of Louisiana* (Baton Rouge: Louisiana State University Press, 1994), 20.

[25] *Cf.* Art. 55 (1685) with Art. 50 (1724).

[26] *Cf.* Art. 9 (1685) with Art. 6 (1724).

[27] Art. 52 (1724) This was part of the policy of restricting emancipations.

[28] Art. 18 (1724). *Cf* art 22 (1685).

from the 1724 version.[29] Already the intervening experience had shown that this commerce was too ingrained and important to be prohibited.

For the moment we will postpone following the customs and their relationship to the *Code Noir* from 1724–1768. These matters will be traced in detail in the next section.[30] It will suffice to note here that the customs relating to the use of the Sabbath, the cultivation of provision grounds, slave hiring out, the establishment of slave public markets, and so forth, sprang up quickly, perhaps within a matter of one or two decades from the introduction of the *Code Noir*. The foundations were already laid down by the time that Spain took control of the colony in 1768.

Spanish Interlude

Upon his arrival in Louisiana, General O'Reilly declared that France's *Code Noir* would continue in force, but this was a temporary decision. According to historians Henry Dart and Hans Baade, once the whole Spanish judicial system became operational, the *Code Noir* ceased to function and the law of Castile and of the Indies was enforced.[31]

From a formal or positive law standpoint, their view is well supported, but I have reservations regarding the true effect and scope of the repeal upon the non-statutory customs that existed outside of it. That subject merits further discussion and investigation.

The changeover to Spain's law of bondage in the area of manumissions is well documented. The numerous *cartas de libertad* in the notarial archives show that voluntary emancipations

---

[29] Art. 5 (1724). A 1751 Regulation of Police decreed by the Governor, the Marquis de Vaudreuil, has been left out of this discussion. This Regulation dealt in part with slavery but with little relevance to my subject. An abstract of it is found in the appendix of Charles Gayarré, *History of Louisiana,* Vol. II *The French Domination* (New Orleans: Gresham, 1879).

[30] *Infra* Section II.

[31] Henry P. Dart, "A Murder Case Tried in New Orleans in 1773," *L. H. Q.* 22 (1939) 623. Hans Baade, "The Law of Slavery in Spanish Louisiana, 1769–1803" in *Louisiana's Legal Heritage*, edited by Edward F. Haas (Pensacola: Perdido Bay Press, 1983), 43–86.

in the Spanish period were made on an unrestricted basis.[32] The *cartas* no longer complied with the requirement, mandated in the *Code Noir*, that voluntary manumissions had to be based on a finding of "legitimate cause" with the need for prior approval by the *Conseil Supérieur*. O'Reilly's abolition of the *Conseil Supérieur* had in fact rendered the requirement an impossibility. Another sign of the changeover was that slaves brought actions in court for involuntary freedom purchases (called *coartación*) against their masters.[33] Such actions were not permitted by the *Code Noir* and had not occurred during the French period. Only Spanish customary law furnished this means of manumission, and it marked a significant transfer of power to the slaves themselves and to the Spanish overlords.[34] Further, in Spanish *Luisiana* slaves had the right to be sold away from a cruel master, a right they did not have in French Louisiana.[35]

Nevertheless not all aspects of the Spanish slave law surface clearly enough in the records to assure they were actually in force. Without further corroboration it might be somewhat speculative to say that the totality of the *Code Noir* was replaced. There is the possibility that much of the French slave law may have simply continued to set the daily standard of plantation life, particularly the

---

[32] Ira Berlin writes that during the period 1769–1779 three hundred *cartas* were registered in New Orleans, which was many times the number issued during French rule. Ira Berlin, *Many Thousands Gone* (Cambridge: Harvard University Press, 1998), 212.

[33] *See* Re Negress Angelica, *Louisiana Historical Quarterly* 11 (March 1772): 37 (Caterall, 426); Blaquet v. Maney, *Louisiana Historical Quarterly* 9 (January 1773): 149 (Caterall, 426); Catalina v. Fazende and Boré, *Louisiana Historical Quarterly* 9 (June 1773): 556 (Caterall, 427); Maria Juana v. Suriray, *Louisiana Historical Quarterly* 11 February 28 (1776): 333 (Caterall, 432).

[34] James McGowan, 175–177. Manumission must have been easier during Spanish rule since the number of free persons increased dramatically. At the end of French rule, there were only one hundred and sixty five freed blacks, whereas by 1785, there were one thousand one hundred and seventy five free blacks out of some fifteen thousand slaves. Shaw, *supra* at 100. The *de facto* closing of the slave trade after 1731 and the resulting scarcity of slaves in the colony, however, was already sufficient reason to discourage manumission in the French period.

[35] The protection reappeared, in somewhat diluted form, in the American period. The Civil Code of 1808 said that where the master was convicted of cruel treatment of his slave, the slave was to be sold at public auction "in order to place him out of the reach of the power which his master has abused." Art. 27, p. 42 (1808).

customs that developed during the French period.[36] McGowan correctly points out that the Spanish accepted the custom of slaves' right to do extra work on Sundays. "Sunday was the slaves' day, not the Lord's, when the merits, either temporal or spiritual, were weighed in civil law."[37] The Spanish also accepted the customs on food and clothing and provision grounds and codified them in 1795.[38] They allowed the slave-operated public markets to stay open and viewed slave commerce as necessary to public subsistence.[39] It is not at all surprising that customs from the French period continued under Spanish slave law. As Professor Baade has pointed out in his penetrating study of marriage contracts, Spanish law did not always replace the ingrained habits of the French people of Louisiana.[40]

We come now to the mid-point of Spanish rule when the Cabildo decided to draft a new slave code. In 1778 it confided the task to two councillors, F.M. De Reggio and Joseph Ducros. The authors, like all the councillors on the Cabildo save one, were planters and slaveholders. Their intent, according to historian Gilbert Din, was "to restore to slaveholders the rights that Spanish law had taken from them."[41] Professor Baade believes that "Many of its 73 provisions reflect literally, or substantially, those of the French *Code Noir*, which obviously served as the model."[42] The

---

[36] For example in 1775 a plaintiff sought to apply the *Code Noir* provisions "ordered to be observed by . . . Count O'Reilly" with respect to the daily amount to be paid in hiring a slave. Chaperon v. Mrs. Dupard, *Louisiana Historical Quarterly*, 11 February 1775, 156 (Caterall, 432).

[37] James McGowan, *Creation of a Slave Society: Louisiana Plantation in the Eighteenth Century* (University of Rochester Doctoral Dissertation, 1976).

[38] *See* Carondelet's Decree of 1795, discussed below in the text accompanying notes 51–54.

[39] The phrase 'necessary to public subsistence' was used in the Cabildo's *projet* of the slave code of 1778–1779, Art.5.

[40] Hans Baade, "Marriage Contracts in French and Spanish Louisiana: A Study in "Notarial" Jurisprudence" *Tulane Law Review* 53 (1978): 1. *See also* my socio-political explanation for the "return" of French law at the end the Spanish period in *The Louisiana Civilian Experience* (Raleigh: Carolina Academic Press, 2005), 75–82.

[41] Din, *Spaniards, Planters, and Slaves: The Spanish Regulation of Slavery in Louisiana, 1763–1803* (College Station: Texas A&M, 1999), 76.

[42] Baade, *supra* at 65.

increased length of the *projet* over its model is mostly due to nineteen new articles regulating slave *marronage* and absenteeism.

The text was never put into effect.[43] It was circulated to the post commandants outside New Orleans and then debated and approved in an extraordinary session of the Cabildo. For reasons never convincingly explained, however, it was not sent to Madrid for the King's approval. Nevertheless it is a valuable link in our understanding of attitudes toward customs and regulatory approaches. In specifically targeting certain liberal Spanish practices for repeal and in reverting to the *Code Noir* as its model, the draft shows that Spanish law was unquestionably in force and its effects displeased the Louisiana plantocracy.[44] For present purposes I do not propose to discuss the text in detail except to highlight the dialectic with the customs.

The *Code Noir ou Loi Municipale Servant de Règlement*, as it was titled, took aim at various customs and practices, including some introduced by Spanish law. In a clear attack on *coartación*, the proposals prohibited manumissions without *judicial* approval, prevented notaries from writing letters of freedom and invalidated self-purchase.[45] It prohibited the practice of hiring out slaves "to themselves" because it was "*un abus*" which led slaves to steal or to prostitute themselves in order to pay the sums due to their master.[46] It forbade marriages between slaves from different plantations, thus attempting to suppress the Spanish law that allowed such marriages.[47] The *projet* required masters to give their

---

[43] This is the consensus view, but Thomas Ingersoll argues from circumstantial evidence that it did go into effect. *See* "Slave Codes and Judicial Practice in New Orleans, 1718–1807," *Law and History Review* 13 (1995): 53–54.

[44] For Thomas Ingersoll, it accurately reflects the inclinations of Louisiana slaveowners and the actual administration of justice.

[45] *Ibid.* The practice of leasing slaves to themselves meant that slaves paid the master a proportion of his earnings and retained the balance, perhaps until he had accumulated enough to purchase his freedom. The practice was considered widespread in New Orleans amongst masters of skilled slaves. John Kendall, "New Orleans' 'Peculiar Institution' " *Louisiana Historical Quarterly* 23 (1940): 864, 872.

[46] Art. 22.

[47] *Las Siete Partidas* stated that slaves could marry even when the master was opposed, whereas the *Code Noir* required the master's approval. *See* Part.4, Tit.5, Law I. In 1772, Governor Unzaga ordered that a marriage ceremony be performed

slaves exactly the quantity of foodstuffs each month "that the usages had determined since the origin of the colony" and prohibited substituting money payments *in lieu* thereof because it resulted in abuses. (Art. 12) The customary ownership by slaves of various animals, particularly horses, is treated as a new practice which needed to be controlled. Article 66 therefore provided:

> To avoid the abuse which has lately reigned among the Slaves, of having Horses belonging to them (*à eux appartenant*); which becomes for them a means to run about at night, to traffic in them, [. . .] it is expressly prohibited for Inhabitants to permit their Slaves to have Horses, Mares, Mules, and Cows. . . .

The next major development came in 1789 when Madrid presented the *projet* of an entirely new *Codigo Negro* to its Spanish capitals in the New World. The *Real Cédula* of 1789 received a hostile reaction almost everywhere and *Luisiana* was no exception. The substantive changes were numerous and, assuming they were enforced and not circumvented, would have curtailed or even suppressed the cluster of customs we have been following. Under its terms, as James McGowan notes, the material conditions of the slaves might have worsened. "The first article of the code denied slaves the right to work on Sundays for themselves and thus undermined their potential to earn sufficient money to free themselves."[48] The *Codigo* was in this respect a return to the model of dependency which the custom of Sunday labor had been continuously undermining. Spanish Governor Miró aptly noted that the slave's right to work on Sunday was a deeply-rooted Louisiana custom that his predecessors and judges had already recognized in *Luisiana*. Other parts of the *projet* would have also increased dependency in an attempt to ameliorate slave treatment. It was required that slaves in the field be separated by age, strength and ability to do hard work, and, in a gallant gesture, it was forbidden to use women as agricultural laborers. This would have also banned

---

between Vicente and Maria Francisca, though this was clearly opposed by Vicente's master. The governor wrote that "our laws allow it, and the King orders, in his most recent royal *cédulas* on the government of this province, that the *negro* can always follow his master and the *negra* hers." Gilbert Din, *Spaniards, Plantations, and Slaves* 57 (1999).

[48] James McGowan, *Creation of a Slave Society: Louisiana Plantations in the Eighteenth Century* (University of Rochester Doctoral Dissertation, 1976) 279.

or reduced female labor in the gardens and provision grounds and thus would have considerably reduced the foodstuffs available for family consumption and/or resale. It also required the presence of chaplains on all plantations for the religious education of slaves, forbade couples from living together unless married in the church, and opened up courts to receive complaints of injustice. "All in all," Jerah Johnson concludes, "it aimed at reducing slaves to a completely dependent caste."[49]

In a petition to the King the planters remonstrated against the *projet,* pleading that the regulations would entail great inconvenience and expense.[50] In a significant display of their local power, the Cabildo planters carried the day and the *Codigo* was never implemented in *Luisiana.*

The final change in the law during Spanish rule came when Governor Carondelet issued a Decree establishing a new set of slavery regulations. The importance of the Decree of June 1, 1795[51] was to give a legislative foundation to the operative customs on slave labor on Sundays, the assignment of provision grounds, the scope of food and clothing rations and more. The Decree is a conservative document that essentially capitulates to deeply-established local practices. In stark contrast to Madrid's desire to halt slave labor on Sunday, the Decree pronounced that "Every Sunday is their [the slave's] own day, but when the crops or other business require it, their masters have a right to make them work on Sundays, paying them four rials per day for the days work."[52] This now codified the custom to which Governor Miró adverted a few years before. Next, the Decree gave official blessing to the system of slave self-provisioning by affirmatively urging masters to assign fields to their slaves for their own cultivation and use.[53] The model

---

[49] Jerah Johnson, *Congo Square in New Orleans* (New Orleans: La. Landmarks Soc. 1995), 17.

[50] The remonstrations by the planters are set forth in Jo Ann Carrigan, "The Spanish Domination and the Cession to the United States, 1969–1803" in *Fortier's History of Louisiana* (1972), 384–386.

[51] Library of Congress, Louisiana Papers, AC 1333. A translated version of the Decree is found in *Louisiana Historical Quarterly* 593–604.

[52] *Ibid.*, 601.

[53] "The Syndics shall persuade the Inhabitants of their District to assign Fields to their slaves, for their own cultivation, and to their use, which will not only put

of dependency in the old *Code Noir* was thus legislatively overthrown. Interestingly, it now set forth the Louisiana custom on food rations and specifically stated that this customary amount was insufficient. It provided that a slave should receive "the barrel of Indian corn per month that is *by the custom of the Colony* his allowance, *for the insufficiency of which,* most masters do voluntarily make up." (emphasis added). Here was statutory admission that the "provision ground system" had become a trade-off for the owners' failure to provide a sufficient amount of food. The same trade-off was recognized with respect to the duty to clothe slaves: "Slaves *who have not fields of their own in cultivation*, shall receive punctually, one Shirt and Trousers, of Linen, for the Summer, one Blanket Capot, and a pair of woolen Trousers for the Winter."(emphasis added).[54] Thus what had heretofore been only a matter of custom was now hardened into Decree: The slave who had a field to cultivate must clothe herself or himself. By converting these customs into black-letter regulations, Carondelet's Decree provided the source for parallel articles in the Black Code of 1806.

Twenty Days of French Rule

As Spanish rule came to an end, France took possession of Louisiana shortly before it was sold to the United States in 1803. The colonial prefect, Pierre Clément de Laussat, was vigorously lobbied by slaveholder interests to reinstate the *Code Noir*. There was still a strong preference for that law and there were continuing objections to Spanish law and custom which even enforced the slave's right of self-purchase. De Laussat acceded to the request and formally exhumed the *Code Noir* in the waning days of his administration.[55] It appears, however, that his last-minute order was

---

them more at their ease, but also increase the mass of the productions of the province, and advantageously employ the time they might otherwise spend in riot and debauchery." *Ibid.*, 601. The Decree also stated, perhaps with an eye to limiting customary rights to possess property, that "No Slave shall be permitted to sell any thing without the permission of his master, not even the production of their own Fields, . . . No slave is permitted to possess a Horse of his own."

[54] *Ibid.*, 601.

[55] Baade, *supra* 71–72. According to De Laussat's memoirs, "the members of the local government tormented me to sanction yet one more decree relative to the

ignored and did not resuscitate the *Code Noir*. Spanish slave law continued in force without interruption at least until 1806 when the territorial legislature enacted a new slave code and slave criminal code. In the following year it enacted a special law on manumission, and in 1808 the legislature passed the Digest of the Territory of Orleans, a civil code that contained many slavery provisions.

American Sequel

The form of the slave laws changed considerably in the American period. The Black Code enacted by the Territorial Legislature in 1806 was a shorter document and did not purport to deal with all subjects. It contained no provisions about manumission, nor did it mention civil disqualifications and slave crimes. Crimes were separately dealt with in a companion law passed in the same session, and manumission was the subject of a special statute in 1807.[56] This last statute abolished the custom of *coartación* by declaring that no person shall be compelled, either directly or indirectly, to emancipate his or her slave and required an owner to obtain judicial authorization for any emancipation.[57] Then in 1808 Louisiana's first Civil Code, properly called the Digest of the Territory of Orleans, accepted the subject of slavery into the civil law itself. The treatment consisted of about forty-five articles stretching across the three books of the Code.[58] This fairly

---

regulation of the Negroes. . . . They came back to the charge several times. I kept refusing on the grounds that this was on the eve of my laying down my ephemeral power. Finally, I gave in." *Ibid.* Interestingly, his *arrêté* of 17 Dec 1803 was careful not to exhume all of the *Code Noir*. He excepted provisions establishing Catholicism as the exclusive religion for slaves and free persons, on the ground that it was contrary to the Constitution of the United States.

[56] Acts of the Second Session of the First Legislature of the Territory of Orleans, Chap. X, 82–86, March 9, 1807.

[57] Sections 2, 3 (1807). *Coartación* was also suppressed by the Civil Code of 1808, Art. 27, p. 42, quoted below, note 58.

[58] For greater detail, see Chapter 3, at note 73 and ff. By way of partial summary, Book One, the law of Persons, defined the condition of slavery and differentiated the condition of manumitted and naturally free persons. Arts. 13, 14, 15, p. 10. In this definition, "A slave is one who is in the power of a master and who belongs to him in such manner, that the master may sell him, dispose of his person, his industry and his labor, and who can do nothing, possess nothing, nor acquire any

extensive treatment broke with the French tradition that had kept slavery outside of the civil law. Nevertheless it was entirely consistent with the Spanish tradition where the corpus of slave law had long been found in Siete Partidas. The decision to include such provisions in 1808 established a precedent that was followed in 1825.

The Black Code was a genuine mixture of the European slave laws and the new American influences pressing upon Louisiana. It resurrected some provisions from the old *Code Noir.*[59] It retained key Spanish rules.[60] It also contained a number of American-inspired articles. This was the first slave code that the inhabitants of Louisiana created and enacted for themselves, in contrast to the codes imposed on them by France or Spain. As a result, three national influences—Spanish, French and American—were quite evident in the same legislation. Louisiana slave law was now a product of its antecedents and its American surroundings.

The Black Code and the Civil Codes clearly reflect the influence of the customs both as a source and a target of legislation. In keeping with Carondelet's Decree of 1795, the custom allowing slaves to work for themselves or to hire themselves out on Sunday was codified. Slaves were entitled to "the free enjoyment of

---

thing, but what must belong to his master." The Civil Code recognized slave marriage with the master's consent but declared such marriage produced no civil effects. Art. 23 p. 40. It prohibited marriage between slaves and free persons, Art 8, p.24, listed the slave's various incapacities, Arts. 17, 18 p. 40, and stated the rule that children inherit the condition of their mother, Art. 24 p. 40. It said that a master may manumit his slave but only in the form required by special laws, Art 25 p. 40, and in an obvious attempt to suppress involuntary manumission or *coartacion*, it declared that "No master of slaves shall be compelled either directly or indirectly to enfranchise any of them [. . .]" Art. 27 p. 42. Book Two, the law of Property, established that slaves are immovables by operation of law, Art 19 p. 99, and by right of accession, slave children are the property of the mother's owner. Art. 19 p. 99. Book Three declared that slaves are incapable of receiving donations and transmitting successions, Art. 64 p. 159, Art. 5 p. 209, cannot witness a will or enter into contracts, Art. 105 p. 232 and Art. 23 p. 265. Masters are responsible for a slave's delicts, Art. 21 p. 323, and the redhibitory action applies to the sale of slaves, Art. 79 p. 358, Art. 80 p. 358.

[59] For example the rule that the master is not discharged from his duty to feed the slaves by permitting them to work certain days of the week for their own account was taken verbatim from the old *Code Noir*. The rule had not been repeated in any statute or draft since 1724.

[60] Such as article 10 declaring that slaves are real estate and subject to mortgage and to be seized and sold as real estate. Most important for the future, Spanish principles would remain the background to fill the lacunae and interpretative gaps in this and other slave statutes.

Sundays" and if a slave were required to work on that day, a fixed wage of fifty cents had to be paid.[61] The customs as to food rations and clothing to be furnished were also codified, as in Carondelet's Decree, and again it took the form of a trade-off between the benefits of the provision ground system for slaves and the owner's reduced obligation toward them. The owner was obligated to furnish clothing only to slaves "who have no lot of ground on owner's property to cultivate on their own account …"[62] Section 7 stipulated that the hours of work and rest in the field followed "the old usages" which it then proceeded to codify.

A novel feature were the provisions attempting to control slave property. Section 38 of the Black Code flatly said that slaves were not permitted to buy, sell, or trade goods of any kind, and it made no distinction whether the goods being sold were the master's or their own. On its face this prohibition had no exception even for slaves who had their master's permission to sell his or their goods. We know, however, that such trading was an everyday occurrence in the markets and the prohibition was disregarded. Apparently trading was customarily allowed under the simple guise that the slave had obtained his master's permission. This fiction provided legal cover, at least in the French period when the old *Code Noir* permitted slaves to engage in market activities *with the master's permission*.[63] Remarkably, however, the slave markets continued to

---

[61] Sec. 1, La. Act of June 7, 1806. This Act is conveniently found in the General Digest of the Acts of the Legislature, 1804–1827, Vol. I (1828) compiled by L. Moreau Lislet. The Legislature, however, restricted this rule to the plantation setting. Slaves employed as servants, carriage drivers, and hospital workers were not covered.

[62] *Ibid.*, Sections 2–3.

[63] Jerah Johnson describes how this fiction operated at Congo Square during the French period: "Throughout the French period the market activities of slaves remained in legal limbo. The *Code Noir* expressly forbade slaves to do any kind of work on Sundays and holy days, to own any kind of property, to conduct any kind of trade on their own account . . . without written permission. On the other hand the slave entrepreneurs provided much needed supplies to a city frequently . . . short of foodstuffs. *The solution was for the authorities simply to do nothing and say nothing, and "assume" that the slave vendors were selling goods for their masters, and with permission.* Hence the absence of any official mention of the market is not surprising." Johnson, *supra* note 49 at 13 (my emphasis). See also Freddi Williams Evans, *Congo Square: African Roots in New Orleans* (Lafayette: University of Louisiana at Lafayette Press 2011), 109 ff.

operate in the American period in the face of a prohibition that no longer recognized a master's right to give such permission, fictional or otherwise. This provision also prohibited slaves from owning horses, mares or horned cattle, "under the penalty of forfeiting the whole" and having the animals sold at public auction. Again the effectiveness of the proscription may have been nil. Another provision stated that, "As the person of a slave belongs to his master, no slave can possess any thing in his own right, or dispose, in any way, of the produce of his industry, without the consent of his master." This effectively restates the concept of *peculium* which the first and second *Code Noirs* already allowed, and arguably seeks to bolster the master's right to control the produce of the slave's free time. Nevertheless the customary claims to slave property were not likely to be called back through recourse to the master's authority since such claims were completely compatible with the *peculium* and the fiction of permission. The drafters of the 1825 Civil Code expressly cited this custom as a reason to adopt a provision authorizing slaves to have a *peculium*.[64] They stated in their *exposé des motifs*: "What is here proposed is by no means new. The Roman law contains similar dispositions; *and we here are in the habit* [*déjà dans l'usage*] *of permitting our slaves to enjoy what they acquire by their industry*." (my emphasis). Thus the *peculium*, far from depriving slaves of the right to hold property, seems to have been a perfect camouflage for the recognition of existing custom.[65]

---

[64] "All that a slave possesses belongs to his master; he possesses nothing of his own, except his peculium, that is to say, the sum of money or moveable estate which his master chooses he should possess." *Projet of the Civil Code of Louisiana of 1825*, Louisiana Legal Archives, Vol. I (New Orleans: 1937), 14.

[65] Professor Baade reads the *Code Noir* (1724) and the later Black Code (1806) as depriving slaves of the capacity to own property without the consent of their masters, and asserts this was in contrast with the freedom enjoyed during Spanish rule. "The Law of Slavery in Spanish Luisiana 1769–1803" in *Louisiana's Legal Heritage*, edited by Edward F. Haas (Pensacola: Perdido Bay Press, 1983), 72, 74–75. For my criticism of this view, *see infra*, section III. His view has been followed by Judith Shafer *Slavery, the Civil Law, and the Supreme Court of Louisiana* (Baton Rouge: Louisiana State University Press, 1994), 6. I disagree to the extent that the learned authors seem to ignore the French custom and the French understanding of *peculium*.

Interim Conclusion

This short overview has illustrated the dialectical interaction between a cluster of customs and subsequent reactions by the lawmaker. Sometimes the decision was to institute a ban and at other times it was to codify these customs. In either event there was a recognition of custom at the legislative level. Even in this limited survey I have noted at least fifteen instances of this recognition. Undoubtedly many more may await discovery.

In the following section we may observe the process by which the customs took root and undermined various provisions in the *Code Noir*.

THE UNINTENDED CONSEQUENCES OF REST ON THE SABBATH

By far the most consequential of the provisions on religion in the *Code Noir* (1685 and 1724) turned out to be the exemption of slaves from Sunday labor. This exemption, or rather the perversion of it, proved to be a path of opportunity, a source of free time, a means to acquire cash or food, and for some slaves, an avenue to manumission. It was a striking instance of customary law development.

The fifth article of the *Code Noir* enjoined every subject, slave and non-slave alike, to observe Sundays and holy days by not working, nor requiring others to work. The cultivation of land and all other works ("*tous autres oeuvres*") was forbidden. Any slaves "surprised" in Sunday labor were to be confiscated.[66]

This day of rest ("from midnight to midnight"), however, soon meant something different than that which the Crown or the Church had intended. Sunday repose took on the unanticipated meaning of freedom from the master's work. It would not ban a slave's

---

[66] There were of course biblical underpinnings: Exodus 20 ". . . the seventh day is a Sabbath to the Lord your God; you shall not do any work—you, your son or daughter, *your male or female slave*, your livestock, or the alien resident in your towns."

Musician and dancers at Congo Square, New Orleans

voluntary labor for his own food or profit. Instead of a day of repose or religious observance, Sunday became a day when slaves could labor for themselves such as by tending to their own planting, by hiring themselves out to other plantation owners to obtain cash, or buying and bartering goods at slave markets in town. The new sense of *rest* also had a tendency to impinge upon what the *Code* said on the subjects of property, capacity, and manumission. Though the *Code* stated that slaves could not own property other than what their masters might permit them to have,[67] the exemption on the Sabbath now furnished the occasion to acquire property which the master had no right to touch. The customary practice included the slave's right to keep all revenues and fruits produced by this free-time activity.

[67] *Code Noir*, Art. XXIII.

It is not possible to identify the moment that this practice took root in Louisiana, except to say that it occurred perhaps as early as the 1730's or 1740's and certainly no later than the 1750's. Le Page du Pratz, who lived in Louisiana from 1718–1734, advocated giving slaves land to farm and for owners to buy their products at an equitable price. He urged that, "It would be better that they do that on Sundays, when they are not Christians, than to do nothing."[68] Jean-Francois Dumont de Montigny who came to New Orleans from Quebec in 1719 and in 1759 published his observations, sketched the outline of this system in his travel memoirs.[69] Probably the formation of the famous slave market at New Orleans in the 1740's or 1750's (the actual date is obscure) is an indication that the provisioning system was already operating in that region and was producing significant food surpluses that were consumed in New Orleans. According to Jerah Johnson, this market was a significant feature of New Orleans' mercantile life and provided "much needed supplies to a city frequently, if not chronically, short of foodstuffs."[70]

The growth of work on Sunday was undoubtedly assisted by the absence of effective enforcement of the religious provisions of the *Code Noir*. The *Code* designated the Catholic religion as the exclusive faith for master and slave. It provided that all slaves were to be instructed and baptized in this faith upon arrival.[71] Slave marriages were to be monogamous and would be solemnized according to Catholic rites.[72] They were to be allowed Sunday observance and were not to be worked on the Sabbath.[73] Overseers

---

[68] Antoine Simone Le Page du Pratz, *Histoire de la Louisiane*, Vol. I, 352, (Paris: De Bure, 1758).

[69] Dumont observed, "Most of the slaves clear grounds and cultivate them on their own account, raising cotton, tobacco, &c. which they sell. Some [masters] give their negroes Saturday and Sunday to themselves, and during that time the master does not give them any food; they then work for other Frenchmen who have no slaves, and who pay them. Those who live in or near the capital generally turn their two hours at noon to account by making faggots to sell in the city; others sell ashes, or fruits that are in season." *Mémoires Historiques sur la Louisiane* (Paris 1753) as quoted in Jerah Johnson, *supra* note 49 at 7.

[70] Johnson, 12–13.

[71] *Code Noir*, Art. II.

[72] *Code Noir*, Art. VII.

[73] *Code Noir*, Art. V.

appointed by the master must be Roman Catholic,[74] and religious services by other churches were expressly prohibited. At death, any baptized slave should be properly buried *en terre sainte*.[75]

Enforcement of these provisions placed heavy responsibility on the Church, but the Church in Louisiana was relatively weak and understaffed. Only five Capuchin priests were present in Lower Louisiana in 1725—three in New Orleans and only two more for the rest of the territory.[76] Over the decade 1720–1730 only nineteen priests served for any period of time within the geographic area. Father Raphael, the first head of the Capuchins, observed with an air of helpless resignation that masters were already working their slaves on Sundays and feast days, in violation of the *Code Noir*. He pleaded in his own defense that the distance of the plantations from the missions and the lack of boats to reach them made it impossible to prevent these abuses. Of course slaves could not be forced to go to church on Sunday (on reasons both of principle and logistics, the nearest church perhaps being ten miles away) and needed no permission to engage in Sunday jobbing or personal work. According to Church historian Roger Baudier, plantation owners were theoretically accountable to the laws on religious instruction, baptism and marriage within the church, but sanctions "were never applied…and the only weapons priests had…was the continued barrage of letters to the Superior Council or to the official in charge of religious affairs for the colony."[77] While denying that the church neglected the spiritual needs of slaves, Baudier conceded that efforts were hampered by the scarcity of qualified teachers, preachers, and ministers, all of which prevented any outstanding

---

[74] *Code Noir*, Art. V.

[75] There is one report of a violation of this provision. Father Mathias, the Curé of New Orleans, and Vicar-General, on learning that a baptized slave girl belonging to the Treasurer-General of New Orleans, had died and been interred in the garden of her owner, filed a formal complaint with the *Conseil Supérieur*. The complaint was founded upon Article XIV of the *Code Noir* which required baptized slaves to be buried in consecrated cemeteries. The *Conseil* fined the Treasurer-General thirty *livres* and ordered that the body be exhumed and reinterred in the cemetery according to the rites of the Church. Vicar-General v. Treasurer-General, *Louisiana Historical Quarterly* 38: 11.

[76] Baudier, *The Catholic Church in Louisiana* (New Orleans: Louisiana Library Association, 1939), 77.

[77] *Ibid.* 140.

evangelization of the negroes.[78] Joe Gray Taylor concludes that most slaves in Louisiana received only a "superficial" degree of religious instruction.[79] The mere veneer of their Catholicism may partly explain why slaves responded so enthusiastically to the Protestant missionaries when they arrived in the 19th century.

Lax enforcement of the Code began early and has been noted by many historians.[80] In a perceptive account Jo Ann Carrigan writes:

> The Catholic Church in Louisiana, always relatively weak in the colonial period, could do little but protest about the treatment of slaves. Occasionally the Spanish governors attempted to force masters to fulfill their obligations. But Spain's tenuous hold on Louisiana required that concessions be made to maintain the support of the wealthy, influential creoles; and their judgments on slavery usually prevailed.[81]

She poses the enforcement problem in terms of the balance of forces—Crown and Church were arrayed against slaveowners and their customs. In her account the discrepancy between the laws and their enforcement resulted from the comparative weakness of the

---

[78] *Ibid.* 128.

[79] Joe Gray Taylor, Negro Slavery in Louisiana (Louisiana: Louisiana Historical Association, 1963), 234. Mary Veronica Miceli credits the Capuchins with devoting considerable attention to slaves, "baptizing thousands." As to reported neglect of religious instruction, she writes, "Despite these complaints, a solid foundation of Catholicism ...had been laid." *The Influence of the Roman Catholic Church on Slavery in Colonial Louisiana under French Domination, 1718–1763* (Tulane University Doctoral Dissertation, 1979), 57. The church registers in fact record many baptisms of slaves, but relatively few marriages. Baudier, *supra* 126–127. The infrequency of slave marriages in the Spanish era, according to Gilbert Din, is explained by the attitude of the planters who preferred to buy and sell black male laborers individually, not in families. Din, *Spaniards, Planters, and Slaves: The Spanish Regulation of Slavery in Louisiana 1763–1803* (College Station: Texas A&M, 1999), 127.

[80] *See* Carl A. Brasseaux, "The Administration of Slave Regulations in French Louisiana, 1724–1766," *Louisiana History* 21: 139. Brasseaux argues that the French Attorney Generals practiced selective enforcement of slavery regulations because of their view that slavery was subject to "two governments", that of public authority and that of domestic authority. This led the Attorney Generals to make concessions to local mores and to ignore code articles which undermined the owner's authority.

[81] Carrigan *supra*, 380.

metropolitan powers *vis-à-vis* planters who ignored the law and followed their customs:

> The basic slave system as it evolved during the French period persisted despite the efforts of Spanish Church and Crown to modify and ameliorate customary practices [. . .] the *Code Noir* had seldom been enforced in French Louisiana. Whenever the Spanish government or the Church sought compliance with its provisions, fierce protests arose from the inhabitants. Louisianians repeatedly referred to their customs and traditions which obviously had become a way of life during those decades when the Code had been ignored. [82]

However since the customs were created in part by the slaves themselves, the triumph of a practice in the face of the code signifies something more than merely the strength of planters or the weakness of government and church. The customs were the emanations of a deeper struggle involving the strength of slaves.

Some are inclined to argue that the planters essentially willed Sunday to their slaves, as if they had made a gift. In my view this misunderstands what actually occurred. The slaves "owned" their rest on Sunday as a matter of law. It was not so much the master's to give as it was to try to subvert through incentives. This would have worked only if the incentives, on balance, were seen by slaves as being in their self-interest. In that regard there was a near-perfect alignment of their respective interests and, rather remarkably, it led to no recorded objections by church or state authorities. It might be a fair statement to say that slaves and owners appropriated Sunday for their mutual material interests.

Only a few years into the Spanish period, the custom permitting slaves to labor for themselves on Sunday (and the inability of masters to interfere with this freedom) was judicially recognized. The decision makes clear that customs sufficiently established in the French period were fully accepted by the Spanish. The case of *Loppinot v. Villeneuve* (1774)[83] is one of the few instances in which a slave custom was judicially tested and

---

[82] *Ibid.*

[83] *See* Laura Porteous, "Civil Procedure in Louisiana under the Spanish Regime as Illustrated in Loppinot's Case, 1774," *Louisiana Historical Quarterly* XII (1929): 33–120. The whole set of documents related to this case is translated into English.

recognized as having the force of law. The planter Villeneuve had hired Mulet, a slave from an adjoining plantation owned by Loppinot, to build a chimney for him on Sunday. Mulet was a highly skilled laborer who worked for wages or in-kind remunerations. After the work on Sunday was completed, Villeneuve paid him, gave him a drink of brandy, and Mulet departed.

In returning home that evening, Mulet drowned while crossing the river, and Loppinot sought to hold Villeneuve responsible for his death. According to him, the slave had been hired without his written permission and became intoxicated from the brandy. Villeneuve answered, "In this Colony it is known that a Negro may, at his free will, dispose of all day Sunday so as to make provisions for himself . . ., and to gain the wherewithal to 'clothe himself.'"[84] The testimony of other planters was introduced into the record to prove and confirm the custom's existence. One witness stated:

> It is because the slaves are not clothed that they are left free of all work on Sunday. On such days some of them go to the neighbors' plantations who hire them to cut moss and to gather provisions. This is done with the tacit consent of their masters who do not know the where-abouts of their slaves on the said day, nor do they question them, nor do they worry themselves about them and are always satisfied that the negroes will appear again on the following Monday for work.

Even an opponent of the practice testified that the "abuse is tolerated because from time immemorial, with the general consent of the masters and connivance of the Superiors, slaves have labored without interruption in the presence of, and with the knowledge and consent of Magistrates."[85] Mazange, representing Villeneuve, argued that in such circumstances the rules of property law had no

---

[84] *Ibid.*, 56. Villeneuve also pointed out that when Mulet crossed the river he was pursuing his own ends. He was not returning home because "my plantation and his master's are on the same side and he did not have to cross." He compared his death to a thunderbolt or some other accidental cause. *Ibid.*, 105.

[85] Quoted from Ira Berlin, *Many Thousands Gone: The First Two Centuries of Slavery in North America* (Cambridge: Harvard University Press, 1998), 202, note 17.

bearing and that being a Sunday, Mulet, like any other slave, was essentially a free agent.[86]

Governor Unzaga, sitting as a single judge, ruled in Villeneuve's favor and Loppinot appealed to the Cabildo where a three-judge panel overruled the Governor. The case was next referred to Havana for learned advice by an assessor. Don Manuel de Urrutia advised that the custom of the colony permitting slaves to work on Sunday with their master's tacit consent was sufficiently proven, but even if no such custom existed, "there is no law nor reason that obligates anyone to answer for a purely accidental and involuntary case such as Mulet's death. At any rate only in the event that he should have perished through [Villeneuve's] fault or fraud would he be responsible for the loss." Urrutia said that fault had not been proven. The giving of one drink of brandy to a slave was only a common courtesy and not considered culpable.[87] On the basis of this advice, the Cabildo ruled in Villeneuve's favor. Loppinot was condemned to pay all costs, which incidentally exceeded the amount he originally sought to recover for the loss of his slave.

The custom recognized in Loppinot's case persisted throughout the Spanish period and into the American era. Frederick Olmstead observed "Sunday jobbing" in Louisiana during his 1852–1853 voyage through the South and noted that proprietors were in the habit of making use of the slaves of the neighborhood, paying them sometimes seventy-five cents a day.[88] The custom was not confined to the plantation. It applied to slaves who worked in the cities or found employment along the river. Those hired to work on steamboats or as stevedores were usually required to work seven days per week, and so it was recognized that "as by law the slave was to have Sunday to himself to earn what he could, the master

---

[86] On this contention, *see* Jerah Johnson, *supra* note 49 at 8.

[87] The Louisiana Supreme Court followed this same principle in interpreting the custom. If a slave died during Sunday work due to the fault and misconduct of the party hiring him, the latter was liable to the owner. Niblett v. White's Heirs, 7 La. 253 775 (La. 1834).

[88] Frederick Law Olmstead, *The Cotton Kingdom* (New York: Modern Library, 1984), 323.

who hired him on the river was supposed to give him one-seventh of the wages earned [. . .]"[89] Historian Thomas Buchanan writes that:

> Just as slaves in other industries bargained for compensation for Sunday work, river workers extracted money for work on their customary day of rest. Steamboat slaves received Sunday wages either from boat officers during the voyage or from their masters after the boat returned.[90]

Olmstead witnessed officers paying slaves a dollar each time they worked Sundays on board, with some slaves receiving "according to custom" higher sums.[91] As seen earlier in Loppinot's case, the principle was that the slave's time and his wages belonged solely to him, so that if he were accidentally to die during this labor, the loss was borne by the slave and his owner, not his hirer. In a similar case arising in 1836,[92] a steamboat stopped at a plantation landing on a Sunday, and engaged the services of a slave to help supply the boat with wood. The slave accidentally died when he came in contact with the flywheel of the boat's engine, apparently without fault on the part of the crew or captain. The slaveowner's suit to recover his value from the steamboat owners was rejected by the Supreme Court, for it was presumed from the circumstances of Sunday labor that the slave had his master's permission to hire himself out. The court stated that:

> The *day* on which the services are rendered is thought to authorize [the work]. According to [...] law, slaves are entitled to the produce of their labor on Sunday; even the master is bound to remunerate them, if he employs them. He, therefore, who [...] on that day [...] does not retain them on his plantation, impliedly permits them to earn money by their labor. [original emphasis]

---

[89] V. Alton Moody, "Slavery on Louisiana Sugar Plantations" (1924) 62, *reprinted from Louisiana Historical Quarterly*, April 1924.

[90] Thomas Buchanan, *Black Life on the Mississippi* (Chapel Hill: The University of North Carolina Press, 2004), 92.

[91] *Ibid.* Other sources of personal income for slaves came from passenger tipping and produce trading wherein slaves benefited from an "ancient marine custom" which allowed boat workers to transport without paying shipping fees a limited amount of their own produce to urban markets along the river. *Ibid.*, 93–94.

[92] Rice v. Cade *et al.* 10 La. 288 (1836).

PROVISION GROUNDS, SLAVE PROPERTY AND THE LOUISIANA ECONOMY

Professor Hans Baade argues that French law, unlike Spanish law, did not permit slaves to acquire property of their own. He believes this explains why the right of self-purchase did not develop during the French domination as it did under Spanish rule.[93] This assertion, however, seems to be a strained reading of the *Code Noir* and it also overlooks the evolution of the customary rights to property discussed above. It is difficult to follow his assertion that the *peculium* was "precluded by inference" under the *Code*,[94] for in fact the slave's *peculium* is mentioned twice in Article XXIII as a permissible form of property that masters could allow their bondsmen. *Peculium* in the *Code Noir* was the same Roman notion found in the *Siete Partidas*.[95] Incidentally, the *Partidas* never admitted that a slave's *peculium* was actually his *de jure,* but insisted instead that "Everything acquired by a slave in whatever manner it may be, will belong to his master."[96] Thus in both systems the derivative ownership designated as *peculium*, which rested solely upon the master's defeasible consent, needed to evolve if it were to result in a slave's "right" to his own property. This evolution, I have argued, occurred first under French rule and continued under the Spanish domination.

---

[93] *See* Hans Baade, "The Law of Slavery in Spanish Louisiana 1769–1803" in *Louisiana's Legal Heritage*, edited by Edward F. Haas (Pensacola: Perdido Bay Press, 1983), 50.

[94] *Ibid.*, 50.

[95] *See* Part. III.5.5 and Part. III.29.13. This is shown by Moreau Lislet's references to Justinian's *Digest* for provisions on *peculium* in the Civil Codes of 1808 and 1825. In the de la Vergne manuscript he refers directly to the Rodriguez translation of the Digest as the source of the provision. In the Louisiana Code of 1825 the authors again embraced the *peculium* in a clear text: "All that a slave possesses belongs to his master; he possesses nothing of his own, except his peculium, that is to say, the sum of money or moveable estate which his master chooses he should possess." Projet of the Civil Code of 1825, p. 14 (La. Leg. Archives 1937). In giving the source for this provision the drafters cited both Roman law and the usages of Louisiana. One therefore finds little justification for the claim that the *peculium* of the Roman-Spanish tradition gave the slave a different property right than that given in the Roman-French tradition. The sources are basically the same.

[96] Part. IV, 21.7.

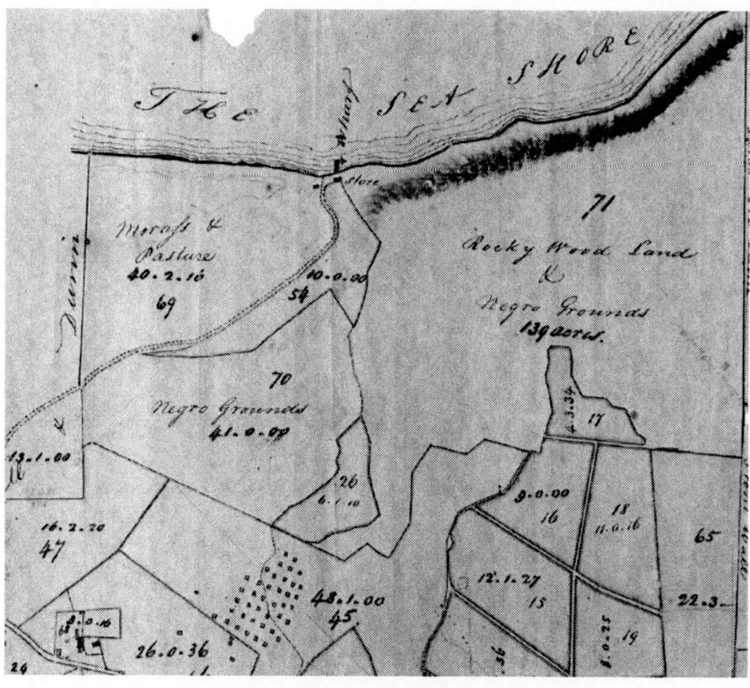

Sketch of plantation showing "Negro Grounds"

As already seen, Sunday labor for the slave's personal account developed *contra legem* into a right to work and to keep the proceeds, as an offset against the master's obligation to provision the slaves adequately.[97] It was a widespread practice to allocate land called "provision grounds" to the slaves so that they might grow crops of rice, corn, and beans for their own sustenance. Slaves received land on the fringes of plantations, within walking distance and accessible during midday breaks and Saturday or Sunday free time.[98] What was not internally consumed on plantations could be sold or bartered in markets or sold to itinerant peddlers. Thus as growers of cash crops, poultry and animals, and indeed as woodcutters, brick makers, coopers, carpenters, and

---

[97] As mentioned earlier, *supra* note 69, the system was already described in Dumont's *Mémoires Historiques sur la Louisiane* (Paris: Bauche, 1753), Vol. II, 15.
[98] McGowan, 141.

blacksmiths in their free time, slaves certainly played a proprietary role in the internal economy of the plantations. They also participated in the economy external to the plantation by selling their cash crops of corn, molasses, moss, and fresh produce on the market.[99] A legal formalist might argue that these sorts of property simply gave new content to the meaning of *peculium* under the *Code Noir*. It is clear, however, that the two are not necessarily linked. The customs would have developed even if the concept of *peculium* were not planted in the law.[100] Such property rights evolved independently of the master's will and went beyond the parameters of that institution.

Studies of the internal economy of Louisiana sugar plantations show various ways in which slaves acquired wealth and improved their lives.[101] They possessed kitchen gardens in which they grew fruits and vegetables, and they typically raised pigs and poultry in the environs of their cabins. As mentioned before, they also were given more extensive allotments elsewhere on the plantation where they generally cultivated cash crops, such as pumpkins, potatoes, hay, and most importantly, corn. (In addition an important traffic in stolen goods contributed to the economic role which slaves played.) By whatever means, enterprising slaves entrenched themselves as producers and consumers within the economy. By the end of the French period slaves had established and operated Sunday markets at the edge of the city of New Orleans to receive and exchange

---

[99] McDonald, 71–72; McGowan, *supra*, at 141. On the circulation of cash among slaves, *see* Larry E. Hudson Jr., "'All That Cash': Work and Status in the Slave Quarters" 77–94 in Larry E. Hudson Jr. (Ed.) *Working toward Freedom: Slave Society and Domestic Economy in the American South* (Rochester: University of Rochester Press, 1994).

[100] As Philip Schwarz points out, a slaveholder like Thomas Jefferson conceded the distinction between his own property and that belonging to his slaves, even without the promptings of Roman law. In a letter in 1778 he stated, "I have ever found it necessary to confine them to such articles as are not raised on the farm. There is no other way of drawing a line between what is theirs and mine." *Supra* note 1 at 46.

[101] Roderick McDonald, *The Economy and Material Culture of Slaves* (Baton Rouge: Louisiana State University Press, 1993); V. Alton Moody, *Slavery on Louisiana Sugar Plantations* (University of Michigan Doctoral Dissertation, 1924).

products and services.[102] Benjamin Latrobe observed that the role of the slave-run markets in provisioning New Orleans was so great that he believed "the city would starve" without them. Trade was reciprocal with the free population. The Cabildo facilitated commerce between the slaves and New Orleans merchants by permitting tradesmen to open their stores on Sundays and holy days, before and after mass, since slaves had no other opportunity to acquire what they needed.[103] As sellers and buyers, slaves were essential actors in the market system. Implicit in this commercial exchange was the community's understanding that the fruit of free-time work actually belonged to the slaves. To this extent they had earned a certain degree of independence within a matrix of dependency relationships. "As managers of their own time and resources, they functioned as self-directed individuals controlling their resources of time, land, and labor to make life more tolerable within the limits of their condition."[104] They decided which crops to plant, how to raise them, how to distribute their time, when to sell, and what to purchase with the proceeds:"the sorts of decisions," writes Roderick McDonald, "not normally associated with an enslaved people whose very being was defined in law by reference to an owner."[105]

Since a slave's free time was his personal currency, it may be asked how much free time a slave might carve out of a weekly schedule. This is difficult to say because motivation and circumstances varied. All owners granted Sunday off, but some granted all or parts of Saturdays off as well.[106] Ira Berlin estimates that highly-motivated slaves on plantations could labor independently for as much as three hours per day, in addition to all

---

[102] Jerah Johnson, "Colonial New Orleans: A Fragment of the Eighteenth-Century French Ethos" in *Creole New Orleans* edited by Hirsch and Logsdon (Baton Rouge: Louisiana State University Press, 1992), 42.
[103] Gilbert Din, *Spaniards, Planters, and Slaves: The Spanish Regulation of Slavery in Louisiana 1763–1803* (College Station: Texas A&M, 1999).
[104] McGowan, *supra*, at 142.
[105] McDonald, *supra*, at 78.
[106] Dumont de Montigny, *Mémoire Historiques sur la Louisiane*, Vol. II (Paris: Bauche, 1753), 241–242.

of Sunday.[107] It would seem possible that such workers could devote up to twenty to twenty six hours (or two to three days per week) for their own account, either to cultivate provision grounds or to work for hire. Again, the circumstances affecting the time available were variable, depending on the crop, the plantation, the system of labor and so forth. When the task work system was used, efficient workers could be rewarded with some time off every day. Those living in the city or working river boats might hire themselves out full time, and repay their owner a fixed sum per week or month. The customary wage for Sunday work was fifty to seventy-five cents per day.[108]

Interim Conclusion

The experience with self-employment on the Sabbath shows that owners and slaves successfully turned the meaning of several provisions of the *Code Noir* inside out. They not only managed to reverse the rule that forbade work of any kind on Sundays, but owners circumvented the injunction which forbade them from discharging their own duty to provide rations and foodstuffs by giving slaves another day off (other than Sunday) to work for their own account.[109]

The provisioning system first took root in Brazil and was in practice in the French Caribbean before the appearance of the *Code Noir* of 1685. The Code drafters wished to suppress the practice, believing that it led to increased theft rather than actual farming or provisioning. They therefore tried to make the master's duty non-delegable and unavoidable. Nevertheless this did not contain the

---

[107] Ira Berlin, *Many Thousands Gone*, 202. Berlin's estimate is consistent with the calculation of an 18th century planter on the isle of St. Vincent who wrote: "On my estate . . . forty-six acres of the richest ground are set apart for the negro gardens, where they work voluntarily in the two hours they have every noon to themselves, on the half-holiday in the week, and Sundays...." Sir William Young, *A Tour through the Several Islands of Barbadoes, St. Vincent, Antigua, Tobago, and Grenada in the Years 1791 and 1792*, (London: J. Stockdale, 1801) 271–272.

[108] Joe Gray Taylor, *Negro Slavery in Louisiana* (Louisiana: Louisiana Historical Association, 1963), 32. Louisiana's Black Code of 1806 stipulated that the Sunday wage would be fifty cents.

[109] *Code Noir*, Art. XIX.

practice.[110] "Voluntary" labor on Sundays was not viewed as a *Code* violation, but became in time the personal right of the slave, though it was arguably the functional equivalent of making the slaves provide for their own maintenance "*à la façon du Brésil.*" The effect was a net gain of freedom for both master and slave which no doubt made it difficult for outside authority to prevent.

The customs regarding free time and provision grounds created a small sphere of liberty within slavery. It amounted to a retrocession of rights to otherwise rightless people. The customs are not reconcilable with the conclusion that slaves had no property and cannot be squared with assertions in the *Code Noir* that the slave had no capacity to contract. Once the slave had property that was needed by society, his capacity to dispose of it within society was difficult to deny.

In the following section we come to a comparative excursus that looks at other slave societies.

COMPARING CUSTOMS IN THE CARIBBEAN AND THE UNITED STATES

The conversion of free-time and provision grounds privileges into a complex of customary rights is not an isolated development. The phenomenon occurred widely in the southern United States and in the Caribbean, even under British laws that did not originally mandate Sunday repose nor seek the conversion of slaves to Christianity. Slaves in Low Country Georgia, where slavery was not legalized until 1751, quickly transformed their day off on Sundays into a right to be compensated by the owner for work on that day. It is said that "what in Georgia had begun in 1751 as the gift or privilege of Sunday as a day of rest from the work demanded by owners, was by 1773 being claimed as a customary right by the colony's bondwomen and men."[111] Any attempt to require Sabbath work without some form of compensation would be met by refusal

---

[110] *See* above, Chapter One: "The Authors and Origins of the *Code Noir*."

[111] Betty Wood, "Never on a Sunday?: Slavery and the Sabbath in Lowcountry Georgia" in Mary Turner (Ed.) *From Chattel Slaves to Wage Slaves* (Bloomington: University of Indiana Press, 1995), 79–80.

and the need for negotiations. In their free time these slaves cultivated their own provision grounds and gardens which were often demarcated with fences made of rails or brush. Wood writes that the fences provided a "visible and explicit assertion of possession, of ownership, by the family or household whose members worked the land in question."[112] In that same period slaves in the Chesapeake also converted the practice of being free from farm and plantation labor on Sunday into a custom that could not be arbitrarily violated. As Lorena Walsh explains, "A master might deviate but only if he compensated for lost free time with extra food or a little cash."[113] The phenomenon was not limited to Sunday time. Free time of any kind, whether after task work or during mealtime, could result in commodities, money or foodstuffs in the hands of slaves. An ex-slave from the Low Country recalled the advantages of the task system: "I could save for myself sometimes a whole day if I could do 2 tasks in a day then I had the next day to myself. Some kind of work I could do 3 tasks in a day."[114]

In Jamaica slaves controlled sizable "provision grounds" where they grew crops for their own consumption for resale on the public market.[115] According to Sidney Mintz:

> Jamaican slaves were producing not only most of their own subsistence but also an astoundingly large surplus of foods, the bigger part of which ended up on the tables of free people, including the planters themselves. In effect, what had begun as a technique for saving the planters the costs of supplying their slaves with food had then become an essential basis for the food supply of the non-slave population.[116]

---

[112] *Ibid.*, 33.

[113] Lorena Walsh, "Work and Resistance in the New Republic: The Case of the Chesapeake, 1770–1820" in Mary Turner (Ed.), *supra*, at 112.

[114] Philip D. Morgan, "The Ownership of Property by Slaves in the Mid-Nineteenth-Century Low Country," *Journal of Southern History* XLIX (No 3) (1983): 399. Olmstead observed that the extent of any particular task was settled by custom and for that reason it was difficult for masters to increase the scope of a task. If the customs were ignored, the planter simply increased the likelihood "of a general stampede to the 'swamp.'" *Ibid.* at 400.

[115] Michael Mullin, "Slave Economic Strategies" in Mary Turner (Ed.), *supra*, at 69–70.

[116] Sidney Mintz, "From Plantation to Peasantries in the Caribbean," in *Caribbean Contours*, Sidney Mintz & Sally Price (Eds.) (Baltimore: Johns Hopkins Press

The property "rights" implicit and inherent in this practice were noted by the island's Governor: "Every settlement on the Low grounds has a Mountain as its appendage, that is parceled out to the Slaves, and every Negro has his particular Lot apportioned to him for raising his provisions, which is *absolutely* his Property, and his whole dependence."(my emphasis). According to Jamaican practice the slaves received Saturday afternoons off to work these grounds. Given these allotments and a fixed time set aside to work them, it must come as no surprise to learn that Jamaican slaves also "owned" flocks of fowl, pigs and goats and other marketable products like fruits and vegetables found in the "slave-dominated markets."[117]

In Antigua, the provision-ground system also operated in conjunction with the reserve of free time on Saturdays and Sundays. According to David Gaspar, the system was a "happy coalition of interests between the master and the slave."[118] Its origins lay in custom and opinion, not in law and statute. The slave markets held on Sundays were not the creatures of laws either—indeed Gaspar points out that the Antigua legislature never passed a single act to recognize and support the Sunday markets during the entire slave period—yet their legal foundation was no less secure. "In this context, Antigua slaves transformed privilege into a right that masters or legislators dared not tamper with, except to regulate the conduct of slaves on Sundays."[119] Antigua's exemption from Sunday labor, it might be noticed, was not embodied in law, as in Louisiana. It rested on tacit acknowledgement. Yet Robertson remarked in the 1720s that if a planter were "so mad as to command his Slaves to work in the field [on Sunday]" they would disobey him and run away in unison. The reason? "Slaves have (or

---

1985), 134; *See also* Beth Fowkes Tobin, "'And there raise yams': Slaves' Gardens in the Writings of West Indian Plantocrats" http:jhu.edu/journals/eighteenth-century_life/v023/23.2tobin.html.

[117] *Ibid.*, 68.

[118] David B. Gaspar, "Sugar Cultivation and Slave Life in Antigua before 1800," in Ira Berlin and P.D. Morgan (Eds.), *Cultivation and Culture: Labor and the Shaping of Slave Life in the Americas* (Charlottesville: University Press of Virginia, 1993), 115.

[119] Gaspar depicts the slaveholders' efforts as "regulating what they could not prevent", noting moreover that these efforts were not enforced and had no lasting effect in any case. *Ibid.*, 118.

which is the same, think they have) some Rights and Privileges, of which they are as tenacious as any Freeman upon earth can be of theirs, and which no Master of common Sense will once attempt to violate."[120]

Rebecca Scott's and Michael Zeuske's treatment of pre-emancipated slaves in Cuba points to customs that permitted slaves to acquire property "rights" in land and animals like pigs and horses. "Virtually everyone," they write, "recognized that enslaved laborers could raise pigs and pocket the proceeds."[121] The "property" to these animals, they note, was in fact a means of escaping from slavery itself. "It was with valuable resources of these kinds that ownership in the legal sense—of the slave by the master—could be brought to an end through the activation of ownership in the customary sense—of the pigs by the slave."[122] The cultivation of *conucos* (provision grounds) by slaves was also a very general practice. Provision grounds were revived and encouraged in the nineteenth century as an amelioration of the slave condition. Rebecca Scott writes elsewhere that the use of the *conucos* "represented opportunity for initiative, relatively unsupervised labor, and a source of funds—a limited 'personal economy.'"[123] More significantly, she shows that the operation of the provision ground system in Cuba was the source of persistent claims to the ownership of the grounds in post-emancipation Cuba. Although originally no more than claims based on customary right, they were later transformed through continuous occupation, possession and pretension into the asserted ownership of these grounds by slaves and their descendants.[124]

The resilience of similar customs on the island of Martinique is most instructive, because as we noted earlier, the original *Code Noir* was specifically tailored for conditions there and expressly attempted to suppress the custom. Before the enactment of the 1685 *Code*, Martinique slaves were commonly granted plots of marginal

---

[120] *Ibid.*, 117.

[121] Scott and Zeuske, "Property in Writing, Property on the Ground: Pigs, Horses, Land and Citizenship in the Aftermath of Slavery, Cuba 1880–1909," 44 *Society for Comparative Study of Society and History* 669 (2002): 674–676.

[122] *Ibid.*, 675.

[123] Rebecca Scott, *Slave Emancipation in Cuba* (Pittsburgh: University of Pittsburgh Press, 1985), 17.

[124] Scott and Zeuske, *supra*, 677–679.

land and a free day on Saturday, so that they would produce all or a portion of their own consumptive needs. According to Dale Tomich, the practice was driven by the introduction of sugar cane into the Antilles. The profitability and dominance of this crop led to the neglect of growing subsistence crops and to the increased expense of provisioning the slaves. The planters adopted the strategy of allotting provision grounds and granting Saturday free as a means of provisioning slaves at a reduced cost. There were, however, critics who thought that the system gave the slaves too much freedom, encouraged theft, and led slaves to hire themselves out rather than farm in their free time. Siding with these criticisms, the *Code Noir* attempted to suppress this practice and make the masters totally responsible for maintaining their slaves. But Tomich points out that there was a persistent failure to enforce these provisions, as demonstrated by the lengthy succession of edicts and declarations "too numerous to recount" that were promulgated during the seventeenth and eighteenth centuries.[125] The colonial authorities, he writes, "lacked the means to enforce this regulation in a society dominated by slaveholders who jealously guarded their 'property rights'...Far from dying out, the practice ...became an established part of colonial life during these years." Indeed when the *Code Noir* was amended in 1784 and 1786, key features of the custom were legitimated and accepted into the text. Free Saturdays were still forbidden, but provision grounds were recognized.[126] Now it was decreed that each adult slave must receive a small plot to cultivate. The yield of the plots, however, was not to discharge the master's duty to provide the ordinary rations (*l'ordinaire*) but only to supplement it. In 1845, however, the Mackau law gave in completely to the provision ground system and recognized certain property rights in favor of slaves. It allowed food grown on

---

[125] Dale Tomich, "Une Petite Guinée: Provisions Ground and Plantation in Martinique, 1830–1848" in *Cultivation and Culture* edited by Berlin and Morgan (Charlottesville: University Press of Virginia, 1993), 223–224.

[126] According to Victor Schoelcher, whether this law intended to make the slave an owner is uncertain, but it is certain that the slaves regarded their gardens as belonging to them. They bequeath them from father to son, mother to daughter and the slaveowners respected this. Victor Schoelcher, *Des colonies françaises: Abolition immédiate de l'esclavage* (Paris: Comité des Travaux Historiques et Scientifiques, 1998), 8–9.

provision grounds to substitute for *l'ordinaire* and said that the produce belonged to the slave. Later, the Superior Council of Martinique declared that the slave is sovereign master over the terrain that the law conceded to him. "This practice has become a custom which cannot be taken away."

By what process had the slave finally acquired "sovereignty" over his terrain? Tomich lays stress upon slave resistance and their refusal to cooperate when their customary acquis were threatened. For example he notes that a master who allotted a provision ground to a slave could not simply reclaim it for his own use. He had first to agree to give the occupants another field. Nor could he simply dispense with a slave's free time, for they felt they had a right to that time and resisted any encroachment. He cites the words of a public prosecutor who wrote in 1844: "It would be almost impossible for a planter to take even a little bit of time belonging to his slave, even if the authorities ignored the situation. There is a spirit of resistance among the slaves that prevents anyone from threatening what they consider to be their rights." [127] Even after the abolition of slavery, former slaves clung tenaciously to their land and homes.

> Attachment to their homes and provision grounds was a fundamental factor in keeping the former slaves resident on the plantations. With the coming of emancipation, the freed population treated such property as their own. Reasserting customary rights established under slavery, they refused to abandon their house and provision grounds or to compensate the planters for their use.[128]

Interim Conclusion

This excursus shows that whether in Louisiana, in Low Country Georgia, or in the Caribbean, the patterns are recurrent. Labor on Sundays coupled with provision grounds, farm animals and slave markets were the entering wedge that produced an

---

[127] *Ibid.*, 236.

[128] Dale Tomich, "Contested Terrains" in *From Chattel Slaves to Wage Slaves* edited by Mary Turner (Bloomington: Indiana University Press, 1995), 245.

incipient form of property rights for slaves. In all the accounts of this phenomenon slave resistance and tenacity toward what they regarded as acquired rights required owners eventually to recognize what they themselves had used as an incentive for cooperation. This resistance, in my view, is the key to understanding the "war without arms," as we see in the section below.

REFLECTIONS ON THE ORIGINS OF SLAVE CUSTOMS—*A WAR WITHOUT ARMS*

The Dutch legal historian R.C. van Caenegem defines custom as a practice "which has become binding through uninterrupted peaceful application over a long period of time, and as such is opposed to law based on legislation or a judicial pronouncement."[129] His definition is agreeable to the usual criteria that courts apply when they are called upon to recognize a binding custom. Another judicially-oriented definition calls custom "a spontaneous norm deriving its force from the concurrence of a uniform practice and a subjective belief that adherence is obligatory."[130] A court will expect proof of the quantitative and qualitative elements in it. Van Caenegem rightly points out, however, that these purely legal definitions of custom are insufficient for the historian attempting to capture what people themselves at any given time felt and considered to be custom, even if it had been introduced through the legislative process. The historian, he says, must take the viewpoint that "What people felt in

---

[129] R.C. van Caenegem, *Law, History, the Low Countries and Europe* (London: Hambledon, 1994) 123.

[130] Francesco Parisi, "The Formation of Customary Law" Paper #01-06 (2001) Law and Economics research Papers Series, http//papers.ssrn.com/paper.taf?abstract_id=262032. *See also* H. Patrick Glenn, "The Capture, Reconstruction and Marginalization of Custom," *American Journal of Comparative Law* 45 (1997): 613. To Glenn, custom consists of long settled practice (repetitive human behavior) and the belief of practitioners that it is obligatory. Malaurie and Aynès speak of "un ensemble d'usages juridiques, devenus obligatoires par une répétition durable, paisible et publique." P. Malaurie and L. Aynès., *Cours de droit civil:- Introduction à l'étude du droit (*Paris: Cujas, 1991), 219.

their bones was customary law; it had grown organically in a piecemeal fashion, constantly building on older native materials and the solid foundations of society itself."

As the reader will have noted, I have taken this wider view as well. I have eschewed a restrictive judicial approach and have used the word in its more popular sense to mean repetitive and consistent human behavior on the part of the relevant actors. I have not been concerned nor realistically able, at this remove, to establish whether a particular custom existed from "time immemorial" or was sufficiently universal to pass judicial muster. I have accepted historical evidence of what was called custom by travelers, legislators, and masters and slaves themselves. To have narrowed the cast of the net to examples actually recognized by courts (obviously very few in number) or to customs which I think might have satisfied judicial criteria though never tested (obviously speculative on my part) would, I believe, leave out most of the customs and obscure their importance. It would not capture the slave customs on their own terms, as a vibrant dynamic system. The difficulty with judicially-recognized "custom" is that it is a static and fictional conception developed by judges with positivist mindsets.[131] The typical common law view that custom should only be accepted as law if its origins were unknown (and thus a date in the 12th century, 1189, would become the presumptive moment in time when all recognized customs were in effect) is symptomatic of this difficulty. It would have been an unworkable starting point for this study, that is to say, for an investigation of an institution which had in some cases a mere one hundred and fifty year existence.

Slavery customs are perhaps an exceptional variety of customary law. The practices did not emanate from the whole of civil society (the majority of free persons did not own slaves) and it is somewhat surprising how quickly these customs took hold. They were created principally by interaction between owners, overseers and slaves, *viz.* between individuals locked together in a violent

---

[131] Leon Sheleff, *The Future of Tradition* 83–84 (London and Portland: Frank Cass, 2000). I agree with Sheleff's point that "Any attempt to relate to customary law must . . . come to terms with the impact of jurisprudential thinking on the manner in which custom is incorporated into the legal system—whether as being of immemorial use and therefore static, or whether as being part of a living group, reflecting changing mores, responding to changing circumstances. . . ." *Ibid.*, 84.

relationship of domination, on the one hand, and resistance on the other. Though everyday slave scenes may have looked peaceful, benign, submissive, paternal, even consensual, slavery's coercive, war-like premise could never entirely disappear from the relationship. Historians have frequently described slavery as day-to-day combat between owners and their unwilling slaves.[132] Norrece Jones speaks of "a grim and endless war."[133] For Orlando Patterson, the operative word is "struggle." ". . .[T]here was a constant struggle between master and slave in the effort of the former to gain as much as possible for himself with the least possible loss, including the self-defeating loss of his slave, and the effort of the latter to minimize the burden of his exploitation and enhance the regularity and predictability of his existence."[134] Struggle and resistance made slavery into a "negotiated relationship." As Ira Berlin notes, the playing field was never level but "the master-slave relationship was nevertheless subject to continual negotiation."[135]

The customs are cultural artefacts that can assist in reconstructing and understanding the struggle. They are like archaeological remnants strewn on the battlefield. They represent complex collective compromises on contradictory goals.[136] Owners generally wished to maximize the output of slaves and extract an optimal return on investment.[137] Slave statutes—law imposed from

---

[132] *See* Jonathan Martin, *Divided Mastery: Slave Hiring in the American South* (Cambridge: Harvard University Press, 2004), 11.

[133] Norrece T. Jones, Jr., *Born a Child of Freedom: Mechanisms of Control and Strategies of Resistance in Antebellum South Carolina* (1990) 11. Jones quotes John Locke's statement that "the perfect condition of slavery…is nothing else but the state of war continued between a lawful conqueror and a captive." *See also*, Alexander Johnston, *supra* note 5, who conceived slavery as placing society on a war footing: "It was a strange society, always on the alert, always with its hand on the sword."

[134] Orlando Patterson, *Slavery and Social Death: A Comparative Study* (Cambridge: Harvard University Press, 1982), 207.

[135] Ira Berlin, *Many Thousands Gone: The First Two Centuries of Slavery in North America* (Cambridge: Harvard University Press, 1998), 2.

[136] On the question of compromise and negotiation with slaves, *see* Richard Follett, *The Sugar Masters* (Baton Rouge: Louisiana State University Press, 2005), 133–135.

[137] Kenneth Stampp correctly saw that "Slavery was above all a labor system [in which] masters measured the success of their methods by the extent to which their

the top—seemingly gave them nearly all the power necessary to obtain such a return. In practice, however, they could not achieve the goal by the use of physical sanctions alone. As Bruce Benson points out, punishment is frequently the threat that induces obedience to law imposed from above, while customs arise when each individual recognizes the benefits of behaving in accordance with other individuals' expectations.[138] Custom develops from the bottom through mutual recognition and acceptance. "Reciprocities" he writes, "are the basic source both of the recognition of duty to obey law and of law enforcement in a customary law system."[139] To some extent reciprocity developed in the field of slavery through the use of incentives. These inducements generated "the tacit commitments that develop out of interaction."[140] Masters could have sought at one level the totalitarian control implied by the words "chattel slavery," but slaves could express their resistance in many ways that escaped the master's control. The vast majority did not run away, rebel or overtly refuse to work, for they had subtler forms of non-cooperation at their disposal. The connection between slave non-cooperation and the formation of custom is explicitly noted in Roderick McDonald's study of Louisiana sugar estates:

> [. . .] As in Jamaica, the modus vivendi on Louisiana sugar estates was not defined solely by the power of the planters. Slaves exercised power by affecting productivity. Although they risked punishment, they applied what control they had to the processes of production, withholding their labor or laboring less efficiently—or more specifically, running away, malingering, working slowly, feigning sickness, ignoring orders or responsibility, and sabotaging crops, tools, and livestock. They thereby got planters to concede better working conditions and

---

interest in a maximum of work of good quality prevailed over the slaves' predilection for a minimum of work of indifferent quality." Cf. Adam Smith's view that because a slave could not own property, he "can have no other interest but to eat as much, and to labour as little as possible. Whatever work he does beyond what is sufficient to purchase his own maintenance, can be squeezed out of him by violence only . . . ." Quoted in Gavin Wright, "Slavery and American Agricultural History," (2003) 3–4, www-econ.stanford.edu/faculty/workp.

[138] Bruce Benson, *The Enterprise of Law: Justice Without the State* (San Francisco: Pacific Research Institute, 1990), 12–13.

[139] *Ibid.*

[140] Fuller, *infra* 234.

> more adequate clothing, food, and shelter. The slaves of Louisiana's sugar plantations sought protection for their economic activities and secured as a customary right the opportunity, during time off from plantation labor, to work on their own, to market the fruit of their labor, and to keep the proceeds. Their internal economy expanded steadily until the Civil War.[141]

In this way slaves sought a sphere of autonomy within the totalitarian structure imposed upon them. The customs are strivings for some middle ground. They were a kind of retrocession of rights to legally "rightless" individuals.

Masters in Louisiana and elsewhere found it useful and necessary to offer a considerable array of incentives, bribes, and 'privileges' by which they effectively relinquished a portion of their power in return for improved performance, cooperation, or loyalty.[142] The *peculium*, which was allowed in all slaveholding societies and had a customary law origin even in Roman times, was one of the best known incentives. According to Orlando Patterson, its universality is not difficult to explain. It "solved the most important problem of slave labor: the fact that it was given involuntarily." Thus the *peculium* was:

> the best means of motivating the slave to perform efficiently on his master's behalf. It not only allowed the slave the vicarious enjoyment of the capacity he most lacked—that of owning property—but also held out the long-term hope of self-redemption for the most diligent slaves.[143]

The Spanish custom of *coartación* or self-purchase may have also originated as an incentive or means to encourage a slave toward increased effort, efficiency and thrift. The fixing of the price in advance and the promise of freedom not on the basis of an

---

[141] Roderick A. McDonald, *The Economy and Material Culture of Slaves* (Baton Rouge: Louisiana State University Press, 1993), 50.

[142] Follett, *supra* at 132 (the identical problem for all slaveholders was: "how could they create a plantation system that tempted the slave to work in his or her owner's interest?")

[143] Orlando Patterson, *Slavery and Social Death, A Comparative Study* (Cambridge: Harvard University Press, 1982), 185.

elapse of time but as soon as the price was worked up was a highly motivating inducement to hard work. The operation of *coartación* of course presupposed that the slave had a protected *peculium* or some protected right to accumulate the price. The practice of hiring out, which permitted slaves to keep the surplus they earned beyond the rate payable to the master, was an incentive that also engendered nascent property rights. Inherent in such actions is the creation of mutual and reciprocal duties between master and slave. The concept of task work carried within it the incentive of free time once the task was completed.

It may be supposed that incentives were originally not forbidden by slave law. The use of incentives would not be so easily proscribed when the law was already permitting masters the right to retrocede all rights through manumission. Thus, as an original proposition, the master's right to offer incentives such as extra free time, provision grounds, cash payments, occasional rations of brandy, the right to own animals and cultivate crops of their own and so forth would have seemed closely connected to the rights of any owner of property and arguably could not be restricted without diminishing property rights. Furthermore, incentives would not necessarily involve the cession of any "rights" since it required a complicated social process to make the practice seem obligatory. Nevertheless, we have seen that at various stages the statutes or codes placed bans on slave ownership of property, *coartación*, hiring out, and the self-provisioning of slaves. These bans were, essentially, attacks on the use of certain incentives. It was not until the later stages of historical development that incentives like self-provisioning, the *peculium*, and payment for Sunday labor were approved of by positive law.

This analysis fits with Lon Fuller's theory of the origins of legal and moral duties. Fuller found there were three conditions for an optimum realization of the notion of duty:[144] "*First*, the relationship of reciprocity out of which the duty arises must result from a voluntary agreement between the parties immediately affected; they themselves "create" the duty." This first condition, I believe, has a surprising degree of support in the historical evidence

---

[144] Lon L. Fuller, *The Morality of Law* (New Haven: Yale University Press, 1969), 23.

on slavery.[145] "*Second*, the reciprocal performances of the parties must in some sense be equal in value." The condition of equivalency is perhaps a feature of all the customs. For instance, Sunday work on behalf of the master had to be paid for in fixed wages; extra labor at harvest time had to be later "repaid" by restoring lost free time and missed holidays. *Third*, "the relationships within the society must be sufficiently fluid so that the same duty you owe me today, I may owe you tomorrow—in other words, the relationship of duty must in theory and in practice be reversible." Fuller thought the last condition was best characterized in a society of economic traders. Among merchants "the reversibility" of roles was greater than in any other context. In a footnote he indeed contrasted traders with the master-slave relationship where a reversal of positions, he thought, could not in fact occur. "It is not much consolation to the slave, for example, to be told that if he had been born a master and his master, a slave, then it would have been his right to command what he must now render." In making this brief allusion to slavery, he argued that "abstract reciprocity" loses some of its appeal. Nevertheless we know that reciprocity and reversible roles did take place between master and slave despite the social distance between them. It is true that slaves and masters could not easily reverse their status and certainly not their racial makeup, but they could and frequently did reverse economic positions in the buyer-seller relationship, as creditors and debtors in the plantation books, and in the leasing of labor and hiring out.

The customs I have examined here relate to particularly contested areas. For example, the master who wishes greater production from slaves may offer them work incentives as a means of inducing increased labor, perhaps time off after task work is completed or yearly bonuses if production targets are met. There are promises in these exchanged performances, implicit promises at least, that are not a necessary part of the master-slave relationship and indeed are not far from a contractual model. Practices such as

---

[145] *See* Norrece Jones's study of mechanisms of control and strategies of resistance in *South Carolina*: *Born a Child of Freedom, Yet a Slave* (Hanover: Wesleyan University Press-University Press of New England, 1990) and Lorena Walsh, *supra* note 113.

granting garden privileges and making provision ground allotments were offered because they were more efficient than other means of provisioning slaves. It allowed the landowner to maximize profit by concentrating acreage on a single lucrative crop for export, like sugar, without the expense of importing the comestibles necessary to support his work force. Because the system was popular and materially beneficial to both master and slave, and due to the fact that others had to follow suit or risk a deterioration in the morale of their own labor force,[146] it proved impossible to stamp out legislatively. Where incentives were put in place and relied upon, they established behavioral benchmarks, or customary settlements of the amount of time and labor that could be exacted, absent increased incentives.[147]

There is the theory that customs generally arise as a matter of human instinct but I think this provides a rather weak explanation for the proliferation of slave customs. According to this view, customs arise from the primordial instincts of man, as filtered by reason. Gilbert Sadler argues that there are three instincts that drive customs: the instinct of self-preservation, the instinct of sex and parentage, and the instinct of sympathy or compassion.[148] Thus the human tendency to appropriate property for oneself, for example, is said not to be the outcome of reasoning—it is prompted by the instincts of self-preservation and self-assertion.[149] Yet even if self-preservation sheds light on the slave's basic urge to appropriate his own labor and to set aside free time and accumulate property, it seems to suggest, misleadingly, that customary slave law would be the product of unilateral instincts, *viz.* those of the slave alone or those of the master only. It gives no scope to the checking actions and competing interests that gave contour to the customs. It traces the source exclusively to personal factors, when in fact many

---

[146] Eugene D. Genovese, *Roll Jordan Roll* (New York: Pantheon, 1972), 538.
[147] *See* Lorena Walsh, "Work Resistance in the New Republic: The Case of the Chesapeake 1770–1820" in *From Chattel Slaves to Wage Slaves,* edited by Mary Turner (Bloomington: Indiana University Press, 1995), 109–110. ("Slaves clung tenaciously to the task requirements and work pace that had become customary on a given plantation. Whenever a new overseer attempted to changed established work routine, he encountered stiff resistance.")
[148] Gilbert Sadler, *The Relation of Custom to Law* (London: Sweet & Maxwell, 1919, reprinted 1986), 10.
[149] Paul Vinogradoff, *Custom and Right* (Oslo: H. Aschehoug, 1925), 69.

customs represent a mixture not just of negotiated behavior but the physical requirements of a given situation or task.[150] The difficulty with the theory of instinctual development, I submit, is that it leaves out of the equation a defining characteristic of the process: the struggle between collective interests. A further deficiency is that it takes no account of the consciousness of the actors, their intellectual awareness of the law and custom. To this I turn in the next section.

The Legal Consciousness of Slaves

An important question about the development of the customs is how much law and custom was known by the slaves. At first glance the question is unpromising for the slave seems to have been at a great disadvantage. The slave laws obviously were not addressed to him or her. They were addressed to their owners, to government officials, the clergy, perhaps to citizens at large who would be expected to play a policing role, but they were not diffused in ways calculated to reach the slaves. That would have required an entirely different kind of promulgation or dissemination of the laws.[151] The

[150] For instance the Louisiana custom regarding the sugarcane harvest season—whereby slaves were worked at a frenzied pace eighteen hours every day, including Sundays and Christmas, until the harvest was complete, with the missed holidays scrupulously made up in January—was largely dictated by the botanical characteristics of sugarcane, the Louisiana climate, and the level of technology available. Rebecca Scott explains that the frenetic pace was a necessary consequence of an objective fact: "Cane had to be cut when the proportion of sucrose in the juice was highest, and, above all, the juice had to be extracted within 24 to 48 hours to prevent spoilage." Rebecca Scott, *Slave Emancipation in Cuba* (Princeton: Princeton University Press, 1985) 24. For a contemporary description of the "great push" at harvest time in Louisiana, *see* Frederick Law Olmstead, *The Cotton Kingdom* (New York: Mason Bros., 1861), 255.

[151] For example in colonial New Orleans under the French, laws and legal announcements were posted on the doors of the St. Louis Cathedral on Sundays at the hour of high mass when the largest number of citizens could be expected to be in attendance. Legal announcements were also made by the *huissier* by marches to the beat of the drum around the city. *See* Sally Kittredge Reeves, "The Notarial Archives Drawings of Adrien Persac" in *Marie Adrien Persac, Louisiana Artist*, edited by H. Parrott Bacot et. al. (Baton Rouge: Louisiana State University Press, 2000), 86.

vast majority of slaves were in fact uneducated and so were many whites,[152] but the difference was that slaves were kept uneducated as a matter of law. It was widely understood they were not to be taught to read and write. Anti-literacy laws in South Carolina (1834) and Louisiana (1830) punished those who attempted to educate slaves.[153] Many slaves, especially the newly arrived and those of the first generation, could not understand the language in which laws were written nor, in view of the diversity of African languages spoken around them, could they always count on fellow slaves to act as informants. Thus we have reason to suppose that most slaves were several steps removed from direct knowledge of the laws. Perhaps the so-called "protective" laws such as minimum weekly rations of food or items of clothing to be furnished or obligatory rest on Sundays were among the first to be grasped and remembered, but such protections were cast as obligations on owners and were left for the sovereign to enforce. They were not intended to instill consciousness of legal "rights" or entitlements in the beneficiaries. Nevertheless, it is submitted that despite these and other handicaps, it is also true that slaves developed considerable legal understanding, carried legal cultures within them, and used the state of the law to their advantage.

The difficulty is that we know little as to how slaves actually perceived the system, their thoughts or feelings, since our basic

---

[152] Down to the end of the Spanish regime perhaps more than half the free adult population of New Orleans was illiterate, according to estimates based on a count of signatures and marks on the oath of allegiance. Daniel Clark said in 1803 that "not over half the inhabitants can read or write the French and not two hundred in the whole country with correctness." Since lawyers were not permitted to practice prior to this time, individuals were deprived of the advice of counselors.

[153] South Carolina Act of 1834, S. 41; Louisiana Act of March 16, 1830, S. 3. For details, *see* Janet D. Cornelius, *When I Can Read My Title Clear: Literacy, Slavery and Religion in the Antebellum South* (Columbia: University of South Carolina Press, 1991); Thomas Webber, *Deep Like the Rivers: Education in the Slave Quarter Community, 1831–1865* (New York: W.W. Norton, 1978); C. Peter Ripley, *Slaves and Freedmen in Civil War Louisiana* (Baton Rouge: Louisiana State University Press, 1976), 126 ff. There was some literacy among blacks, though not much. It appears to have been higher among domestic slaves and free persons of color in urban centers. It is known for example that the Ursuline nuns in New Orleans taught slaves, Indians and free persons of color to read and write. Laws actually banning the teaching of slaves to read and write were not enacted in the South until fairly late.

source materials yield mostly white perceptions.[154] Legal records are basically silent on slaves' legal consciousness and it is difficult to develop what Kenneth Pike calls the "emic" or inside point of view.[155] Based on the writings of ex-slaves, Ariela Gross argues that slaves were "keenly aware of the law's influence on their lives." Those who fled and went on to write or narrate their stories commented on the injustice of the law, listed the ways the law deprived them of their rights, "sometimes quoting statute books by section number and page." Quoting Jon-Christian Suggs, she notes that ex-slave narratives are "obsessed" with the law and with legal status. Solomon Northup's story, for example, reflects strong awareness of the operative legal rules that worked for and against him.[156] The difficult question, however, is whether slave authors were necessarily exceptional in their knowledge and interest of the law, or were they simply more articulate about it.

Ordinary slaves could certainly display a high level of legal awareness and often bargained and negotiated on the basis of legal rights in order to improve their quality of life.[157] As mentioned earlier, it is unlikely that this awareness derived from first-hand understanding of the printed word tacked to the church or from proclamations read in the public square. They must have used other means of acquiring knowledge, including their own experience with what was considered customary treatment or negotiated behavior, their own inquiries, and undoubtedly a network of information that passed by word of mouth from plantation to plantation, from parent to child, and from whites and free persons of color with whom they were in contact. Their knowledge of customary law could have been more immediate and first hand

---

[154] Jo Ann Carrigan, "The Spanish Domination and the Cession to the United States, 1769–1803" in *Fortier's History of Louisiana*, Vol. II (Baton Rouge: Claitor's, 1972), 386.

[155] *See* Wolfgang Fikentscher, *Modes of Thought: A Study in the Anthropology of Law and Religion* (Tubingen: J.C.B. Mohr, 1995), 118–120.

[156] Ariela J. Gross, *Double Character: Slavery and Mastery in the Antebellum Southern Courtroom* (Princeton: Princeton University Press, 2000), 42–43.

[157] In her fine study of manumission in Louisiana, Judith Schafer comments that some slaves found ingenious and remarkably sophisticated ways to use the law, lawyers, judges and court proceedings to gain their freedom. *Becoming Free, Remaining Free: Manumission and Enslavement in New Orleans, 1846–1862* (Baton Rouge: Louisiana State University Press, 2003), xii.

since they were physically present in the formative give-and-take and to some degree played the part of lawmaker and law enforcer. It is not unreasonable to assume that some slaves were more current than even governmental officials, priests or the general public as to the developing customs on the ground. Although the matter cannot be conclusively shown, there is a foundation for this assertion in the historical examples given below.

In the summer of 1774 an incident occurred which led the Comandante at Pointe Coupée to discover that slaves were "very much aware of their rights and ready to travel to New Orleans to complain if these rights were violated." This situation arose when the Comandante seized and sold a quantity of horses belonging to slaves and used the proceeds to repair the fort. The Comandante justified his action on the ground that it was illegal for slaves to own horses. His view was correct in terms of a literal reading of the *Code Noir*, but it took no account of the prevailing customary pattern which permitted slaves to own various kinds of property and animals, including horses. Three of the dispossessed slaves promptly left for New Orleans—a journey of several days and a distance of more than a hundred miles—to see Governor Unzaga and demand that the money from the sale be returned to them. On arrival they were promptly placed in jail for traveling to the capital without passport or permission of their masters. Within a few weeks, however, they returned to Pointe Coupée boasting to their friends of their success, claiming that the Comandante would be replaced.[158] Why was it that they regarded themselves as the actual owners of the horses? The *Code Noir* stated that a slave might have a "*pécule*" (*peculium*) with the permission of his master. Such permission to own horses may have in fact existed, or might easily be inferred in this case, in which case the Comandante's confiscation of the property had interfered with the master's ownership.[159] Yet the ownership issue had evolved well beyond the provisions of the *Code Noir*. Slaves had acquired and here asserted a direct property right for themselves deriving from the customs in Louisiana. The legal force of this custom can be seen in Governor

---

[158] Gwendolyn Midlo Hall, *Africans in Colonial Louisiana* (Baton Rouge: Louisiana State University Press, 1992), 305–306.

[159] *Code Noir* art. 29 speaks of "le pécule desdits esclaves que les maitres auront permis d'avoir en sera tenu . . . ."

Unzaga's disposition of the case. He had the money refunded directly to the slaves, and not to their master. According to historian Gilbert Din, "The slaves who lost their steeds but did not travel to New Orleans received their money. This case illustrates that slaves, in addition to owning horses, were accumulating sums of money, although usually modest, and spending them as they saw fit."[160] We have earlier seen that similar property rights developed in many Southern states and in the Caribbean as well. These permitted slaves to amass property in the form of pigs, chickens, horses, crops from provision grounds, and pay for Sunday and free-time labor. Such wealth was frequently passed through inheritance to their descendants, relatives and friends.[161]

In 1773 the negress Françoise left Pointe Coupée for New Orleans to see Governor Unzaga to insist that her mulatto children, aged six or seven, were not to be sold and separated from her. She may have known of a protective provision in the *Code Noir* declaring that the husband, the wife and their children under the age of fourteen could not be sold separately if they belonged to the same master.[162] Sales in violation of this provision were in theory null. However all depended upon the interpretation of the words "husband" and "wife." It had been the practice of French officials and owners to extend the protection to couples not formally married in the church. This was a pragmatic approach because, as church historian Roger Baudier noted, most slaves lived in concubinage: "that most of their children were natural children, cannot be denied."[163] The old French parish registers confirm that

---

[160] Gilbert Din, *Spaniards, Planters, and Slaves: The Spanish Regulation of Slavery in Louisiana, 1763–1803* (College Station: Texas A&M Press, 1999), 64.

[161] Thus Rebecca Scott and Michael Zeuske note that in Cuba virtually everyone recognized that enslaved laborers could raise pigs and pocket the proceeds and that "almost every negro on the estate owns a horse [. . .]" "Property in Writing, Property on the Ground: Pigs, Horses, Land and Citizenship in the Aftermath of Slavery, Cuba, 1880–1909" 44 *Comparative Study of Society and History* 669 (2002).

[162] *Code Noir* art 43. According to Robert Shaw, this was the only provision of its kind in North America. "It was only in Louisiana that there was any statutory restriction upon the breakup of slave families." *A Legal History of Slavery* 165 (Potsdam, N.Y.: Northern Press, 1991).

[163] Roger Baudier, *The Catholic Church in Louisiana* (New Orleans: Louisiana Library Association, 1939), 206.

relatively few slave marriages took place *en face de l'église*. The flexible French approach, which Gwendolyn Midlo Hall characterizes as a "strong pro-family" approach,[164] disappeared when the Spanish took over Louisiana. The Spanish administration took the view that only families in which the parents were formally married within the church need be held together.[165] Yet slave marriages within the church were highly exceptional events during Spanish rule as well.[166] This strictness therefore struck hard at the slave family. Françoise's children were probably her natural children and thus might be separated from her. Comandante Villiers wrote to the Governor "I was good enough not to take away the youngest from her, but she is not satisfied . . . . I beg you to state your intentions . . . to serve me as a rule for sale of *nègres* in the future." [167] Whether Françoise received relief is not known, but she made an arduous journey to press her case. Was she conscious of the rules under French law? Was she caught in the shifting protections of different regimes?

The speed with which Louisiana slaves grasped the details even of obscure slave laws is also remarkable. A striking example was how quickly they grasped the implications of the Spanish administration's policy toward freedom purchase. As Thomas Ingersoll notes, the complex regulations of *coartación* were never officially publicized in Louisiana. They were not found among the slave provisions of *Las Siete Partidas* nor in the *Récopilación de las Indias* and they had no basis in the French regulations. It was an unwritten, imported custom and Louisiana slaves had not played a part in its creation. It allowed a slave to have his value appraised and fixed, even over the objection of his master, so that the slave might purchase his own freedom. An owner who refused to

---

[164] G.M. Hall, *supra*, 168, 183, 304.

[165] "The Spanish identified husbands and wives not legitimately married in church —and very few were— as unrelated pieces of property, and the children followed the mothers as 'bastards, father unknown. . . ." James McGowan, *Creation of a Slave Society, Louisiana Plantations in the Eighteenth Century* (University of Rochester Doctoral Dissertation, 1976), 273.

[166] Gilbert Din notes that between 1767–1777 there were only forty recorded marriages among blacks, both free and slave, at St. Louis Cathedral in New Orleans, as compared to two hundred and sixty five marriages for whites. Over the period 1782–1791, the clergy married merely forty black couples. *Supra* note 41 at 127.

[167] Letter from Villiers to Unzaga, April 6, 1773, quoted in Hall, *supra*, 305.

negotiate could be carried before a judicial tribunal which would fix the purchase price and cause forced execution, though in the great majority of cases this was unnecessary.[168] As described by Aimes, "The process of coartación consisted in fixing the value, by agreement between master and slave, of a slave definitely, so that at no time thereafter could a larger sum be exacted for his or her liberty."[169] The institution presupposed the slave's capacity to enter a binding freedom contract with his master. It further assumed a patrimonial separation between master and slave wherein the latter had private property of his own. Actually, as we have seen, this patrimonial separation had been established in Louisiana during the French colonial period as a matter of custom resulting from the independent slave economy that had grown up around market day, sale of produce and handicraft, free-time work, and contract jobbing. This custom was admitted by the drafters of the Civil Code of 1825 who recognized the slave's right to a *peculium* consisting of all property acquired through his own industry.[170] A system of compulsory purchase was of little use if slaves did not have the wherewithal to use it.[171]

How did this unusual custom enter the legal consciousness of Louisiana slaves? *Coartación* seems to have developed first in Cuba, possibly also in Puerto Rico, and then spread to Louisiana

---

[168] Ira Berlin, *Many Thousands Gone* (Cambridge: Harvard University Press, 1998) 213–214. When the owner refused to negotiate, a slave or any interested party could petition the court to have a *carta de libertad* issued. Berlin estimates that only about 1/5th of all freedom purchases were ever contested.

[169] H.S. Aimes, "Coartación: A Spanish Institution," *Yale Review* (1909): 414. *See also,* E.V. Goveia, *The West Indian Slave Laws of the 18th Century (Barbados:* Caribbean University Press, 1970), 14; Herbert Klein, *Slavery in the Americas: A Comparative Study of Virginia and* Cuba (reprint Chicago: Ivan Dee, 1989), 196–199.

[170] The principle they proposed in the Civil Code was "All that a slave possesses belongs to his master; he possesses nothing of his own, *except his peculium. . . .*" (emphasis added) In their *exposé des motifs* they partly base the *peculium* on local custom: "We here are in the habit of permitting our slaves to enjoy what they acquire by their industry." Projet of the Civil Code of 1825, Vol. I (1937), 14.

[171] Berlin estimates that blacks spent over ½ million Spanish dollars on self-purchase, most of it coming in the last two decades of the 18th century. This says as much about their determination and sacrifice as about the considerable resources generated by the independent slave economy. Between 1769–1803 some fifteen hundred purchased their liberty or that of their family and friends in New Orleans. Ira Berlin, *supra*, 332.

with the arrival of the Spaniards.[172] In Cuba the number of *coartados* was never large by comparison to the overall number of slaves, and more than forty percent of them were concentrated in the urban center of Havana.[173] In New Orleans between 1769–1803, about one thousand five hundred slaves purchased their freedom or had it purchased by others.[174] It was of course known to lawyers and government officials since it was enforceable in the colonial courts. How Louisiana slaves learned to take advantage of it, however, is not perfectly clear. They had played no role in the creation of this custom and their understanding did not initially derive from everyday experience. Ingersoll maintains that this unpublished custom was "universally understood" by Louisiana slaves and free blacks and they used it with great sophistication. It has been said the word spread from freed blacks and via the grapevine that slaves could buy their freedom and that owners could not stop them.[175] Perhaps the first informants were within the batallion of free black militiamen who came with O'Reilly from Cuba. These were about one hundred and sixty soldiers regimented in New Orleans. O'Reilly was accompanied by two legal officials who would have known of this custom, the *licensiado* Don Félix del Rey and the *escribaño* Francisco Javier Rodríguez.[176] They, or their successors, may have served as conduits to other government officials.

Conclusion

The living, unwritten rules that owners and slaves jointly authored were some of the most vital parts of slave law and played

---

[172] There is also reported evidence of *coartación* or a close equivalent in Brazilian slavery. *See* Mary C. Karasch, *Slave Life in Rio de Janeiro 1808–1850* (Princeton: Princeton University Press, 1987), 356.
[173] Rebecca Scott, *Slave Emancipation in Cuba 1860–1899* (Pittsburgh: University of Pittsburgh Press, 1985), 11.
[174] Berlin, *supra* 332. Ingersoll's estimate is a total of about 1,100 for the period 1769–1807. *Supra* 42–43.
[175] Gilbert Din, *supra* note 47, at 65.
[176] Taken from details of the expeditionary force from Cuba. *See* Bibiano Torres Ramirez, *Alejandro O Reilly en las Indias* (Sevilla: Escuela de Estudios Hispano-Americanos, 1969), 101–102.

a significant role in legal evolution. The authors of this spontaneous creation were an invisible collectivity. They did not sit in the legislature, the sovereign councils or colonial ministries and apparently did not use political rights to assert their will. They were simply anonymous individuals in the field who struggled, exploited, compromised, and used all means to advance and defend their interests.

Slaves tenaciously held on to and asserted their "rights" to family life, marriage, provision grounds, homes, regularly accorded free time, their Sunday markets, and so forth. They were cognizant not only of norms that their own resistance or acquiescence had helped establish, but they were capable of taking advantage of customs developed by others and of turning them to their use and benefit. Their legal awareness contributed to the durability of custom and to the instability of the positive law.

Louis Casimir Elisabeth Moreau Lislet,
Codifier of the 1808 Digest and 1825 Civil Code
(*Courtesy of Grand Lodge of Louisiana*)

CHAPTER 3

The Strange Science of Codifying Slavery

Moreau Lislet and the Louisiana Digest of 1808

INTRODUCTION

The Digest of 1808 was the first European-style code to be enacted in the Americas—the cause of our present celebration[1]—but it was also the first modern code anywhere in the world to incorporate slave law, and that distinction is the cause of this study. The decision to combine the two subjects in a single code is curious and intriguing, and has not been explained. It is as if the Digest was to be the simultaneous expression of two contradictory impulses or perhaps two contrasting blueprints. It was, on the one hand, a code of enlightenment and natural reason,[2] drafted shortly after the French and American revolutions, and embodying therefore all the *acquis* of those revolutions—the end of feudalism, the monarchy, the power of the church, the privileged orders and social differences. Thus it heralded the beginning of liberal society, equality, freedom of contract and property rights.[3]

---

[1] This chapter was presented at the Bicentennial Conference celebrating the two hundredth anniversary of the Digest of 1808. The Conference was held under the auspices of the Eason Weinmann Center for Comparative Law at the Tulane Law School.

[2] This faith in universal reason permeated the philosophy of the redactors of the French Civil Code. As Portalis expressed it, "*Il existe un droit universel et immuable, source de toutes les lois positives, il n'est que la raison naturelle en tant qu'elle gouverne tous les hommes.*" Portalis, *Ecrits et discours juridiques et politiques* (Aix-en-Provence: Presses Universitaires d'Aix-Marseille, 1988).

[3] Of course revolutionary aspirations were not instantiated in all European codifications of this period. The Prussian Landrecht of 1794, for instance, confirmed a stratified society organized into three "estates"—the nobility, the bourgeoisie and the peasantry, in which each sector had its own laws, differing

On the other hand the Digest embodied slavery and was therefore a code of darkness, a code *contra naturam*, dedicated to the continuance of human bondage. Ever since Roman times, slavery had been defined as an institution of the law of nations that was contrary to nature.[4] In the *Siete Partidas* we read denunciation after denunciation of slavery: "Servitude is the vilest and most contemptible thing that can exist among men . . . for the reason that man, who is the most noble and free among all the creatures that God made, is brought by means of it under the power of another, so that the latter can do with him what he pleases, just as he can with any of the rest of his property living or dead."[5] The Digest of Orleans, in contrast, omitted sentimental, conscience-salving statements and certainly made no apology for treating slavery. It has the tone of those who are comfortable in the right. Of course, the issues facing the legislature and redactors were not on that account any less problematic. Would not the juxtaposition of slavery in a liberal code produce a Janus-faced figure at war with itself? Was it possible to reconcile and unite the principles of liberal society with those of a slave-holding society? How would the slave be presented, as a person without rights or as human property without personality? How to reconcile the everyday contradiction that a slave could purchase his freedom, yet was supposedly incapable of owning property, including that which he used in purchasing his own freedom? Or how to reconcile that slaves were at times paid laborers (such as the wages from Sunday labor or hiring out in free time) but remained enslaved the rest of the time? Could the code distinguish between the civil rights enjoyed by free whites and those rights held by free persons of color? Were those graded distinctions even settled or understood in 1808 and what could be codified about them? One imagines that these must have been only some of the challenges facing Louis Moreau Lislet, the principal draftsman.

---

capacities, legal privileges and degrees of liberty. *See* Manlio Bellomo, *The Common Legal Past of Europe, 1000–1800* (Cochrane trans.) (Washington, DC: Catholic University Press, 1995), 6.

[4] *See* Florentinus' definition of slavery, D. 1.5.4. Alan Watson believes this to be "the only instance in Roman law in which a rule of the law of nations—defined as the law which all nations obey—is said to be contrary to nature. *Roman Slave Law* (Baltimore: Johns Hopkins University Press, 1987), 7.

[5] *Partida* IV, tit. V, Concerning the Marriages of Slaves.

Historians tell us that in Brazil the codifiers had great difficulty drafting the nation's first civil code so long as slavery was extant in the land. Codification attempts foundered for nearly a hundred years because the drafters could not find the ways and means of stating clear definitions and consistent rules.[6] In marked contrast, Louis Moreau Lislet and James Brown produced the Digest in a record breaking twenty-one months.[7] The speed and efficiency with which they worked suggest that they were unencumbered by policy disagreements or drafting difficulties.[8] The task was undoubtedly facilitated by two favorable circumstances. The law of slavery had just been comprehensively restated by the Legislature shortly before their appointment, and the members of the Legislature were apparently united behind the decision to draft an integrated document. This investigation of their efforts, however, is somewhat hampered by the meager materials at our disposal: the jurisconsults themselves left no notes or *motifs* to explain their thinking; and the Legislature kept no journal of its debates. There will be gaps and uncertainties on various points in this account. Nevertheless we are fortunate in that the era 1806–1825 affords an acute angle of historical observation. In 1806, 1808 and 1825 the Legislature took three consecutive general positions on slavery, thus allowing us to follow the expression and the evolution of the legislative will.

---

[6] Keila Grinberg, *Slavery, Liberalism, and Civil Law: Definitions of Status and Citizenship in the Elaboration of the Brazilian Civil Code* in Caulfield, Chambers & Putnam eds., *Honor, Status and Law in Modern Latin America* (Durham, N.C.: Duke University Press, 2005), 109–127.

[7] A first draft was ready in merely nineteen months. In January 1808, the *Moniteur* reported that the draft was ready for examination by legislative committees. *Le Moniteur*, Jan. 27, 1808.

[8] Brown's intellectual contribution is unclear. Some historians, such as Professor Batiza, believe that Moreau produced the Digest by himself. This view rests upon the statement in the Preliminary Report (February 13, 1823) that "the unaided exertions of one person [Moreau] were not sufficient for the completion of the task." *See* Rodolfo Batiza, "The Louisiana Civil Code of 1808: Its Actual Sources and Present Relevance," *Tulane Law Review* 46 (1971): 4. John Cairns, however, finds the sole-authorship theory to be improbable and unconvincing. *The 1808 Digest of Orleans and 1866 Civil Code of Lower Canada: An Historical Study of Legal Change* (1980), 110.

THE TWIN ASPIRATIONS OF THE DIGEST

The Digest is usually, and rightly, presented as a profoundly conservative and preservationist document in which the Creoles attempted to perpetuate their own legal culture and to avoid imposition of the common law. What has not received sufficient attention, however, is that the decision to enact a *slavery-inclusive* Digest involves a separate and distinct political goal. By introducing slavery into the civil law, the Creoles apparently intended to make an equally important political and cultural statement. After all, there was nothing absolutely necessary or historically inevitable about the decision to introduce slavery into the Digest. Technically speaking, nothing required it. Indeed it would have been the easier path to leave all slavery matters confined in the Black Code, as they always had been, and simply proceed to draft a new Digest of civil law strictly for free persons.

Whether the idea for an integrated code originated with Moreau Lislet and Brown or originated with a legislative committee or the Legislature as a whole, we actually do not know because of a lack of surviving records. However, it would not be fully persuasive, in my view, to attribute such a decision merely to the choices at the discretion of the redactors or to the legal models (French or Spanish) influencing their choices. Important and consequential as redactorial choices were, and there are many examples of important choices, the basic decision to showcase and entrench slavery in the social constitution of Orleans seems also to reflect the dominance of the planters in the legislature and their visceral attachment to slavery. Ascribing the primary decision to them is a thesis that should surprise no one. They had shaped slave laws for decades during French and Spanish rule by virtue of their preponderant influence in the *Conseil Supérieur* and the Cabildo.[9] In the absence of the Crown, they now had even tighter control over the Legislature than in the past, and the decision to merge slavery into the Digest was consistent with their self-interest and their own contemporaneous actions to preserve the institution in the territory.

---

[9] On the earlier efforts under Spanish rule to draft a new slave code, *see supra* Chapter Two: "War Without Arms, The Customs of Slavery." *See also* Gilbert Din, *Spaniards, Planters and Slaves: the Spanish Regulation of Slavery in Louisiana, 1763–1803* (College Station: Texas A&M, 1999).

Two indications of their resolve were the enactment of the Black Code in 1806 and the sending of the Memorial (also called the Remonstrance) to Washington to protest Congress's embargo on the further importation of slaves into Louisiana.

At this remove I do not pretend to prove the actual intent behind the Digest, but I would suggest, based on the planters' predominance in the Legislature and the biographical details of the primary drafter, that this thesis is quite plausible.

Influence of the Planters in the Legislature

The legislators who enacted the Digest of 1808 were generally large landowners and slaveowners. The bicameral legislature established in 1805 by Act of Congress was an all-white, exclusively male body. It consisted of twenty-five members in the House of Representatives (the lower house) and five members in the Legislative Council (the upper house).The qualifications for election to the House of Representatives were citizenship, residence and two hundred acres of land; for the Legislative Council, the qualification was higher: five hundred acres of land.[10] These leaders largely owed their prominence to the ownership of land and slaves. In the lower house sat such notables as Etienne de Boré, Charles Bouligny and Julien Poydras. Poydras was reputedly the wealthiest and most influential man in Louisiana. There were also a few physicians serving in this body, but they too had diversified landed interests.[11] The five members of the upper house—Joseph Bellechasse, Jean Noel Destréhan, Augustin Macarty, Pierre Sauvé and Evan Jones—owned plantations and large entourages of

---

[10] These property qualifications for elected representatives were taken from the Northwest Ordinance of July 13, 1787 (secs. 9 and 11) and were made applicable in the Territory of Orleans by the Act of Congress of March 2 1805 (Sec. 2). *See also* Charles Gayarré, *History of Louisiana: The Spanish Domination* Vol. 4 (2d ed.) (New Orleans: Gresham, 1879), 66–67.

[11] For instance Dr. John Sibley was a physician, planter, cattle raiser and salt manufacturer. Dr. John Watkins, who in 1805 served concurrently as Speaker of the House and as Mayor of New Orleans, owned enough land (according to Henry Clay) "to form a respectable state." *See* Jerah Johnson, "Dr. John Watkins, New Orleans' Lost Mayor," *Louisiana History* 36 (1995): 187–196.

slaves.[12] Leading men of this kind had served in the administration set up by De Laussat just before the transfer of Louisiana to the United States, and then served in the transitional legislature of 1804 set up by Governor Claiborne. They were known as warm advocates of the slave trade and two of them had been chosen to carry the Creoles' Memorial to Washington which, among other things, took exception to Congress's ban on further slave importation into the territory.[13] One of the very first projects undertaken by the Legislature was to enact the most detailed and repressive slave codes that Louisiana had ever had.[14] In their world view slave law was not some variety of special legislation merely regulating the hours and working conditions of field hands. Rather, it was essential to social order, agriculture and way of life, as much a part of their *droit commun* as the civil law itself.[15] In this light the Digest expressed their twin aspirations. They were not only trying

---

[12] While visiting Washington in 1804, Pierre Sauvé related to Senator Plumer that he had 150 acres of sugar cane under cultivation. Jean Noel Destréhan reported that he had two hundred acres of sugar cane under cultivation and that it took sixty negroes to manage his crop. Everett S. Brown, *Constitutional History of the Louisiana Purchase, 1803–1812* (Berkeley: University of California Press, 1920), 156.
[13] According to Judith Schafer, *Slavery, the Civil Law, and the Supreme Court of Louisiana* (Baton Rouge: Louisiana State University Press, 1994), 4: "Louisianians saw this prohibition as a violation of the language and spirit of the treaty of cession and possibly the first step toward abolition of slavery itself." Moreover, she argues that the Act of 1806 declaring Spanish law to be the law of the land, which did not go into effect because of Claiborne's veto, was intended to prevent the establishment of English common law in civil matters but also intended to protect slavery in the territory.
[14] They were not unfamiliar with slave insurrection. The revolt in Pointe Coupeé in 1795 began at Julien Poydras's plantation. The slave uprising near New Orleans in January 1811—the largest in American history—began on the plantation of Manuel Andry, a member of the House of Representatives.
[15] The Memorial, which Edward Livingston drafted, contained an apologia for the necessity of maintaining slavery in Louisiana:

> To the necessity of employing African laborers, which arises from the climate and the species of cultivation pursued in warm latitudes, is added a reason in this country peculiar to itself. [Levees were needed and could not be built or maintained except] by those whose natural constitution and habits of labor enable them to resist the combined effects of a deleterious moisture and a degree of heat intolerable to whites.

Quoted in Gayarré, *supra* note 10, vol. iv, at 62.

to preserve and entrench civil law, but were asserting their identity as a slaveholding society.

A Glimpse at Moreau

The man to whom the Legislature turned to co-draft a mixed code may be the most important legal figure in the history of the state. The details of his life remain somewhat sketchy, but his legal achievements were monumental.[16] An extraordinary jurist, linguist and scholar, Louis Casimir Elisabeth Moreau Lislet [b. 1766-d. 1832] was born in St. Domingue, educated in Paris, and served in the public administration up until the last days of the Haitian revolution.[17] How he escaped that calamity and safely emigrated to Louisiana owed something to the fickle winds in the French isles *sous le vent*. According to Moreau's own deposition,[18] he was a passenger on the falouche *l'Alexandrine* en route to Cap Français on official business in 1803 when the ship was driven off course by contrary winds and then pursued by enemy cruisers. The captain was forced to seek safe haven in Santiago, Cuba, where Moreau found himself spared from danger, stranded for a year, and conversing in Spanish. Unable to return to St Domingue, which by then was consumed in flames, he and his family set sail for New Orleans in 1804 to launch a new life.

Moreau Lislet was born into a prosperous family at Cap Français in St-Domingue. His father was a militia officer but the basis of the family's wealth appears to have been coffee plantations. Moreau eventually inherited two plantations and along with them, one would assume, a large quantity of slaves. His vocation however

---

[16] *See* Alain Levasseur, *Louis Casimir Elisabeth Moreau Lislet: Foster Father of Louisiana Civil Law* (Baton Rouge: Louisiana State University Law Center, 1996). Further details of his life have been uncovered by Augusta Elmwood. *See* Saint-Domingue Newsletter, vol. 20, nos. 1 & 2, Jan.–Apr. 2008.

[17] He was initially appointed the *premier substitut de procureur général au conseil supérieur de Saint-Domingue*, a position equivalent to that of first assistant public prosecutor. In 1803 he served as the curator of vacant successions. Saint-Domingue Newsletter, *supra* note 16, at 2.

[18] *See* the Declaration of Moreau-Lislet 3 May 1804 given at Santiago, Cuba, as translated *id.*

was not that of a planter but rather that of jurist and public official. He was sent to study law at the Sorbonne in Paris and in 1789, at the age of twenty three, he married Mlle de Peters. Moreau de St. Méry, the famous statesman, served as his tutor and attended his wedding. Returning to St Domingue he was appointed assistant public prosecutor and served in various government capacities. Some sources indicate that at some point during the Haitian upheavals he served as personal secretary to Toussaint l'Ouverture,[19] a position that would have been consistent with his gifts as a linguist and translator. Fluent in French, Spanish, English and Latin,[20] he immediately found employment in New Orleans as official translator to the Territorial Legislature.[21] His talents as a lawyer soon came to the fore[22] and in 1806 he and James Brown were officially nominated to draft a civil code for the Territory of Orleans. In the course of his career in Louisiana he held nearly every office of public trust, from parish judge to state representative, state senator, attorney general and, most important for present purposes, he was selected to draft both the Digest of 1808 and the Civil Code of 1825.[23] He also engaged in an extensive private practice which involved him in the greatest cases of the day.[24]

---

[19] *See* G. Debien & R. le Gardeur Jr., "Les colons de St.-Domingue refugiés à la Louisiane, " 1975 *Bulletin de la Société de l'Histoire de la Guadeloupe*, No. 1, at 99; Frederick Starr, *Bamboula: The Life and Times of Louis Moreau Gottschalk* (Oxford: Oxford University Press, 1995), 27. Levasseur, *supra* note 16, at 84–88, is doubtful of any link to Toussaint, though he does not cite the preceding authors.
[20] His library contained more than one thousand books in French, English Spanish and Latin. *See* Mitchell Franklin, "Libraries of Edward Livingston and of Moreau Lislet," 15 *Tulane Law Review* 399 (1941). For comparative perspectives on these collections, *see* Florence Jumonville, "Formerly the Property of a Lawyer: Books That Shaped Louisiana Law," *Tulane European & Civil Law Forum* 24 (2009): 161.
[21] The earliest record of his employment as a translator appears in October 1804, letters from Casa Calvo (in Spanish) to Claiborne.
[22] He argued the pivotal case of Paul v. Succession of Carriere (1806) (*citation unknown*), which recognized the civil law as the law in force in the Territory.
[23] An indication of the esteem in which he was held was that in the balloting to select three jurisconsults to draft the Civil Code of 1825, he received nearly twice the number of votes received by Livingston and Derbigny. Levasseur, *supra* note 16, at 140.
[24] He was, in his legal practice, the partner of Pierre Soulé. According to Levasseur's research, he appeared as counsel before the Supreme Court in two hundred and eight cases over the years 1809–1832.

Of the philosophical or inner mind of Moreau Lislet we know very little because there are no surviving letters. He was, however, by every indication a legal conservative who was committed not only to the civilian tradition but to the institution of slavery. There is no evidence that he had any qualm about the morality of slavery. After losing plantations and slaves in St. Domingue, he acquired domestic slaves in New Orleans and at his death his estate contained several slaves.[25] As a state Senator, he opposed a bill that would have set a time limit for the emancipation of slaves.[26] He was probably very comfortable with the task of integrating slavery into the civil law and certainly carried out the task with alacrity.

THE STATE OF SLAVE LAW ON THE EVE OF THE DIGEST

To understand the task that Moreau Lislet entered upon, we should bear in mind the slave laws that Louisiana possessed at the end of the colonial period and shortly after the Louisiana Purchase. That law was now encapsulated in a new Black Code passed by the Territorial Assembly in 1806. It represented the first slave law ever drafted and enacted by the Louisianians themselves and its character departed sharply from laws formerly in force. It was the best expression of what white Louisianians thought about and wanted in a slave law.[27] To understand this sharp departure, however, we must briefly revisit the antecedents of Louisiana's slave legislation.

---

[25] Olographic will, 6 Dec. 1832. There are at least nine notarial acts containing sales or purchases of slaves by L. Moreau Lislet. *See* Levasseur, *supra* note 16, at 281 ff.

[26] Journal of the Senate, 8th Legis., 1st Sess., at 13, cited in Levasseur, *supra* note 16, at 147.

[27] The pen behind the Black Code of 1806 is unknown. It might have been Moreau Lislet, for he had been working for the Legislature as a translator since 1804. Nevertheless the generally inelegant style of the document, and its heavy reliance upon verbatim borrowings from the slave statutes of sister states tends to suggest a less distinguished provenance. The authors may have simply been members of an internal committee of the Legislature.

The French and Spanish Background

The oldest roots of slave law, chronologically speaking, dated from the French *Code Noir* first decreed in 1685 and directly introduced into Louisiana in 1724. The 1685 edict had been written in the time of Louis XIV by his on-the-scene colonial administrators in the French Islands. They were non-lawyers, who sought the advice of the planter class and applied their own administrative experience to confect the provisions. Their *oeuvre* consisted of sixty provisions divided into seven titles denominated Religion, Police, Nourishment, Status and Incapacity, Crimes and Punishment, Seizures and Slaves as Movables, and Emancipation. In my view it was in large part the product of France's own fifty years' experience with plantation slavery. It did not owe its inspiration—except perhaps for certain instances in the rules on manumission—to the ancient slave law of Rome.[28] When this code was introduced in Louisiana under Governor Bienville in 1724, it was an organic transplant of a distant Caribbean experience. It had been drafted long before Louisiana had slaves or any need for slave law.[29]

By the time of the Louisiana Purchase, however, very little of this old law was still extant. It had been superseded by Spanish law. Governor O'Reilly kept the old *Code Noir* in effect for a time, but by proclamation on November 25, 1769, he repealed and replaced it with Spanish law. The actions and declarations of later governors, notaries and courts leave little doubt as to the effectiveness of this repeal.[30] This is not to say that the French law was ever entirely

---

[28] *See* supra, Chapter One: "The Authors and Origins of the Code Noir."

[29] Amusingly, in their haste, or perhaps in their ignorance of geography, the King's scribes referred to Louisiana in the preamble of the Code as a set of islands ("*des esclaves dans lesdites isles*").

[30] Justice Derbigny recognized the repeal of the *Code Noir*, at least *pro tanto*, in Poydras v. Beard, 4 Mart. (O.S.) 348 (1816). Professor Baade, "Law of Slavery in Spanish Luisiana 1769–1803," in *Louisiana's Legal Heritage*, edited by Edward F. Haas. (Pensacola:: Perdido Press, 1983), 54–55, produced evidence of the repeal (though some parts may have remained 'living law') during the Spanish period. His argument is supported not only by the archives, but by the instances in which fundamental Spanish rules running contrary to rules of the *Code Noir* were enforced, including involuntary freedom purchases (*coartación*) and manumissions without prior government permission. He notes that the Courts,

forgotten. To begin with, there had always been considerable overlap between the Spanish and French versions of slave law. There was also a certain amount of mutual influence and interaction: The *Code Noir* had been studied and imitated by Spanish jurists, for example in confecting the 1784 *Código Negro* in Santo Domingo.[31] There were at least two attempts by Creole forces to revive the *Code Noir*, once by the Cabildo around 1777,[32] and on a later occasion when they prevailed upon Pierre Clément de Laussat to resurrect it only days before the transfer of Louisiana to the United States. These resuscitation attempts failed, but they tended to show that the Creoles preferred the *Code Noir's* planter-friendly provisions over Spanish law. In drafting the 1806 legislation, the Legislature reinstated a few provisions from the old Code, but it was by no means a significant influence any longer.[33]

---

when professionally advised, did not apply the *Code Noir*. Yet the question of the *Code Noir's* repeal is not uncontested. Manuel Lucena Salmoral, *Los codigos negros de la América Española* (Alcalá de Henares/Paris: University of Alcalá/UNESCO Publishing, 1996) holds to the thesis that Governor O'Reilly, instead of repealing the code, simply appropriated it as Spanish law. This created an exceptional situation in which this Code was "*el único que tuvo vigencia in las Indias españolas.*" His research is supported by archival evidence. The weakness of his claim, however, is that, unlike Professor Baade, he made no investigation of the contrary practices and declarations of the colonial officials.

[31] The policy there was "*Hacer un Código como el 'francés.*'" Lucena Salmoral, *supra* note 30, at 61–94.

[32] Historians generally agree that the Cabildo's draft *Code Noir* of 1777 did not go into effect. Nevertheless its long-term influence was considerable. At least eight of its provisions were copied directly into the 1806 statute. It was, inter alia, the original source of provisions stating that slaves cannot be hired to themselves, that the slave's condition was a "passive one" in which he/she owes "a respect without bounds" to the master, and that free people of color ought never "presume to conceive themselves equal to the whites." *See Code Noir ou Loi Municipale*, 14 Mai 1777, Arts. 18, 29 and 72.

[33] It appears that at least five provisions in the Black Code of 1806 were actually borrowings from the old *Code Noir* of 1724. For example under the old *Code Noir* it was a capital offence for a slave to strike the master and cause "a contusion or effusion of blood." That crime with its unique wording reappears verbatim in the Black Code of 1806. (*Compare* §9, Crimes and Offences, 7 June 1806, *with* Art. 33 of the *Code Noir* of 1724.) Another instance is that the old *Code Noir* stated that the master was not discharged from his duty to feed the slaves by permitting them a day off to work for their own account, nor from his obligation to care for disabled and sick slaves for life. The latter rule probably endured because much of the French slave law, even if repealed by the Spanish, continued to set the daily standard of plantation life. It is known that the Spanish accepted and continued a

Spanish slave law also seemed to be in decline. One of the first statutes passed in the American period explicitly called for the use of Spanish law in the punishment of slaves,[34] but this provision was abrogated in 1806. Only two monuments of Spanish slave law were still standing, and one would be kept in force and the other would be suppressed. The retained law stated that slaves were reputed to be immovable property ("real estate" according to the Black Code[35]) and were subject to be mortgaged. This law was based upon an Ordinance by Governor Unzaga in 1770, and it required all transactions involving slaves to be in writing. This resulted in a treasure trove of notarized documents, the boon of future historians.[36] The immobilization of the slave also turned the slave into a somewhat higher form of property which perhaps brought more stability to the slave condition.[37] In Spanish *Luisiana* the slave was not technically a chattel; his importance rivaled that of the land.

The slave rule suppressed by the Black Code was a liberal form of manumission called *coartación*. It had led to a considerable increase in the number of free persons of color in the late 18th century. *Coartación* permitted a slave to have his value appraised and fixed, even over the objection of his master, so that he might purchase his freedom. An owner who refused to negotiate could be

---

variety of customs that were started under the French, and ended up codifying such customs in their Regulations of 1795 (Carondelet's Decree of June 1, 1795, Library of Congress, Louisiana Papers, AC 1333).

[34] By section 47 of the Crimes Act, May 4, 1805, "every slave accused of any crime shall be punished according to the laws of Spain for regulating her colonies, provided however, that no cruel or unusual punishment shall be inflicted."

[35] Art. 10, Black Code 1806.

[36] The Mortgage and Conveyance Ordinance is published in Gayarré, *supra* note 10, vol. 3, at 631–632, and discussed in Baade, *supra* note 30, at 60–61.

[37] Jean Carbonnier has pointed out that the slave, when defined as movable, could be deracinated at will by his master and was subject to unrestricted transfer at every credit seizure or division of the community. As an immovable he was less likely to be ripped from his social and family environment where he had always lived. *See* J. Carbonnier, "L'Esclavage sous le régime du Code civil," in *Annales de la Faculté de Liège* (1957), 53, 54. Nevertheless in Louisiana, apparently due to nonenforcement of the principle, designation as immovable oftentimes did not protect father, mother and child from being separated. *See* Ann Patton Malone, *Sweet Chariot—Slave and Household Structure in Nineteenth-Century Louisiana* (Chapel Hill: University of North Carolina Press, 1992), 213–216; *see also* Thomas Morris, *Southern Slavery and the Law 1619–1860* (Chapel Hill: University of North Carolina Press, 1996), 76–77.

carried before a tribunal which would fix the price and order forced execution, though this was usually not necessary.[38] This form of manumission had always been offensive and unpopular with slaveowners, and once they secured control of the territorial legislature, the institution was eliminated.[39] With its disappearance the influence of Spanish slave law appeared to reach low ebb, and yet the tide was just about to rise again due to the enactment of the Digest merely two years later.[40]

The Black Code of 1806

Four Characteristics

The Black Code is really an amalgam of three statutes passed in 1806-1807.[41] I refer to these laws as the "Black Code," as others have done, because there has been a dismemberment of the subjects that used to be treated in a single law by that name.[42] Since there is no space to describe this law in meaningful detail, I will condense my remarks into four characteristic features.

---

[38] *See* Ira Berlin, *Many Thousands Gone* (Cambridge: Harvard University Press, 1998), 213–214; H.S. Aimes, "Coartacion: A Spanish Institution," XVII *Yale Review* 412–431 (1909); Herbert Klein, *Slavery in the Americas: A Comparative Study of Virginia and Cuba* (Chicago: University of Chicago Press 1967), 196–199.

[39] The provision read, "That no person shall be compelled either directly or indirectly, to emancipate his or her slave or slaves, but in the case only where the said emancipation shall be made in the name and at the expense of the territory, by virtue of an act of the legislature of the same." Act to Regulate the Conditions and Forms of the Emancipation of Slaves §1, Mar. 9, 1807.

[40] *See* the discussion below, The Advancing Spanish-Roman Influence.

[41] The first statute, the only one actually entitled the Black Code, consists of forty sections and prescribes "the rules and conduct to be observed with respect to Negroes and other Slaves of this Territory." The second statute has twenty-two sections setting forth "Crimes and Offences." The third has eight sections and deals solely with the manumission of slaves. *See* Black Code, Act of June 7, 1806, as amended April 14, 1807; Crimes and Offences, Act of June 7, 1806; and Act to Regulate the Conditions and Forms of the Emancipation of Slaves, Mar. 9, 1807.

[42] Judith Schafer refers to the three parts of the Code in this generic sense as well. *See* Judith Schafer, "Under the Present Mode of Trial, Improper Verdicts Are Very Often Given: Criminal Procedure in the Trials of Slaves in Antebellum Louisiana," 18 *Cardozo Law Review* (1996) 635, reprinted in *The Louisiana Purchase Bicentennial Series in Louisiana History,* vol. XIII.

(150)

CHAPTER XXXIII.

BLACK CODE.

AN ACT

Preſcribing the rules and conduct to be obſerved with reſpect to Negroes and other Slaves of this Territory.

Slaves to have the enjoyment of Sundays, & be paid when they work on that day.

Sec. 1. *Be it enacted by the Legiſlative Council and Houſe of Repreſentatives of the territory of Orleans, in general aſſembly convened,* That the inhabitants ſhall leave to their ſlaves the free enjoyment of Sundays, and ſhall pay them for their labor on ſaid day, when they will employ them, at the rate of fifty cents; *Provided,* That the preſent ſection ſhall not be conſtrued ſo as to extend to ſlaves employed as ſervants, carriage drivers, hoſpital waiters, or to thoſe employed in carrying proviſions to market.

Proviso.

Their rations.

Sec. 2. *And be it further enacted.* That every owner ſhall be held to give to his ſlaves the quantity of proviſions hereafter ſpecified, to wit: one barrel of Indian corn, or the equivalent thereof in rice, beans, or other grain, and a pint of ſalt, and to deliver the ſame, to the ſaid ſlaves, in kind, every month, and never in money, under a penalty of a fine of ten dollars for every offence.

Penalty for delivering them money instead of rations.

Sec. 3. *And be it further enacted,* That the ſlaves who ſhall not have on the proper.

Black Code of 1806, first page

The first characteristic is that it was a broad retrenchment from the more liberal dispositions of earlier laws. For instance, as already mentioned, the liberal form of manumission under Spanish law, called *coartación*, was expressly suppressed. The slaves' *peculium*, which law and custom had once recognized, was also suppressed. A less obvious form of retrenchment resulted from the sudden secularization of the master-slave relationship, apparently as a result of American constitutional requirements. Prior laws granted religious rights to slaves and imposed religious duties on owners that they usually sought to avoid. Under the 1724 *Code Noir* slaves were to receive baptism and instruction in the Catholic faith and to have the opportunity to marry within the Church. They were guaranteed Sunday rest and Christian burial. It appears, however, that under cover of the American concept of separation of Church and State, the Creoles systematically purged the Black Code of these spiritual rights and duties. The concept of the slave's 'moral personality' was probably lost in the process,[43] along with some of the more humane and protective rules that had been placed there for religious reasons.

The second characteristic is a new urgency in the laws on the question of public safety, reflecting a society on high alert against the danger of uprisings, revolts and slave criminality. This can be seen in the provisions controlling slave assemblies, unpermitted movement and the amassing of weapons. The Code's protective mechanisms were the use of citizen informers, a system of written permits, and, for the first time, a special court was established to deal with slave crimes. There was wider reliance upon the citizen as informer and vigilante. Any slave away from his usual place without a white person accompanying him could be questioned, seized and subdued by any "freeholder."[44] A model permit to be carried by slaves was set forth in the law.[45] An unusually high number of provisions dealt with the capture and return of runaway slaves.[46] Property found in the hands of slaves for buying selling or trading could be confiscated, as well as any barge, pirogue or boat or horses under their control.[47]

Insurrection was not a distant or theoretical menace at this time, and history tends to show that the stronger the fear of insurrection, the more likely restrictive laws will be passed which specifically target free people of color. The Louisianians witnessed a major slave uprising at Pointe Coupée in 1795, and experienced three slave plots in 1804–1805 that were aborted (one involving a plan to kill all city officials in New Orleans and take over the city).[48] In 1811 the largest slave rebellion in the history of the

---

[43] Carbonnier, *supra* note 37, at 59.
[44] Black Code of 1806 §32.
[45] *Id.* §30.
[46] *Id.* §§26–29, 34–37.
[47] *Id.* §38. Slaves on horseback were viewed as a social menace. *Id.* §25.
[48] *See* James H. Dormon, "The Persistent Specter: Slave Rebellion in Territorial Louisiana," *Louisiana History* 18 (1977): 389, 392–393; Jack D.L. Holmes, "The Abortive Slave Revolt at Pointe Coupée, Louisiana, 1795," *Louisiana History*

United States unfolded a few miles from New Orleans and was ruthlessly suppressed.[49]

The third characteristic is that a massive amount of American slave law was directly introduced into the Black Code. Six provisions in the statute on "Rules and Conduct" were copied from the South Carolina Act of 1740,[50] and more than half of the Code's "Crimes and Offences," were taken bodily from that Act as well.[51] The South Carolina Act, as we know, was a reactionary slave code passed just after the Stono insurrection of 1739, which in turn, traces its roots to borrowings from the laws of Barbados, which were notorious for their severity. Whatever we may have heard or believed about the deep and abiding antipathy of the Louisianians toward common law does not seem to hold true in this context, for the drafters of 1806 did not stand upon cultural pride or protocol when it came to their slave law. The Territorial Legislature chose an American model that suited its objectives and its nervous mood. Borrowed American texts were simply reverse translated into French on the facing page. There was no pretense of civilian drafting. Everything was borrowed including the common law terminology (for instance, terms such as 'freeholder' entered the Louisiana vocabulary; the slave is not designated as immovable property but as 'real estate') and the centerpiece of the legislation was also borrowed—a special slave court composed of justices and freeholders with jurisdiction over slave crimes.[52]

11(1970): 341; Gilbert Din, "Carondelet, the Cabildo, and Slaves: Louisiana in 1795," *Louisiana History* 38 (1997): 5. Governor Claiborne wrote to James Madison that he had received a petition from notables of New Orleans. "You will discover there is some apprehension of an insurrection among the Negroes and that much alarm exists, although I am not myself of opinion that we are in as imminent danger. I have nevertheless taken every means of precaution in my power. Letter of Sept. 20, 1804, reprinted in Dunbar Rowland, editor, *Official Letterbooks of W.C.C. Claiborne (1801–1816)* Vol. 2 (Jackson, Miss: State Department of Archives and History, 1917).

[49] The story is compellingly told by Daniel Rasmussen, *American Uprising: The Untold Story of America's Largest Slave Revolt* (New York: HarperLuxe, 2011).

[50] *See* Black Code, Act of June 7, 1806, §§30–32, 34, 38–39.

[51] The first provision on Crimes and Offences is taken from the preamble to the South Carolina Act and acknowledges due process as a natural right even of slaves ("As the natural purport of justice forbids that any person, let their situation in life be what it may, should be condemned without a legal hearing. . . ."). The other borrowed provisions are §§2–7 and 11–15.

[52] These were partly lay tribunals, composed of a judge (or two Justices of the Peace in his place) and differing numbers of "freeholders" depending on whether

Great slave revolt of 1811 near New Orleans
(*Courtesy of Lorraine Gendron*)

A final characteristic of the Black Code is that it effectively recognized a three-caste society and targeted free persons of color in new discriminatory ways.[53] Free people of color appeared early

---

the offence was capital or non-capital. It has been suggested that this special court was modeled upon Virginia law, perhaps reflecting the influence of WCC Claiborne, a native Virginian who had practiced there. Schafer, *supra* note 13, at 450. In my view, however, this is unlikely since Virginia's 1786 act called for a court composed of at least five justices and did not include freeholders, whereas South Carolina's special court provided the precise model. The use of a freeholder court appeared first in the Barbados Code of 1661. Barbados and other island legislatures rejected the premise that the regular courts and the protections of English common law applied to slaves. *See* Richard Dunn, *Sugar and Slaves* (Chapel Hill: University of North Carolina Press, 1972), 239–240; E.V. Goveia, *The West Indian Slave Laws of the 18th Century* (Barbados: University of West Indies, 1970), 32–33.

[53] To be sure the caste structure progressively hardens during the American period. The oppressive legislation passed in 1830, for example, was a major watershed. (*See* Act Mar. 16, 1830 requiring newly manumitted persons to leave the state and forbidding immigration of free people of color into Louisiana and requiring slaveowners to post $1000 bond for each slave upon his emancipation to ensure removal from the state within thirty days.) *See* Schafer, *supra* note 13, at 181–184; Brown, *supra* note 12, at 139–140. Nevertheless, the point I am making in the text

in Louisiana history,[54] but they were not a distinct and sizable class until the late 18th century. Their number doubled between 1803 and 1806[55] and by 1810 it had doubled again. In New Orleans they were nearly on a par with the size of the white population.[56] The two Code Noirs of 1685 and 1724 promised that the manumitted slaves would receive full citizenship and equality of rights, without the necessity of letters of naturalization. "We grant to the manumitted the same rights privileges and immunities that persons born free enjoy. . . ."[57] That guarantee of equality, however, quickly became meaningless in the French isles, as the list of discriminatory measures against *gens de couleur libres* lengthened and their grievances festered.[58] If Louisiana was comparatively slower to develop and institutionalize its three caste society, one reason was the intervening period of Spanish rule in which the administration had restrained racial stratification by more tolerant policies toward free persons of color.[59] However self-government

---

is that the seeds of the repression of 1830 (and thereafter) were already planted in the Black Code of 1806.

[54] According to Donald Everett, their presence dates from the year 1722. *Free Persons of Color in New Orleans 1803–1865* (unpublished Tulane University Doctoral Dissertation, 1952), 16. Alice Dunbar-Nelson notes that free black officers commanded Negro troop regiments as early as 1735. "People of Color in Louisiana," in *Creole,* edited by Sybil Kein (Baton Rouge: Louisiana State University Press, 2000), 12.

[55] There is some discrepancy in the numerical counts. According to Laura Foner, their number rose from 1,566 in 1803 to 3,350 in 1806. "The Free People of Color in Louisiana and St. Domingue: A Comparative Portrait of Two Three-Caste Slave Societies," *Journal of Social History* 3 (1970): 406, 422. But Donald Everett indicates that their number in 1806 was only 2,312, and in 1810 rose to 5,727. "Emigrés and Militiamen: Free Persons of Color in New Orleans, 1803–1815," *Journal of Negro History* 38 (1953): 377.

[56] According to Logsdon and Bell, by 1810 there were 4,950 free persons of color living in New Orleans, as compared to 6,331 whites, or 27.7% *versus* 36.7% of the population, respectively. "The Americanization of Black New Orleans 1850–1900," in *Creole New Orleans, Race and Americanization*, edited by Hirsch & Logsdon, (Baton Rouge: Louisiana State University Press, 1992), 206. About two thousand had come in the 1809 migration from St. Domingue. Only a small percentage lived outside of New Orleans. Jerah Johnson, "Colonial New Orleans," in *Creole New Orleans, Race and Americanization, supra*, at 53.

[57] *See* Arts. LII and LIV, *Code Noir* (1724).

[58] Gabriel Debien, "Gens de couleur libres et colons de Saint-Domingue devant la Constituante" *Revue d'Histoire de l'Amérique Française* 4 (1951), 3–6.

[59] Under Spanish rule, there was an "official" egalitarianism in the rhetoric regarding the treatment of free people of color. Governor Carondelet's Regulations (1795) declared: "The Free People of every color enjoy by Law, the same

in the Territorial Period now removed the Crown as an impediment, permitting racial sentiment to be translated directly into law. The Government's immediate denial to them of the right to vote, to seek public office and to freely assemble now opened a cleavage that was not obvious during colonial government. Previously comparisons between these classes were more in terms of their equal rights to hold property, enter contracts, access the courts, establish legitimate families and so forth. In those respects the *état civil* of the two classes was somewhat comparable. By monopolizing political rights for themselves, however, whites in the American period opened a new division in racial separation.[60]

In the wake of the Haitian rebellion free people of color were increasingly seen as natural allies of slaves and as potential leaders of slave revolts. An 1806 Louisiana statute barred entry to all free *men* of color from Hispaniola and said such persons "shall be considered suspicious, and treated as such, until [they find] a conveyance to quit the territory." Those already residing in Louisiana and "pretending to be free" had to prove their status before a magistrate and obtain a certificate, or otherwise be regarded as fugitive slaves.[61]

---

privileges as the other members of the Nation, to which they are subject, and therefore are not to be molested in their possessions, or persons, nor injured, or abused, under penalty of the punishment prescribed by the Law." Decree of June 1, 1795, Library of Congress, Louisiana Papers, AC 1333, XX La. Hist. Q. 593, 604–605 (1937). Benjamin Morgan in 1803 recalled that the Spanish government accorded them "rights in common with other subjects." Letter to Chandler Price (Aug. 7, 1803), *quoted in* Everett, *supra* note 55, at 377.

[60] Article III of the Treaty of Cession provided that the *inhabitants* of Louisiana would enjoy "all the rights, advantages, and immunities of citizens" of the United States. On the basis of this language "free persons of color contended for the next sixty years that they should have been invested with the full rights of citizenship." Everett, *supra* note 55, at 377. Under the 1812 Constitution, Louisiana was the only state which specifically required a legislator or an elector to be a "free white male citizen of the United States." Philip Uzée, *The First Louisiana State Constitution: A Study of its Origin* (unpublished Louisiana State University Doctoral Dissertation, 1938), 26.

[61] The inability to produce this documentation caused many to be arrested and subjected to forced labor. Everett, *supra* note 55, at 164. Free women of color and children under fifteen years were not covered by the embargo of 1806. In 1807 the scope was enlarged to prohibit all free negroes or mulattoes, whatever their former residence, from emigrating or settling in Louisiana. Act of Apr. 14, 1807.

The Black Code was written amidst distrust and fears of this kind. The Code openly declared that free persons of color were legally inferior and subordinate to the whites. They must never insult or strike a white person, nor "presume to conceive themselves equal to the white. . . and never speak or answer to them but with respect."[62] The Code also required free blacks to carry certificates attesting to their status.[63] Certain provisions lumped free persons of color in the same category as slaves. Capital crimes theretofore reserved for slaves were now made into capital crimes for free people of color as well, though these were lesser offences for whites. A slave's testimony in a criminal matter was admissible against a free person of color, but remained inadmissible against whites.[64] At the same time all intermarriage between whites and free persons of color was prohibited,[65] and notary publics were obliged by law for the first time to insert racial markers ("f.m.c." and "f.w.c.") after their names in all public documents. Printers and auctioneers at public sale were similarly required to use these identifiers in their announcements.[66]

---

[62] On the origin of these phrases, *see* Lucena Salmoral, *supra* note 30.

[63] Black Code, "Rules and Conduct" Act of June 7, 1806, §§21, 40. As mentioned earlier, the source of these provisions was §§72 and 36, respectively, of the Cabildo's draft *Code Noir* of 1777, which never went into effect. *See* discussion *supra* note 30.

[64] To maliciously set fire to stacks of rice or grain, to burn buildings or to rape a white woman were treated as capital crimes for free persons of color and slaves, but not for whites. §§6–7, Crimes and Offences Act.

[65] The 1807 marriage statute forbade free persons to intermarry with slaves. Act of April 6, 1807, §13. This did not expressly forbid marriages between free whites and free persons of color, and such marriages had taken place during Spanish rule. *See* Kimberly Hanger, *Bounded Lives, Bounded Places* (Durham: Duke University Press, 1997), 92. The 1808 Digest, however, made the ban complete by forbidding whites to intermarry with free persons of color. Digest of the Civil Laws, Territory of Orleans (1808), Art. 8, at 24. It is not clear why or by what authority the Digest enlarged the marital restriction. As mentioned, the 1807 statute did not reach so far, and the *Partidas* freely allowed intermarriage between slaves and free persons, provided they were Christians. *See* tit. 5, L. 1, at 4. This is one of several examples showing that Moreau Lislet quietly made significant policy changes in the course of redacting the Digest. For another example, see the elimination of the ban on donations to manumitted persons (*cf.* Art. LII, Code Noir (1724), *with* Digest (1808) Art. 5, at 209).

[66] Act To Prescribe Certain Formalities Respecting Free Persons of Color, Mar. 31, 1808.

Here then, on the eve of the Digest, were a host of measures delineating the castes and opening the laws to unequal treatment.

THE INSERTION OF SLAVERY INTO THE CODES

As mentioned earlier, there was nothing absolutely necessary or historically inevitable about the decision to introduce slavery into the Digest or Code. Technically speaking, nothing required it. Indeed it would have been the easier path to leave all slavery matters confined in the Black Code, as they always had been, and simply proceed to draft a new Digest of civil law strictly for free persons. This would have produced a clean division *á la Française*: one law for slaves and another law for all free persons, including free persons of color. If speed were a consideration, a policy of strict separation would in fact have offered the fastest approach, and the French model was close at hand. There is of course a long-running debate over how deeply Moreau and Brown borrowed from French law,[67] but here is certainly an instance in which they could not follow the French model. It was incompatible with the decision to confect a hybrid *slave-and-civil* Code.

An Unavailing French Model

France possessed a vast and lucrative overseas slave empire, but there was not a single word about slavery or empire in the Civil Code of 1804, nor in any of the preparatory *projets*. Slavery had not been recognized in France proper since medieval times. A proud and ancient maxim declared the Freedom Principle: "*Nul n'est esclave en France*."[68] French slavery was essentially overseas; its

---

[67] *See* John Cairns, "The de la Vergne Volume and the Digest of 1808," *Tulane European & Civil Law Forum* 24 (2009): 31.

[68] Marcel Garaud, La *Révolution et l'égalité civile* (Paris: Recueil Sirey, 1953), 35. Loisel wrote in Inst. Cout., I, 24: "*toutes personnes son franches, en ce royaume, et sitost qu'un esclave a attaint les marches d'icelui, se faisant baptiser est affranchi.*" A considerable number of African slaves were brought into France as servants in the 17th and 18th centuries, and according to Sue Peabody, there are

day-to-day inhumanity was out of sight, and the regulations pertaining to slaves were conveniently compartmentalized in what was called "colonial law." French slavery, we might say, was both geographically and juridically confined. The *Code Civil* was essentially a *droit de cité* for a single class of persons: those who were deemed to be French citizens. The *Code Civil* declared that every Frenchman would enjoy civil rights under the Code, and it established an elaborate set of civil registries to identify the beneficiaries.[69]

The decision to exclude slavery from the *Code Civil* suited the design and fit the philosophy of the French redactors. They systematically resisted the incorporation of special legislation of all kinds into the Code civil, but in this case their objection was indeed more than technical. Slavery was an embarrassment to the professed ideology of the Republic. For slavery was more than "contrary to reason" in the Roman law sense. It was a glaring violation of the principles of the French Revolution. As Robespierre, a member of *Les Amis des Noirs*, told the National Assembly: "From the moment you pronounce the word 'slaves,' you will have pronounced either your dishonor or the reversal of your constitution. . . . Let the colonies die if you must keep them at that price."[70] Napoleon feared no such dishonor and sought

---

hundreds of cases in which they obtained their liberty in the courts. Sue Peabody, "*There Are No Slaves in France*": *The Political Culture of Race and Slavery in the Ancien Régime* (Oxford: Oxford University Press, 1996), 3–4. Nevertheless, certain edicts permitted slaves to enter France on a temporary basis, without altering their status, to learn a trade or receive religious instruction. *Id.* at 6.

[69] It is very suggestive that the authors of the Digest omitted inclusion of all provisions in the French Code Civil dealing with civil registries. Moreau and Brown otherwise followed the structural outline of the Code civil, but when they came to these provisions (Arts. 7–111), they were forced to skip nearly 100 articles, apparently because no civil registries yet existed in Louisiana (the first recording of Births and Deaths was introduced in 1811) and probably because there was no clear resolution of the question whether free people of color were considered citizens or not. The 1812 Constitution required a legislator or an elector to be a "free white male citizen of the United States" but it did not take up the question whether free persons of color were citizens. After the Civil War, in Walsh v. Lallande, 25 La Ann 188 (La 1873), the Louisiana Supreme Court ruled that *gens libre de couleur* in Louisiana had been admitted to U.S. citizenship all along "by the treaty whereby Louisiana was acquired," which was a convenient position to take in 1873 but was unclear in 1808.

[70] Marcel Garaud, *La Révolution et l'égalité civile* (Paris: Recueil Sirey, 1953), 44. Moreau de St. Méry had told the National Assembly that abolishing slavery would

militarily to reimpose slavery in the colonies. Yet to mar the Code named after him with the baseness of slavery would have been unthinkable.

The Castilian Alternative

Moreau and Brown could not have easily produced an integrated *slave-and-civil* Code using the French model, but Castilian law provided an alternative. Slave laws had been seamlessly integrated into Spain's famous code, the *Siete Partidas* some 500 years before. No fewer than forty *Leyes* were devoted to the subject, the greatest number being clustered in the Fourth *Partida*.[71] Additionally Moreau and Brown had general legislative instructions to follow the "existing law" which probably inclined them toward the Spanish alternative to begin with. Then too, in the de la Vergne manuscript, Moreau-Lislet made repeated reference to the *Partidas* in his annotations to the Digest provisions, which some scholars would have us understand to mean, "Here are the actual sources of the provisions."[72] In translating the *Siete Partidas* a few years later, he translated virtually all of its rules connected to

---

cause France to lose her Caribbean colonies: "You must renounce your wealth and commerce or declare frankly that the Declaration of Rights is not applicable to the colonies."

[71] *See* tits. V, XXI, and XXII.

[72] Do the provisions sufficiently agree in substance with the references he provides so that the latter may be regarded as a set of "sources"? If we compare the thirteen provisions in Chapter III with these references, the answer must be equivocal for Moreau's references are not always substantively compatible with the Digest provision he drafted. In this Chapter he lists the *Partidas* as a reference twelve times, the Spanish author José Febrero four times and Louisiana's Black Code (1806) five times. His Spanish law citations are in some cases examples of concordant material, such as for the proposition that the slave is entirely subject to the will of his master, short of murder or mutilation. References to the master's near boundless power may indeed be found in passages in the *Partidas*, though Moreau left out important accompanying qualifications on that power, such as the slave's right to seek protection against a cruel master. On the other hand, in instances such as the treatment of slave marriages, Moreau refers us to Spanish rules that are directly opposed to those in the Digest, with no warning of any contradiction. To one in search of sources, the reference is self-contradictory. This must cast doubt on the view that these citations were meant to be a disclosure of actual sources. His true purpose must have been more complex than that.

slavery, and made some comparative observations about the Louisiana rules. Thus in a general sense, when Moreau and Brown drafted a mixed *slave-and-civil* code, they necessarily rejected the French example, and followed an old Spanish tradition.

Codifying the Castes

To merge slavery with the Civil Law required no superficial intervention. About forty-five articles were involved, and these appear in each of the Digest's three Books and run the length of the document.[73]

In approaching the task Moreau used two self-limiting techniques. Firstly, he did not try to codify the whole law of slavery. He concerned himself mainly with private law rules and left most of the public law aspects in the special statutes.[74] Secondly, even with respect to the private law aspects, he was highly selective. He seems to have chosen for inclusion the more stable and important private law ideas, and, more importantly, he deliberately excluded any rules that contradicted the 1806 Black Code. In effect the Black Code was his substantive guide to the right balance to strike in the master-slave relationship.

Near the beginning of Book One on "Persons" Moreau presents provisions of a quasi-constitutional nature called the "Distinctions Among Persons" established by law.[75] In three brush strokes he delineates the classes or castes in antebellum society—the slaves, the former slaves and the free persons. The slave is defined as "one who is in the power of a master and who belongs to him in such a manner, that the master may sell him, dispose of his person, his

---

[73] *See* the following provisions of the Digest of 1808: Arts. 13–15 (p. 10); 8 (p. 24); 15–27 (p. 38–42); 47 (p. 65); 30 (p. 50); 19 (p. 98); 4 (p. 103); 114 (p. 114); 24 (p. 115); 72 (p. 124); 64 (p. 159); 5 (p. 209); 105 (p. 230–32); 5 (p. 232); 23 (p. 265); 21 (p. 322); 34 (p. 328); 47 (p. 331); 50 (p. 335); 16–17 (p. 348); 78–80 (p. 358); 114 (p. 367); 3 (p. 447); 24–25 (p. 451); 36 (p. 459); 3 (p. 453); 41 (p. 460); 74 (p. 488).

[74] He begins Chapter III "Des Esclaves" with the following provision: "The rules prescribing the police and conduct to be observed with respect to slaves in this territory, their enfranchisement and the punishment of their crimes and offences are fixed by special laws of the legislature." Art. 15 (p. 38).

[75] *See* Arts. 13–15 (p. 10).

industry and his labor, and who can do nothing, possess nothing nor acquire anything, but what must belong to his master." Manumitted persons are defined, tautologically, as "those who having been once slaves are legally made free." Free men are defined as "those who have preserved their natural liberty, which consists in a right to do whatever one pleases, except in so far as one is restrained by law." One might have expected Moreau, having stated these distinctions, thereafter to build an elaborate inequality around them, with differentiated provisions applicable to each stratum of Louisiana society. That does not, however, turn out to be altogether true. From the standpoint of differentiated treatment, there are basically only two castes: slaves and free persons (including the manumitted). The Digest has few particularized rules differentiating the condition of free persons of color from free white persons.[76] This confirms the impression of most observers that, while equal *political* rights were denied to the manumitted, they enjoyed practically the same *private law* rights as white citizens.

In setting up these social tiers, Moreau dexterously refrained from using racial adjectives and he did not disclose the origins or causes of the castes. As Rebecca Scott aptly noted, the definition of a slave in the Digest is simply ostensive, pointing out rather than analyzing its object. To all appearances, Moreau might be legislating for a non-racial society in another time and place. His definitions have the sheen of classical purity, which is understandable because he obtained them from classical sources. All three provisions were taken verbatim from the 17th century French author Jean Domat,[77] who had in turn had taken them from Justinian's 6th century Digest.

As a consequence of his classical approach Moreau's reader cannot know on what basis persons in society became slaves or stayed free, because the enslaved are not called blacks, Indians or mulattoes; the manumitted are not called *gens libre de couleur*, and free persons are not called whites. Why one group was enslaved and others were free is left to the imagination. Domat listed two

---

[76] There are very few instances in which the rules apply differently to free persons of color: *See* Art. 30 (p. 50); Art. 8 (p. 24). In the 1825 Civil Code, *see* Art. 221.
[77] Jean Domat, *Les Loix civiles dans leur ordre naturel* (1689–1694) tit. II (Des Personnes), § II, L. i, ii, iv. I have consulted the 1777 Paris edition.

causes of slavery, but those causes did not account for African bondage in Louisiana, so Moreau simply deleted Domat's explanation.[78]

Yet Moreau's ability to suppress all use of racial adjectives and historical identifiers,[79] though it produces neutral drafting, leaves a puzzling impression. From what we know of Moreau's background, it was not a reflection of personal *pudeur*, nor of his inability to devise clear definitions. A few years later he himself penned a frank racial definition of slavery, the very kind he had shunned placing in the Digest.[80] If he was deliberately disguising or minimizing reality, it was much in the same way the Founding Fathers strained to keep slavery by name out of the American Constitution, using the euphemisms they needed to count slaves for purposes of taxation and political representation.[81] Indeed, this guise was adopted in Louisiana's first Constitution of 1812 which was drafted without

---

[78] The causes of slavery were basically capture in war and descent from a female slave:

> *Les hommes tombent dans l'esclavage par la captivité dans la guerre, parmi les nations où c'est l'usage que le vainqueur sauvant la vie au vaincu, s'en rend le maître, & en fait son esclave. Et c'est un suite de l'esclavage des femmes, que leurs enfans sont esclaves par la naissance.*

Id. L. iii. The *Partidas* repeated the first two and added a third cause: the sale of oneself into slavery. *See Partidas* I. 21. IV.

[79] One exception is Art. 8 (p. 25), forbidding intermarriage between whites and persons of color. *See also* Art. 30 (p. 50) allowing illegitimates to bring a paternity action only if they are free and white.

[80] "Slavery in this state, is confined to negroes, brought immediately from Africa, or their descendants; with the exception of certain Indiens [sic] who were taken as captives in war; or who were sold as slaves while Louisiana was held by the French." *The Laws of the Siete Partidas* Vol. I, at 582 n. (a) (Moreau Lislet & H. Carleton trans., 1820) (Reprint, Madrid: Colegio de Abogados, 1996).

[81] "Throughout the debates," Paul Finkelman writes, "the delegates talked about 'blacks,' 'Negroes,' and 'slaves.'" But the final document avoided these terms. The change in language was clearly designed to make the Constitution more palatable to the North." *Slavery and the Founding Fathers* (Armonk, NY: Sharpe, 1996), 3. For instance, Art. I, §2 (1789), provided that "Representatives and direct Taxes shall be apportioned . . . by adding to the whole Number of free Persons, including those bound to Service for a Term of Years, and excluding Indians not taxed, three-fifths of all other Persons."

mentioning 'slave' or 'slavery' in the entire document.[82] Was Moreau's reticence a similar strategy? Perhaps he was only laminating the Digest with the veneer of respectable antiquity or perhaps this was how a cultivated Paris-educated jurist would naturally execute his legislative instructions. At this remove it is difficult to make reliable judgments, but clearly this recourse to classical sources had effects which went beyond the Digest itself. The Romanization that he embarked upon, for whatever reason, turned out to be more than a mere ornament. It brought classical rules and concepts into a field previously dominated by the Black Codes, and soon the courts, lawyers and litigants began to make use of this classical learning to develop and expand that law. This is a point to which I will return.

Slave Rules in the Three Books of the Digest

The core of the treatment in the Book of Persons comes in Chapter III, entitled "On Slaves." There is no space to cover each provision in detail, so I will provide a brief overview.[83] The first article in the series is merely a cross-reference to the provisions of the Black Code, thus informing the reader that the Digest does not contain the entire law of slavery.[84] The second article in the series describes the intensity of the master's power over his slave. The relationship is conceived as an entire subjection to the master's will, with no limits on mastery other than to avoid the mutilation or death of the slave. The next articles plunge the slave into an abyss. Almost every aspect of civil personality is denied. The slave is incapable of contracting engagements, incapable of owning or possessing any property or of having a succession, incapable of holding public or private office, incapable of serving as tutor, attorney, witness or appearing in court as a litigant. He may appear in court in but one instance—"when he has to claim or prove his

---

[82] Uzée, *supra* note 60, at 28, 32. The stated reason for the omission was that the 'slave code' in force in the territory made adequate provision for that class of society.

[83] *See* Arts. 15–27 (p. 38–42).

[84] *See* discussion *supra* note 74.

freedom," which is at least a fleeting glimpse of the slave's civil existence. Slaves may marry provided the master consents, but the marriage has no civil effects.[85] Children born of a mother in a state of slavery, whether she be married or not, are slaves. Slaves may be manumitted by the master through acts *inter vivos or mortis causa* provided the forms and conditions of the special laws were followed, but it is stressed that no master shall be compelled either directly or indirectly to enfranchise a slave. Here was the express repeal of the doctrine of *coartación*. Insofar as a slave's criminal responsibility is concerned, Art. 19 authorized direct prosecutions against slaves for their crimes and misdemeanors, without the necessity of joining their masters to the proceedings.

Book Two (Property) provided, following the Spanish tradition, that slaves were reputed to be immovable property by operation of law.[86] Slaves were therefore mortgageable, and creditors could execute on their mortgage though the slave had passed into the hands of third parties, provided the instrument was registered.[87] Book Three (Actions) provided that the slave was an "effect of commerce" and was subject to all manner of contracts and transactions.[88] He could be bought, sold, leased, and loaned and donated. When slaves were sold, the Roman remedy of redhibition (or *quanti minoris*) provided a guarantee to the buyer against latent defects and vices in the slave. The Digest gave surprisingly detailed treatment to this remedy in the sale of slaves,[89] allowing rescission for hidden vices of the slave's disposition or temper, such as the

---

[85] Thus slave marriages under the Digest were conceived as non-binding relationships. That view is not based upon any explicit provision in the Black Code of 1806, but was consistent with the French view in the original 1724 *Code Noir*. Pothier wrote in his *Traité du contrat de mariage* vol. I, pt. I, ch. III, Art. I, §III (Paris 1813), that "*Les esclaves n'ayant aucun état civil . . . c'était un mariage destitué de tous les effets civils, et qui n'en avait d'autres que ceux qui naissent du droit naturel. On appelait ce mariage contubernium.*" In Girod v. Lewis (La. 1819) Mathews J. held that a marriage between slaves gave forth no civil effects during their enslavement, but upon emancipation their marriage would produce full civil effects. Certain passages in the *Siete Partidas* would indicate that Spanish law followed the church tradition which gave civil effect to slave marriages, but the matter is doubtful. *See* Gayarré, *supra* note 10, vol. IV, at 292–293.

[86] Digest Art. 19 (p. 98).

[87] *Id.* Art. 41 (p. 460).

[88] *Id.* Arts. 16–17 (p. 348).

[89] *Id.* Arts. 78–80 (p. 358).

habit of running away or committing theft, as well as vices of the body, such as illnesses like leprosy and epilepsy. It stated that the principle of lesion beyond moiety did not apply to the sale of slaves.[90] The principles of prescription, however, did apply and ownership of a slave could be acquired by prescription.[91]

One other matter covered in Book Three is civil liability. The Digest provided that the master was civilly responsible for the damage caused by his slave to others. The liability was strict, applying even though the master was not negligent and could not have prevented the injury. However, he was entitled to give up the slave to the injured party or have the slave sold, in complete satisfaction.[92]

Conception of the Slave's Legal Nature

These articles may permit some insight into Moreau's conception of the slave. At first glance the placement in the law of "Persons" would suggest that the slave is viewed as a person since his status is defined and discussed under that rubric. Yet the actual content of the articles could throw that impression into disarray. It becomes apparent, as we read through, that virtually all the attributes of being a person in a legal sense (what French law would call "l'état civil") are systematically withheld. The slave resembles someone who has suffered the equivalent of civil death. The utter absence of rights suggests that it would have been alternatively possible, and perhaps conceptually clearer, had Moreau merely defined the slave as property under the Second Book, and dispensed with any genuflection toward the law of persons.[93]

---

[90] *Id.* Art. 114 (p. 367).

[91] The periods for acquisitive prescription, however, were half the length of those normally applicable—*viz.*, five years with just title, as compared to fifteen years without. *Id.* Art. 74 (p. 488).

[92] Curiously, the rule of noxal surrender is stated twice in the Digest. *See id.* Art. 21 (p. 322), Art. 22 (p. 40).

[93] As Buckland points out, the Romans had always been ambivalent in their description of the slave, stating that a slave is a Res, but in other places referring to slaves as persons. "It is clear that the Roman lawyers called a slave a person, and

Curiously, it was the provision that made the slave subject to criminal prosecutions (Art. 19) which tempted Louisiana jurists to conclude that slaves were both persons and property at the same time.[94] For purposes of public law, he was seen as a responsible human being who must expiate his crimes, a moral actor in that regard and no mere piece of property.[95] This suggested that the slave really had two natures under Moreau's approach. Interestingly, this dual nature was acknowledged by F.X. Martin, then the Attorney General, when he was asked for an opinion on the question whether slaves possessed any constitutional rights under the Constitution of 1812. The question had arisen whether the Governor had the power to reprieve the criminal sentence of a slave, and it was objected that the Governor could not have that power since slaves were not "parties to the Constitution." Martin's opinion disagreed: "If there be. . . no mode pointed out by which the Governor is to act toward them when they are the object of the clemency of the State, he must act toward a slave as he would toward another human being." He concluded that "although, in civil cases, slaves are considered as things, in criminal cases they are considered as men."[96]

The Paradox of the Digest

It has already been suggested that Moreau used the Black Code as his policy guide and never contradicted a position or a policy expressly taken there. This would explain the selective nature of his borrowings from Roman-Spanish rules. In the de la Vergne volume he cited the *Partidas* frequently, as if that law were his main inspiration, but actually he carefully bypassed rules in the *Partidas* that were incompatible with the Black Code. He ignored passages which recognized the slave's *peculium* (*cf.* Art. 17) and he passed over provisions allowing slaves to marry without their masters' permission. Likewise, he ignored provisions giving civil effect to

---

this means that for them 'person' meant human being." *The Roman Law of Slavery* (Reprint, Union, N.J.: The Lawbook Exchange, Ltd., 2000), 4 (Cambridge 1908).

[94] *See* Schafer, *supra* note 13, at 21.

[95] *See, e.g.*, State v. Seaborne, alias Moore, 8 Rob. 518 (La 1843).

[96] Gayarré, *supra* note 10, vol. 4, at 292–293.

slave marriages and those allowing interracial marriages.[97] (*cf.* Art. 23). He spurned rules allowing slaves to complain in court of cruelty by their masters (*cf.* Art. 18) and those permitting manumissions without governmental approval or over the opposition of their master (*cf.* Art. 27).[98] His selectivity perhaps sheds little light on the Pascal/Batiza debate about the sources of the Digest, except perhaps to show, in this one area at least, that the Black Code was more important to the substantive choices he made than either Spanish or French law. The greater importance of the Black Code was not clear until Moreau's work was evaluated not by the slavery regime he actually codified, but in comparison to the regime he could have codified if he had been allowed to follow Spanish law in its full dimension. That comparison reveals the paradox of the Digest. Moreau's choices turn out to be both a repudiation and a revival of Spanish slave law.

Moreau the Realist?

It is worth asking, however, whether Moreau was in fact codifying the law of his own time and place, or was he blithely inserting rules with little normative connection? The question arises because he must have noticed the singular irrelevance of some of the rules he drafted. He could not have been oblivious to the contrast between the slave law on the books and the slave law in action. In the Digest he broadly declared that slaves had no legal capacity to enter contracts, which meant they could not legally sell their labor or goods to others. But that was not the reality of slavery

---

[97] The *Siete Partidas* followed the church tradition that even in subjection the slave retained a sphere of autonomy and could marry without his master's knowledge or consent. Thus Aquinas, quoting Seneca, maintained, "It is wrong to suppose that slavery falls upon the whole man: for the better part of him is excepted. His body is subjected to the master, but his soul is his own." *See* Paul Cornish, "Marriage, Slavery, and Natural Rights in the Political Thought of Aquinas," Rev. Pol. 60 (1998): 545, 550. According to Kimberly Hanger, marriages between whites and free blacks were allowed in the Catholic Church in New Orleans during Spanish rule. Hanger, *supra* note 65, at 92.

[98] For contrasts between Spanish and French slave law in Louisiana, *see* Baade, *supra* note 30, at 50–53; Lucena Salmoral, *supra* note 30, at 52–59.

in the Territory of Orleans. It was an everyday experience, supported by legal custom, for slaves to hire themselves out in their free-time and to sell their own goods for profit in the markets. In other words, they already possessed the legal capacity that the Digest withheld from them in principle.[99] Similarly, the Digest declared that a slave could own no property, that everything a slave might acquire or possess belonged to his master. This too defied reality and was in contradiction of positive law. Provisions in the Black Code indicated that wages paid for work on Sunday belonged securely to the slaves and could not be taken away.[100] Custom further held that the pigs, horses, chickens and fowl raised by slaves were theirs exclusively. Crops grown on "provision lands" for personal consumption or sale to others belonged to slaves as well. When slaves sold and exchanged goods within the plantation economy or in public markets, they generated wealth which they were allowed to keep. Savings accrued in the process were in fact used to buy their freedom and the freedom of other slaves.[101]

One imagines Moreau as hard pressed to explain away the daily reality of slavery. If his definitions of "slavery" "property" or "capacity" appear stable and logical it is only because he glossed over inconvenient truths on the ground. A more realistic approach would be later adopted in the Civil Code of 1825 which made important concessions to the slave law in action. It recognized that the slave's entitlement to the *peculium* was a custom that pre-existed the Codes. It also bestowed limited forms of contractual capacity.[102] In this way, the slave law in the Civil Code advanced in a slightly liberal direction, even as the Black Code had tilted toward repression.

---

[99] For further details, *see supra* Chapter Two: "War Without Arms, The Customs of Slavery."
[100] Black Code 1806 §1.
[101] In theory these contracts were enforceable in the courts, but actions by slaves could be stymied by problems of proof. Owners sometimes accepted their money and later denied the existence of a contract. *See* Judith K. Schafer, *Becoming Free, Remaining Free: Manumission and Enslavement in New Orleans, 1846–1862*, at (Baton Rouge: Louisiana State University Press, 2003), 45–58.
[102] *See* text accompanying infra note 110.

THE ADVANCING SPANISH-ROMAN INFLUENCE *FROM THE DIGEST TO THE CODE*

The interim years between the codes (1808-1825) saw constant resort to Spanish and Roman authorities in the courts, and the law of slavery expanded well beyond what was contained in the statutes and the Digest. The decision to include slavery in the Digest now bore Spanish and Roman fruit. The subject of slave law was also swept up in the general revival of Spanish law occurring at that time, a revival that would not have been conceivable had slavery remained isolated in the Black Code. The famous reasoning of the Louisiana Supreme Court in *Cottin v. Cottin*[103] was instrumental in furthering this new direction. The *Cottin* reasoning stressed the limited footprint and porous design of the Digest (emphasizing it was a *Digest*, not a Code)[104] and permitted the recrudescence of Spanish slave law. Segments of Spanish law that the Digest had not specifically displaced or abrogated were viewed as waiting in the wings, ready for application, and could be used as a rule of decision in the unprovided-for case. This was actually the method by which a novel and unanticipated means of manumission—emancipation by prescription—found its way into the jurisprudence. A slave could gain his freedom if his master failed to exercise dominion over him for a certain period of time. Justice Derbigny recognized

---

[103] Cottin v. Cottin, 5 Mart. (OS) 93 (La. 1817). On the importance of this methodology, *see* my Tucker Lecture at Louisiana State University (November 17, 2011), "The Quest to Implant Civilian Method and Restrain Judicial Lawmaking in Louisiana: Tracing the Origins of Judicial Methodology" (*publication forthcoming in the LSU Law Review*). *See* further Vernon Valentine Palmer, "The Death of a Code—The Birth of a Digest," *Tulane Law Review* 63 (1988): 226.

[104] In the statutes commissioning the work, the Legislature twice referred to the future *projet* as a "Code," but when it emerged, it bore the title of a Digest. This last-minute change has been the cause of much debate. In Cottin, Justice Derbigny used the distinction as indicative of the way it must be interpreted:

> It must not be lost sight of, that our civil code is a digest of the civil laws, which were in force in this country, when it was adopted; that those laws must be considered as untouched, wherever the alterations and amendments, introduced in the digest, do not reach them, and that such parts of those laws only are repealed, as are either contrary to, or incompatible with the provisions of the code.

this "liberative" prescription solely on the authority of the *Partidas*, never mentioning that it arguably conflicted with the strict controls on manumission established under the Black Code.[105] It was thereafter accepted bodily into the Civil Code of 1825.[106]

A more dramatic example of the power of the incoming tide of Spanish-Roman law was the appearance of the *statuliber*, a class of slave not contemplated by the Digest.[107] *Statuliberi* had been recognized as anciently as the Twelve Tables. According to Buckland, they were "persons to whom liberty has been given by will under a condition, or from a day, which has not yet arrived."[108]

In terms of the three castes, the *statuliber* fell somewhere between the categories, so perhaps it could be considered a fourth caste. The codifiers of 1825 reformulated this Roman idea as follows: "Slaves for a time or statu-liberi, are those who have acquired the right of being free at a time to come, or on a condition which is not fulfilled, or in a certain event which has not happened;

---

[105] *See* Metayer v. Noret, 5 Mart. (OS) 566 (La. 1818); Metayer v. Metayer, 6 Mart. (OS) 16 (La. 1819). In the latter case, the court held that a slave who had lived as a free person for more than twenty years, out of the presence of her master, was liberated. (A ten-year period would have sufficed if the master were present.) The court relied upon the authority of L. 23, tit. 19, Part. 3 and L. 7, tit. 22, Part. 4. The special statute of 1807 on manumission subjected all cases of manumission to a judicial inquiry with exacting requirements. For a valuable account of the plaintiff's struggle in these cases to litigate her freedom, *see* Rebecca J. Scott, "'She . . . Refuses To Deliver Up Herself as the Slave of Your Petitioner:' Emigrés, Enslavement, and the Louisiana Civil Code of 1808," *Tulane European & Civil Law Forum* 24 (2009): 115.

[106] Art. 3510 (1825). In 1862 in the case of Rosalie f.w.c v. Fernandez, the District Court in New Orleans declared Rosalie and her daughter (born 1845) to be free, since Rosalie had enjoyed freedom for the past twenty years. Daily Picayune, Nov. 13, 1862.

[107] Poydras v. Beard, 4 Mart. (OS) 248 (La. 1816), may have been the first case to recognize the *statuliber*. *See also* Catin v. D'Orgenoy's Heirs, 8 Mart. (OS) 218 (La. 1820); Moosa v. Allain, 4 Mart. (OS) 98 (La. 1825); Jun, f.m.c. v. Livaudais, No. 1292, 5 Mart. (NS) 301 (La. 1827); Dorothee v. Coquillon, 7 Mart. (NS) 350 (La. 1829); Valsain v. Cloutier, 3 La. 170 (La. 1831). Moreau and Livingston participated as counsel in many of these cases. James Brown purchased a husband and wife and their two-year-old child, Harcles, in 1807 and promised the seller that he would grant the child its freedom in the year 1829, thereby making Harcles a *statuliber*, and he further agreed to pay a penalty of $500 if he failed to do so. *See* Everett, *supra* note 55, at 138.

[108] Buckland, *supra* note 93, at 286; Watson, *supra* note 4, at 25.

but who, in the mean time, remain in a state of slavery."[109] Other provisions made clear that the *statuliber* had significantly different rights and capacities than an ordinary slave. The person of the *statuliber* could no longer be sold by his master; only his time of service could be sold. By virtue of this status the slave temporarily remained a slave, but was clearly no longer an object of property. He could not be transported out of the territory. While awaiting his emancipation he could receive testaments and donations in his favor. The child born of a female *statuliber* acquired her condition, automatically becoming free at the time when his or her mother should be free.[110]

The Civil Code of 1825 attenuated the severity of the Digest in several other respects as well. The slave was now accorded the capacity to enter into a contract for his own emancipation and could enter contracts as agent for his master.[111] Slaves could also own personal property acquired through their own industry, which was accomplished by adding an exception: "The slave possesses nothing of his own, except his *peculium*." The drafters explained that the slave's *peculium* was an old Roman institution that was already recognized by Louisiana customs. Finally the Civil Code provided that succession rights might pass through the slave to a free descendant. This allowed property that a slave would have inherited, had he been free, to pass to a free descendant or relative.

Conclusion

In the years 1806–1807 the Territorial Legislature passed a series of statutes called the Black Code which reflected, for the first time, the kind of laws that Creole slave owners preferred. The Black Code, while retaining rather few rules inherited from the past, now borrowed heavily from American slave statutes. What emerged was a security-conscious Code that established new slave courts and new criminal offences, recognized a three-caste society,

---

[109] La. Civ. Code Art. 37 (1825).
[110] *Additions and Amendments to the Civil Code of the State of Louisiana* (New Orleans: Levy & Co. 1823), 3–4, 15.
[111] Arts. 174 and 1783 (1825).

tightened requirements for manumission and eliminated all references to Christianity.

It was at this juncture that Moreau Lislet was called upon to insert slavery provisions into the Digest of 1808. He did not attempt to codify the entire law. It is clear that he left the bulk of the police and criminal matters in the special law or Black Code, thus allowing him to focus upon the private law aspects at a fairly high level of generality. By borrowing non-racial Roman definitions and principles he created the outward appearance of a racially neutral law that was in contrast to social reality as well as the white-supremacist "Black Code" by which he was guided. Although substantively compatible, Moreau's opuscule on slavery in the Digest was formally different than the core slave law of the Black Code. The effects of his work certainly resonated beyond the Digest. The provisions proved to be something more than an ornamental façade. In the interim period between the codes, the Louisiana judges and lawyers went back to Spanish-Roman sources and retrieved various non-codified slave rules and principles to resolve unanswered questions. Some of these tended to soften the rigor of slavery. The drafters of the second code continued the resurgence of Spanish-Roman law by introducing new concepts like the *statuliber* and by reviving older ones like the *peculium*. On the whole the Romanization of Louisiana's slave law in its private law aspects tended to produce a regime considerably more favorable to the slave than the Black Code enacted a few years before.

From a purely technical and legal point of view, the most notable effect of this strange desire to include slavery in the Codes was that it ultimately created the conditions for a systematic and coherent jurisprudence of slavery. It helped transform slave law into lawyer's law; it brought slavery center stage into the courtroom and forced judges to write hundreds of legal opinions which attempted to mould and reconcile the slavery articles with the civil law of Louisiana. Slavery-related civil litigation would become the largest single category of the Louisiana Supreme Court's jurisdiction. The constant references to Roman and Spanish civil law made this a learned jurisprudence that, although now understandably forgotten, was quite exceptional in its day, not merely in the United States but abroad as well. This jurisprudence far eclipsed the French colonial jurisprudence under the *Code Noir* which, in comparison, ventured no further than the confines of the statute and produced little more than a set of simple maxims and skeletal answers. The next chapter will attempt to explain Louisiana's remarkable jurisprudence and the systematic thinking and classical learning which made it unique.

Pierre Auguste Charles Bourguignon Derbigny
Justice of the Supreme Court and Governor of Louisiana
(*Courtesy of the Louisiana Supreme Court Library*)

CHAPTER 4

Slave Law under Digest and Code, 1808–1860

Systematic Thinking and Classical Learning[1]

INTRODUCTION

By codifying their laws Louisiana Creoles attempted to entrench and preserve their culture and heritage, at least those parts of the heritage that they considered most important. Oddly enough slave law was considered sufficiently important to include in both of the 19th century civil codes. This was an unprecedented step whose effects have been somewhat overlooked by the historians. Here were the first modern codes to weave slavery in a systematic way into the fabric of the civil law. The effort was an unexpected extension of the codifiers' task that they were not technically bound to undertake, either by virtue of their instructions or due to the civilian tradition. Indeed, as mentioned earlier, the French Civil code was obviously a model expression of the civil law which the drafters held in view, but it did not treat slavery and in this respect the codifiers could not follow its example. They seem to have been following instead the example of quite ancient laws like Justinian's Digest and Spain's *Las Siete Partidas*, which built slavery provisions into the rules of private social relations. The Louisiana codifiers integrated slavery provisions into the law of persons, property, successions, sales and prescription. In approximately forty five provisions strewn across the titles and books of the codes, black slavery was built into the private law rules without any use of

---

[1] This chapter was presented in May 2011 at the Edinburgh Conference on Louisiana Legal History.

racial identifiers, much as the United States Constitution had concealed its own slavery provisions.[2]

At first glance it may not have been apparent that this event marked any momentous turn in the history of this subject, and yet it opened new vistas for outward expansion and systematic reasoning unlike any preceding period. It produced broad and long-lasting legal effects in several ways.

Firstly, this integration into the code moved slavery from the edges of the legal system into the heart of private law relations. It brought the subject out of an obscure corner to center stage in the courtroom. The law of slavery would become for the first time "lawyers' law." Civil litigation over slaves became probably the largest single category of the courts' jurisdiction. In the antebellum period about one thousand two hundred slavery-related appeals came before the Louisiana Supreme Court and in some years it was not uncommon for twenty to twenty five percent of all cases on the docket to be slavery-related.[3] Slavery would therefore no longer be identified merely with a special statute that contained mostly public law provisions.

The importance of this litigation was partly responsible for the rapid growth of the legal profession. French and Spanish colonial rule had not permitted lawyers to practice before the courts, but as soon as the first court in the Territory opened in 1804, Governor Claiborne began to issue licenses to practice. The minute book of the Court of Common Pleas for 1804 shows that about twenty lawyers were immediately admitted to practice, and the entries are rather evenly divided between American and Creole surnames.[4]

---

[2] Similarly, there were no racial references in the Louisiana Constitution of 1812.

[3] "Slavery-related" would encompass all civil cases in which slaves were either objects or subjects of the litigation. *See* Judith Kelleher Schafer, Slavery, the Civil Law, and the Supreme Court of Louisiana 13–15 (Baton Rouge: Louisiana State University Press, 1994). In the years 1810, 1816, 1817 and 1820, slavery-related cases ranged from 19.3% to 25.9 % of the Supreme Court's appellate docket. *Ibid.* 14. Such figures are impressively high, considering that they only include *civil* cases involving slaves. All criminal cases involving slaves, a large number, are excluded. The Supreme Court's jurisdiction for most of this period was confined to civil cases of a value exceeding $300 (the Court had no criminal appellate jurisdiction until 1845). The Court had no discretion to refuse civil appeals above that value.

[4] Court of Pleas (New Orleans), Index to Minute Book, 1804. Available at http://nutrias.org/~nopl/inv/court%20of%20pleas%20index.htm. This estimation

Slave cases alleging hidden defects in slaves at the time of their purchase were among the first to be tried in this court.

Furthermore, this integration would build a more principled and systematic slave law which needed to be compatible with the general concepts found in the civil code. It presupposed that slave rules would be interpreted in the same way that civil law was generally interpreted. Compatibility actually ran in two directions, not one: slave provisions had to be internally consistent with adjacent articles of the Digest, but the same provisions were also examined for external consistency with the Spanish, Roman and French law of the *ius commune*. The Digest of 1808 was, in the view of the courts, only a condensed version of the civil law of Spain, France and Rome. The provisions in the Digest, both slave and non-slave, were an outline or convenient summary that could receive modification and supplementation from all compatible Spanish-Roman laws. Integration in the Digest meant therefore that the reigning "Digest Methodology" utilized by the courts of Louisiana in the years 1808–1828,[5] would play an important role in the interpretation of slavery provisions. It would permit the courts to go beyond the Digest itself and delve into ancient, far-flung rules of slavery. As we shall see, it produced surprising new avenues of manumission, even at a time when the public policy toward

---

of the number of American and Creole lawyers is somewhat conjectural, since it is based solely on inference from their surnames. The growing American presence at the bar became more evident in 1813 when they numbered around sixty per cent of those sworn in before the Louisiana Supreme Court. By 1839, their numbers reached seventy eight per cent of those admitted. Elizabeth Gaspard, "The Rise of the Louisiana Bar: The Early Period, 1813–1839" *Louisiana History* 28, (1987) 183, at 187.

[5] The best articulation of the "Digest Methodology", as I have called it, was in Cottin v. Cottin (1817) in which Judge Derbigny defined the meaning of natural birth by going beyond the Digest's definition and adding a test peculiar to Spanish law. The justification for this modification was that "It must not be lost sight of, that our civil code is a digest of the civil laws . . . ; that those laws must be considered as untouched, wherever the alterations and amendments, introduced in the digest, do not reach them, and that such parts of those laws only are repealed, as are either contrary to, or incompatible with the provisions of the code." For a demonstration that the method had been in place well before *Cottin*, indeed from as early as 1809, *see* my Tucker Lecture at Louisiana State University (November 17, 2011), "The Quest to Implant Civilian Method and Restrain Judicial Lawmaking in Louisiana: Tracing the Origins of Judicial Methodology"(*publication forthcoming in the LSU Law Review*).

manumission was manifestly repressive.[6] Slave rules stored in old Spanish reservoirs such as the *Partidas* served to supplement that outline, and permitted uncodified Roman slave concepts to be introduced. The overall result was that Louisiana slave law was Romanized and, in consequence, tempered in ways that had not occurred before.[7] The jurisprudence of the period 1808–1825 fundamentally altered Louisiana's second codification, the 1825 Civil Code, which incorporated revived Spanish ideas into its provisions.[8] A key area in which this occurred was the law of manumission.

Manumission

The legislature's policy toward the subject of slave emancipation in the antebellum period was one of escalating repression. It was generally feared that too many freed slaves posed a grave threat of insurrection and instability. Free persons of color were inevitably suspected of assisting or masterminding slave revolts such as the great uprising of 1811 near New Orleans, the largest slave revolt in United States history.[9] Many different ways of limiting the numbers of free persons of color were tried. The Black Code of 1807 restricted the emancipation of slaves to those thirty years of age and above who had demonstrated "honest conduct" (had not run away, robbed, and so forth) during the preceding four years.[10] An owner desiring to free his slave had to

---

[6] This was prompted by a noticeably greater anxiety over public safety and a new alertness to the danger of uprisings, revolts and slave criminality. Massive amounts of American slave law and terminology were directly introduced into the Black Code of 1806/1807. *See* above Chapter Three, "Strange Science of Codifying Slavery—Moreau Lislet and the Louisiana Digest of 1808."

[7] The reader will recall that, according to Professor Watson, there was considerable Roman influence in the provisions of the original French *Code Noir* of 1685, a proposition that I disputed in Chapter One, *supra*: "The Authors and Origins of the *Code Noir*." With respect to the 19th century antebellum period, however, the Roman influence is conspicuous and uncontested.

[8] Slave provisions also entered into the Code of Civil Procedure. *See* Art. 103, and Art. 114, of the *projet*.

[9] *See* Daniel Rasmussen, *American Uprising: The Untold Story of America's Largest Slave* Revolt (New York: Harper, 2011).

[10] Acts 1807, Chap. X, 82.

petition a parish judge and show that these age and conduct-related conditions were met. A public notice needed to be posted, allowing time for others in the community to file opposition to the enfranchisement if they had reason to do so. Age-wise, this law was by definition highly restrictive. It meant, for example, that a slaveowner could not free an entire family with small children. A free woman of color could not purchase and liberate her children if they were underage. In 1827 the legislature "softened" the age requirement by allowing the master of a *native-born* slave under thirty years of age to petition the police jury of his parish, and manumission could be granted if he or she obtained the approval of three-fourths of its members.[11] In 1830, however, the legislature added a drastic qualification. It ordered that all manumitted slaves had to leave the state immediately and required the owner to post a $1,000 bond to ensure the departure, *unless* the police jury ruled that the slave did not have to leave.

The actual exercise of the police jury's discretion to excuse this deportation requirement gives an insight into the ambivalent feelings that must have existed toward these severe laws. Kotlikoff and Rupert's study of the petitions presented to the police jury in New Orleans over the years 1827–1846 shows invariable support for freeing slaves regardless of their age and without requiring them to leave the state. Of 1,166 petitions in the study, 1,159 were approved by the police jury. A total of 1,770 slaves were manumitted. Each minute entry ended with the routine statement, "without being compelled to leave the state."[12] Thus it seems clear

---

[11] Acts 1827, 12–14.

[12] Laurence J. Kotlikoff and Anton J. Rupert, "The Manumission of Slaves in New Orleans, 1827–1846" *Southern Studies* (1980), 172–181. The study revealed that free people of color served as the catalyst for a large number of these manumissions. About 37% of all the petitions *were filed by free-black owners*, who accounted for six hundred and forty six of the one thousand seven hundred and seventy slaves manumitted. Considering the number of free black households in New Orleans at the time, this meant that one in every eight households was engaged in the emancipation of one or more slaves during the period. In 1846, the ending year of the cases studied, the legislature abolished the Orleans Parish Police Jury and transferred jurisdiction over emancipations to the "Emancipation Courts of the Council of the Three Municipalities." Judith Schafer notes that the petitions to the Emancipation Courts continued to request permission to remain in the state and the Councils allowed these requests. *See* Judith Schafer, "Forever Free

that these laws, despite their apparent rigor, were ineffectual in slowing down the numbers of free people of color. In 1820 the number of free people of color in the state was 10,476. By 1840 the figure had soared to 25,502.[13]

In view of these mounting numbers a vacillating legislature countered with stronger restrictions. In 1842 it prohibited the importation into Louisiana of slaves "entitled to freedom at a future period" (a *statuliber*), and it ordered that those *statuliberi* presently in the state must, upon gaining their freedom, be deported at the owner's expense.[14] It resorted to a more desperate measure in 1852 by ordering all manumitted slaves to be sent to Liberia at the owner's expense.[15] This deportation requirement only stayed on the books for three years. In 1855 the legislature required that all instances of emancipation would be tried by jury, and the jury's decision would include whether an emancipated slave must leave or could remain in the state. Thus the deportation question was once again to be decided by popular decision, which, as we saw in the case of police jury determinations under the 1830 law, was favorably inclined to excuse deportation. According to historian Judith Schafer, a sudden and dramatic increase in emancipations took place in New Orleans in 1855 and 1856 as a result of this law, and this prompted the most desperate measure of all.[16] In 1857, the legislature closed all loopholes and enacted a total prohibition on emancipations.[17] The effects were apparently significant. By 1860 the number of free persons was reduced to 18,647, about 7,000 less than the highpoint in 1840.

This history of these manumission statutes, however, strongly contrasts with the trajectory of the jurisprudence under the codes. While the legislature was concerned with reducing the avenues to emancipation and reducing the number of free persons of color, the courts discovered several new forms of manumission in the Roman-Spanish laws of the *ius commune*.

From the Bonds of Slavery: Emancipation in New Orleans, 1855–1857" in W.M. Billings and M.F. Fernandez (eds.), *A Law Unto Itself?: Essays in the New Louisiana Legal History* (Baton Rouge: Louisiana State University Press 2001), 142.

[13] *Encyclopedia of Louisiana*, verbo "Free People of Color," www.knowla.org.

[14] Acts 1842, 316.

[15] Acts 1852, No. 315, 214.

[16] Schafer, "Forever Free From the Bonds of Slavery," 142.

[17] Acts 1857, No. 69, 55.

Emancipation by Prescription

This was a type of manumission neither contemplated by the Digest of 1808 nor allowed by the special statutes of Louisiana. The idea was first discussed by the Supreme Court in two cases decided in 1818–1819. In *Metayer v. Noret*,[18] Noret claimed that Adelaide Metayer was his slave and had her and her children seized and imprisoned. Adelaide countered with a lawsuit for false imprisonment and sought damages. Adelaide contended that she had purchased her freedom from her master in St. Domingue in 1801, and had been living as a free person ever since. A jury of eleven men found in her favor and awarded her freedom, but the jury did not award her damages against those who had seized her. Noret appealed to the Supreme Court. The Court did not base its ruling on the contested papers Adelaide presented as evidence of her status, but focused instead upon a Spanish rule of prescription found in the *Siete Partidas*. Judge Derbigny wrote that "By the laws of Spain, a slave can acquire his freedom by a possession of ten years, in the presence of his master, or of twenty years in his absence."[19] The Digest of Orleans had no comparable rule. It contained a rule that dealt with the "acquisition" of slaves by prescription, as between the competing claims of two rival owners, but this rule, said the court, "cannot be construed to embrace the prescription of liberty by [slaves] themselves."[20] Obviously the Digest's provision did not control the question of Adelaide's manumission and equally clearly it did not conflict with or repeal

---

[18] 5 Mart. (OS) 566 (1818).

[19] The rule is stated in *Partida* 3.29.23. A related rule in *Partida* 3.29.24 laid down that "If a man be free, no matter how long he may be held by another, as a slave; his state or condition cannot be thereby changed; nor can he be reduced to slavery, in any manner whatever, on account of the time he may have been held in servitude." This rule on the imprescriptibility of freedom was applied in plaintiff's favor in the case of Delphine v. Deveze, 2 Mart. (n.s.) 650 (1824).

[20] Rather remarkably, the repeal issue entertained by the court was restricted to possible conflicts between prescription rules. It did not consider whether the prescription rule in the *Partidas* was in conflict with a special statute on manumission which laid down strict conditions (minimum age and proof of good behavior for four preceding years) which would be circumvented by the Spanish rule.

the prescriptive rule of liberty found in the *Partidas*.[21] This was clearly an occasion where the Court employed the Digest methodology and treated unrepealed Spanish laws to be in force to the same extent as if they had been enacted by the Louisiana legislature. Based on its reading of the facts, however, the court did not agree that Adelaide had gained her freedom under the Spanish rule, nor that she could recover on her main claim for damages from defendant for causing her to be wrongfully seized. She had failed to show that she had been living as a free person for the requisite twenty years in the absence of her master. She left St. Domingue in 1803 for Cuba and had lived in New Orleans since 1809, or a total of only fifteen years. In *Metayer v. Metayer*,[22] however, Adelaide Metayer's case reappeared a year later before the Supreme Court, and the Court recalculated the years she was in possession of her freedom outside of the presence of her master. Justice Derbigny was now willing to take into account the revolutionary decrees of the French Commissioners who had abolished slavery in St. Domingue in 1793. Accordingly he began the prescriptive period in 1793 and concluded that Adelaide had lived in possession of her freedom for more than the requisite twenty years.[23]

These two cases illustrate the process by which the law of slavery was progressively Romanized during the antebellum

---

[21] *See* Digest 1808, Art. 74, 488: "Slaves may be prescribed for in half the time required for the prescription of immoveable estate and in the same manner and subject to the same exceptions."

[22] 6 Mart. (OS) 16 (1819).

[23] In contrast to the prior calculation, the court now included certain years before she left St. Domingue as fulfilling part of the prescriptive period. "[T]he evidence, in the present case, shows that she was in Hispaniola when the general emancipation was proclaimed by the commissioners of the French government, and remained there until after the evacuation of the island by the French in 1803, a period of about ten years. It is further proved, that she continued in the enjoyment of her freedom, without interruption until 1816; so that she has lived as a free person during twenty-three years . . . three years more than the time required by law for a slave to acquire his freedom, by prescription in the absence of his master." *Ibid.* 18. For details of the remarkable life of Adelaide and her courageous struggle to establish her free status and her children's as well, *see* Rebecca J. Scott, " 'She . . . Refuses To Deliver Herself as the Slave of Your Petitioner': Emigrés, Enslavement, and the 1808 Louisiana Digest of the Civil Laws," *Tulane European & Civil Law Forum* 24 (2009): 115.

period. As a first step it needed to be ascertained whether the Digest's provisions on prescription were in conflict with the Spanish law of emancipation by prescription. If the rules were in conflict, the Spanish rule was considered repealed and could not be used. The highly discretionary question of repeal was in fact the linchpin of the Digest method. It was an *a priori* determination upon which all else depended.[24] Normally the judges used the strictest of tests to judge implied repeals (interestingly, they relied upon common law authorities of repeal in this period), and in consequence the maximum amount of Spanish law was kept potentially relevant. Here the court concluded that the Spanish law was not impliedly repealed because the two laws could stand together without logical contradiction. Then the Court drew directly upon the prescriptive rule stated in the *Partidas* and applied it to the facts presented by plaintiff, concluding that she had become a free woman of color by the elapse of twenty three years. A further step in the Romanization process took place a few years later. The codifiers of the Civil Code of 1825 took cognizance of these precedents and added a new provision to the code. That code article provided: "If a master suffer a slave to enjoy his liberty for ten years during his residence in the State, or for twenty years while out of it, he shall lose all right of action to recover possession of the slave unless the slave be a runaway or fugitive."[25] The circularity of this development could not be more striking: A rule originally found in the *ius commune* and not the Digest, was recognized by the judges and passed into the jurisprudence, after which it was received in the Civil Code.

The *Statuliber*

The concept of the *statuliber* furnishes a second illustration of the circular process of Romanization. The *statuliber* was a slave in

---

[24]Vernon Valentine Palmer," The Quest to Implant Civilian Method and Restrain Judicial Lawmaking in Louisiana: Tracing the Origins of Judicial Methodology" (Tucker Lecture at Louisiana State University November 17, 2011, *publication forthcoming in the LSU Law Review*).
[25] Civil Code Art. 3510 (1825).

350 CASES IN THE SUPREME COURT

East'n. District. *May* 1816. BEARD *vs.* POYDRAS.

We contend that she is what is in the Roman law called a *statuliber*, and not a free woman. On this we are at issue.

A little closer examination of the title of the digest *de manumissis testamento*, commented upon by the plaintiff's counsel, would have convinced him that the general principle of the Roman law, in respect to conditional enfranchisements, is quite the reverse of what he argues it to be, and the laws which he has cited, are exceptions only to the general rule, which are not susceptible of extention.

Freedom may be given absolutely or conditionally, or to be enjoyed at a future day. When the slave is manumitted absolutely, he becomes free as soon as the succession is accepted; but if either a condition or time be added to the manumission, the condition must be performed or the time must elapse, before the freedom is enjoyed, *ff* 40, 4, 23, § 1, 3 *Pothier's Pand. Just.* 55. 14 *Rodriguez's dig.* 187.

According to the Spanish law, all legacies may be absolute or conditional, or at a future day, *Part.* 6, 9, 31. 1 *Febrero contratos, ch.* 1, *n* 46.

In legacies under a condition or at future day, the condition must be performed, or the day must arrive before they have any effect. *Part.* 6, 9, 21. *Febrero id. n.* 47 48.

Slaves manumitted by will, under a condition, or on a future day, were called at Rome *statu liberi* until they acquired their freedom. *ff* 40, 8, 1. 14, *Rod. dig.* 287.

STATULIBER. By this word was designated the slave manumitted, under a condition, or at a future epoch; it came from *statuta libertas*, *conditio statutæ libertatis*. 1. 81 *ff de legatis* 2 *Dict. du Dig. n.* 1667.

Till the condition was performed or the day arrived, the *statuliber* was considered as a slave. No body is ignorant that the *statuliber* is in the interim the slave of the heir. *ff* 40, 7, 9. 14 *Rod. Dig.* 315.

Children born from a woman *statuliber*, are the slaves of the heir. 40, 7, 16. 14 *Rod. Dig.* 321, 322.

We read in the books of Gaius Cassius, that what is acquired by a *statuliber*, before the performance of the condition, added to the manumission, does not enter into the *peculium* which is bequeathed, unless the legacy be made for the time when he should be free. Yet it is to be observed that the *peculium* being susceptible of increase and decrease, the increase ought to make part of the legacy, *provided the heir has not*

East'n. District. *May* 1816. BEARD *vs.* POYDRAS.

Classical sources in the Louisiana jurisprudence
(Brief of Moreau Lislet, 1816)

transition toward freedom. This intermediate status could be created by the juridical acts of the master—such as by making a will, a contract or giving a unilateral promise—in which he declared the terms and timetable for his slave's future freedom.[26]

[26] Thus in Valsain v. Cloutier, 3 La. 170 (1831) a free woman of color purchased her own daughter in 1796 and held her as a slave. By notarial act in 1797 the mother declared that from maternal love and affection her daughter would become free at her (the mother's) death, which occurred in 1815. On the basis of Roman

According to a passage from Paul in Justinian's Digest, "The *statuliber* is one who has freedom arranged to take effect on completion of a period or fulfillment of a condition. Men become *statuliberi* as a result of an express condition, or by the very nature of the case."[27] Pending the arrival of the term or the fulfillment of the condition, the slave remained in a state of slavery, and still subject to the absolute domination of his master, and yet his future status was settled and could not be unilaterally revoked by the master. No longer a perfectly rightless individual, the slave possessed the capacity to receive such declarations and promises (the terms of which were no doubt negotiated in many cases), to make payments of self-purchase and perform acts in discharge of any conditions, and generally to enforce the juridical act in court if necessary, even by specific performance. Though temporarily a slave, he was clearly no longer a simple object of property. His person could no longer be sold by his master; only the remaining time of his service could be sold. He could not be transported out of the territory, and while awaiting his emancipation he could receive testaments and donations in his favor. The child born of a female *statuliber* acquired the same status as his or her mother, and became free at the same time as the mother obtained her freedom.[28]

The Digest of 1808 did not mention this institution in any of its provisions, and indeed the absence of such a transitional path out of slavery, which Roman and Spanish rules had long before recognized and elaborated upon, was no doubt a gap in the Digest.

It was a gap, however, that was easily filled in by Louisiana's *ius commune*. If the Digest originally described a three-caste society, the new institution added a fourth caste, for the *statuliber* fell neatly between the social position of the slave and that of the former slave (free persons of color). [29] *Poydras v. Beard* in 1816 marked the first in a series of cases recognizing the *statuliber* under

---

and Spanish authorities, Judge Porter held that the daughter became a *statuliber* as of the act in 1797, was then emancipated by her mother's death in 1815, and instantaneously acquired the capacity to inherit her mother's estate.

[27] Digest of Justinian (Statuliber) 40.7.1 *See also* 40.7.6.

[28] *See* above, Chapter Three, "Strange Science of Codifying Slavery."

[29] *Ibid.* at 104, 112.

Louisiana law.[30] In *Cuffy v. Castillon,*[31] an owner had agreed to free certain slaves for the fixed price of $3,400 but had received only $316, an amount that was imputed to the freedom of another slave rather than to the plaintiff. Nevertheless plaintiff argued on the basis of Roman authorities (Dig. 50, 17, 20; 40, 1.40) that even when the whole price agreed upon has not been paid, the slave may still acquire his freedom if the deficiency was afterwards supplied "in-kind" through his labor or industry. Counsel further argued that any doubt as to whether this was the proper interpretation of the agreement should be resolved in favor of liberty. *Quoties dubia libertatis interpretation est.* Judge Mathews did not deny that the plaintiff enjoyed the status of a *statuliber*, but insisted that a *statuliber* must fulfill the condition on which he is to be entitled to his freedom. He declared that "Freedom must not be so favored by interpretation, as to depart entirely from the intention of the contracting parties, apparent on the contract itself." This *statuliber* lost his case, but the institution was nevertheless recognized.

It was only a few years later that the legislature placed the following provision in the Civil Code of 1825: "Slaves for a time or *statu-liberi*, are those who have acquired the right of being free at a time to come, or on a condition which is not fulfilled, or in a certain event which has not happened; but who, in the meantime, remain in a state of slavery."[32] Here again the pattern and process of legal development is familiar. A slave rule which had never been previously codified or applied in Louisiana is found among the Spanish-Roman sources. It is recognized by the Court, passes into the jurisprudence, and is eventually incorporated into the positive law.

---

[30] *See* Catin v. D'Orgenoy's Heirs, 8 Mart. (OS) 218 (1820); Moosa v. Allain, 4 Mart. (OS) 98 (1825); Mathurin v. Livaudais, 5 Mart. (n.s.) 301 (1827); Dorothee v. Coquillon, 7 Mart. (n.s.) 350 (1829); Valsain v. Coutier, 3 La. 170 (1831).

[31] 5 Mart. (OS) 494 (1818).

[32] Civil Code Art. 37 (1825). An 1838 act added, "The child born of a woman after she has acquired the right of being free at a future time, follows the condition of its mother and becomes free at the time for her enfranchisement, even if the mother should die before that time."

THE SYSTEMATIC INTERPRETATION OF SLAVERY ARTICLES

The insertion of slavery rules into a logically-arranged and conceptually-consistent civil code sometimes provoked internal contradictions and interpretational difficulties. After all there was no ready template for a rigorously logical slave law. Ideally the slave provisions should have been as systematic and coherent as all other provisions, and yet, as the practical problems arose, slave law had to be adjusted. Indeed to find its place it had to become self-generative and interactive, by virtue of its association with the entire civil code framework of which it formed a part. For instance the action in redhibition to rescind the sale of a slave with a hidden defect seemed, according to the Digest, to carry a short prescriptive period of only twelve months, and this rule certainly applied when the vendee was a plaintiff asserting the action. The Supreme Court ruled, however, that when the seller sued the buyer on the price, the buyer could always raise the slave's redhibitory vice as a defence for an unlimited period of time.[33] That distinction, between the buyer asserting the action as opposed to his interposing a defense, was not explicitly stated in the Digest. Here the tradition and framework of the civil law gave added understanding or value to the rules which they would not necessarily have had in statutory isolation.

Rules that seemed simple and clear in most contexts proved problematic when applied to slaves. For example the provisions in the Digest declaring that the slave is an immovable and that any contract to alienate an immovable must be reduced to writing gave rise to significant problems of interpretation. Article 241, page 310 of the Digest stated, "Every covenant tending to dispose by a gratuitous or incumbered title of any immoveable property *or slaves* in this territory, must be reduced to writing and…no parol evidence shall be admitted to prove it [the covenant]." (emphasis added) The reason for such a requirement was clear enough with

---

[33] *See* Thompson v. Milburn, 1 Mart. (n.s.) 468 (1823). The Court referred to Febrero, 2, lib. 3, cap. 1, sec. 6 for this interpretation: "*Lo que tiene tiempo limitado para demandarse in juicio, es perpetuo para exceptionarse.*"

respect to a sale of land from one owner to another or for title-passing transactions in which the object of the contract was a slave. But was that requirement meant to apply to transactions of self-purchase in which the slave himself was a party? Was self-purchase envisioned by the rule, and should an illiterate slave be expected to comply with it?

When the matter first arose Judge Mathews held that the same rules ordinarily applicable to buyers and sellers, mortgagors and mortgagees and so forth would also govern cases in which slaves sought to establish their freedom. Parol evidence ought not to be exceptionally admitted to prove the contract because a contract of manumission "tends to dispose of a slave."[34] He recognized that a contract of manumission under Spanish law (*Partida* 3.2.8) might be oral and proven by witness testimony, but he asserted "We are, however, of opinion that the latter laws are virtually repealed by the civil code." In an 1848 decision, however, the Supreme Court re-examined this question and read the Code differently.[35] It reasoned that the rule of the Civil Code authorizing slaves to contract for their emancipation was originally derived from the *Partidas* and Justinian's Digest and did not literally require any particular formality. The court now advanced a subtle distinction to the effect that while the act of emancipation itself would have to be in writing, this did not mean that an earlier contract under which "the right" to emancipation was acquired required the same formality. In other words, the contract by which the slave became a *statuliber* might be oral but his actual emancipation must be written. The distinction permitted the court to uphold the requirement of a writing, while at the same time to uphold the validity of oral promises of freedom received by a slave. The court thereupon concluded in favor of plaintiff, who was declared free.

A related question was whether a contract of manumission needed to be publicly recorded in order to affect the claims of creditors. In *Doubrere v. Grillier's Syndic*,[36] a bankrupt had (at an earlier time when he was solvent) manumitted his slave and was paid $1,800 purchase money. This act of emancipation was not

---

[34] Victoire v. Dussuau, 4 Mart. (OS) 212 (1816).
[35] Gaudet v. Gourdain 3 La.Ann. 136 (1848).
[36] 2 Mart. (n.s.) 171 (1824).

publicly recorded. By a provision in the Digest no "sale or exchange of immoveables or slaves" could have effect against third persons unless it was publicly recorded, and no exception was made for contracts of manumission.[37] The bankrupt's creditors seized and sequestered the manumitted slave (then enjoying his freedom), on grounds that an unregistered act of emancipation could have no legal effect against third parties. The Court held against the creditors and in favor of the former slave. The Court conceived a slave's self-purchase to be an ordinary contract of sale, but it reasoned that this was a *bona fide* sale with delivery which caused no injury to the creditors' interests. It created no false credit, did not mislead and did not diminish the common fund. The creditors "cannot make an honest purchaser give up what he has bought and come on the estate for the price." The Court effectively made an exception to the general requirements of the code where a slave's self-purchase was involved.

Although the official theory was that Spanish-Roman law, if unrepealed, had the force of statute in Louisiana, in actuality this theory was sometimes disapplied because of racial considerations. The Spanish and Roman law of slavery was thought to be color blind and had no discriminatory rules specifically directed at particular *races* of slaves. How therefore could such a background law be applied to the racial slavery in Louisiana? The historical record shows that when it could not be squared with local conditions it could be ignored. In its place the judges could simply create or borrow rules drawn from other sources, including American slave law. An important example of this is the landmark case of *Adelle v. Beauregard*[38] which was frequently cited and followed in succeeding years. The plaintiff Adelle was a woman of color asserting her free status, while defendant claimed her as his slave. Neither side had documents of title proving her true status, and the issue was whether the burden of proving the ultimate question of freedom or slavery rested upon plaintiff or defendant. The Digest of Orleans certainly provided no rule establishing a presumption one way or the other. The *Partidas* on the other hand addressed the issue specifically with a rule placing the burden on

---

[37] Digest, 306, Art. 228.
[38] 1 Mart. (OS) 183 (1810). *See* further Mary, f.w.c. v. Morris, 7 La. 135 (1834).

the master to show proofs of ownership.[39] It is however significant that the Court did not apply the rule of the *Partidas* on the burden of proving slavery, though one might have supposed it was bound to do so since it had not been repealed. Instead Judge Martin declared that whenever the plaintiff is a black person he is presumed to be a slave until he can prove otherwise. The burden of proof was upon the black slave to destroy that presumption. Blacks had been brought to Louisiana to be slaves and "their descendants may perhaps be presumed to have continued so, till they show the contrary. On the other hand, white persons and persons of color, such as plaintiff, were presumed free. They may have descended from Indians on both sides, from a white parent, or mulatto parents in possession of their freedom." In a related passage the court added: "Considering how much probability there is in favor of the liberty of those persons [whites and persons of color], they ought not to be deprived of it upon mere presumption, more especially as the right of holding them in slavery, if it exists, is in most instances capable of being satisfactorily proved. *Gobu v. Gobu*, Taylor 115." The court did not disclose to the reader that the entire paragraph just quoted was taken verbatim from the North Carolina case of *Gobu* decided by the North Carolina Supreme Court in 1802, which was the leading national case on the subject.[40] The Louisiana Supreme Court thus rejected the color-blind evidentiary rules of the *Partidas*, which were biased in favor of freedom for all slaves, and opted *sub silentio* for discriminatory rules dependent upon skin color.[41] In other words, in place of the *Partidas*, the court covertly instituted the racial presumptions of American law. Those racial

---

[39] *Partidas* 3.14.5 (Moreau Lislet and Carleton transl. 1820) states, "[W]e say that where the plaintiff claims as his slave the defendant who is in the enjoyment of his liberty, and who replies that he is free; that it will be incumbent on the plaintiff, to prove what he alleges, and not the defendant who is in possession of his freedom, unless he choose. But where the plaintiff in a cause alleges that he is free, and brings a suit for his freedom against his master, who holds him in his power, and claims him as his slave; and the master produce any title, document of other proof, to shew that he had possession of the plaintiff in good faith, and not by force or fraud; it will then be incumbent on the plaintiff to prove that he is free. . . . "

[40] *Gobu* was followed in Virginia: Hudgins v. Wrights (1806) 11 Va. 134. For a chronological list of the cases following this decision, *see* Wilbert Moore, "Slave Law and Social Structure," *Journal of Negro History* 26 (1941): 171, 187.

[41] *See* Frank Sweet, "Essays on the Color Line and the One-Drop Rule," (2004) http://backintyme.com/essays/item/7.

presumptions were designed for a three-caste society. They protected persons who were visibly of mixed blood, like the plaintiff Adelle, but instituted enslavement by default for all black persons.[42]

A different example of judicial creativity arose in connection with the effects produced by a slave marriage upon spouses who were later emancipated. In *Girod v. Lewis* (1819)[43] the Court treated such marriages as creating a natural obligation that would give forth full civil effects after emancipation. It is probably no coincidence that the Court's opinion was extremely short and devoid of citations to authorities. Judge Mathews began by noting that slaves have no legal capacity to assent to contracts of any kind, yet they may undoubtedly marry with the consent of their master. Their marriage, while in a state of slavery, cannot produce any civil effect, because slaves are deprived of all civil rights. Yet, he concluded, their marriage received retroactive validation upon emancipation. "Emancipation gives to the slave his civil rights, and a contract of marriage, legal and valid by the consent of the master and moral assent of the slave, from the moment of freedom, *although dormant during the slavery*, produces all the effects which result from such contract among free persons." (emphasis added) As mentioned, the Court used no authority and deployed no reasoned basis, and yet it seems clear from its reference to "dormant" civil rights that it was regarding a slave marriage as constituting a natural obligation which may be converted into civil obligations once the obligor acquires *un état civil*. If that is a fair reading, it is another instance in which we find that slave law, through interaction with surrounding legal ideas and institutions, gained new substance.

---

[42] Adelle v. Beauregard was controlling authority in the famous "white slave" case of Morrison v. White, 16 La. Ann. 100 (1861) which resulted in a jury verdict for the plaintiff. *See* Walter Johnson, "The Slave Trader, the White Slave, and the Politics of Racial Determination in the 1850's," http//www.uvm.edu/psearls/johnson.html.
[43] 6 Mart. (OS) 359 (1819).

REDHIBITION AND THE LAW OF SALES

The *Code Noir* did not address the question of slave sales, and the French civil code, although dealing with sales, did not apply to slaves. On the other hand, the *Partidas* provided for the remedy of redhibition in the case of the sale of defective slaves. Its provisions, however, were weighted in favor of sellers and were perhaps unacceptable to the codifiers. A seller under Spanish law could not be forced to take back the slave from the buyer unless he had *actual* knowledge of the slave's defect at the time of the sale.[44] The solution preferred by the Louisiana redactors was to create a blend out of these French and Spanish sources: they borrowed the French rules about the seller's state of mind (which held the seller strictly accountable for latent defects, regardless of his ignorance of their existence), thus offering strong buyer protection, and merged them with the well-developed Spanish rules about the types of defects that were actionable, (which they now split into defects of character and defects of body). The spliced-together rules produced a unique design and a prodigious jurisprudence.[45] Judith Schafer points out that redhibition for defective slaves came before the Louisiana Supreme Court more often than any other slave-related issue.[46] As many as one hundred and sixty six appellate cases involved diseased slaves (frequently tuberculosis) and an additional fifty cases involved vices of character, such as being a habitual runaway or addicted to crime.[47] Louisiana was the only state to codify the vices in a slave with any particularity, and it was one of a handful

---

[44] The Spanish source in question was *Partida* 5, 5, 64 while the French source was *Code Civil* Arts. 1641–1646. Partida 5, 5, 64 stipulated: "When a slave that is sold has any vices or defects, as if he be a thief, or were in the habit of running away from his master, or had any other similar defect, *to the knowledge of the seller*, and he did not make them known to the buyer, he will be obliged to take back the slave and restore the price to the buyer and pay him for all the loss and damages . . . *But if he were ignorant of his defects, then the buyer must keep the slave,* and the seller restore so much of the price as the value of the slave is diminished . . . And so we would say it would be if the slave were badly affected with any hidden disease."

[45] *See* Digest 1808, 358, Arts. 78–80.

[46] Judith Schafer, 147. As noted, of the 1,200 slavery cases decided by the Supreme Court in the antebellum period, roughly one in six was redhibition-related.

[47] Schafer, 132.

of jurisdictions (along with North Carolina and South Carolina) to protect the purchasers of slaves through implied warranties.[48]

As a related development, New Orleans became the largest slave trading center in the Old South.[49] In 1860 it had thirty four permanent slave dealers in residence, not to mention any number of visiting dealers on the scene at any one time. Interestingly, none of these traders was originally from Louisiana. The exchange sold some six to eight thousand slaves annually, worth $8 million. It was four times the size of the Natchez exchange which had seven or eight dealers and sold one and a half to two thousand slaves yearly.[50] Judith Schafer argues that this was an instance where the law of slavery acted as a force to strengthen Louisiana's civil law tradition rather than to Americanize it. Her point is well taken, and I would further argue that redhibition actually spurred the success of the New Orleans slave market. Louisiana was a net importer of slaves, and the guarantees of redhibition would have been attractive to local purchasers.[51] Records show that some New Orleans traders, such as Bernard Kendig who landed in court thirteen times in ten years, sometimes sold defective slaves knowingly and were found guilty of fraud, but, more importantly, at other times they were strictly liable for defects of which they had no knowledge.[52] Elsewhere in the country, the rule was generally *caveat emptor,* unless unquestionable cheating had taken place.[53] In the New Orleans slave exchange, however, the rule was *caveat venditor.*

---

[48] Thomas Morris, *Southern Slavery and the Law, 1619–1860*, (Chapel Hill: University of North Carolina Press, 1996), 109–113.

[49] For detailed description, *see* Walter Johnson, *Soul By Soul: Life Inside the Antebellum Slave Market* (Cambridge: Harvard University Press, 1997); Reinders, "Slavery in New Orleans."

[50] Richard Tansey, "Bernard Kendig and the New Orleans Slave Trade" 23 La. Hist. 159 (1982); Walter Johnson, *ibid.* at 49–57.

[51] Schafer, 148, points out that many transactions on the slave exchange actually involved two sales: the first from the out-of-state seller to the trader, and the second from the trader to the purchaser in New Orleans. The second sale would be governed by Louisiana's law of redhibition.

[52] Robert H. Gudmestad, *A Troublesome Commerce: The Transformation of the Interstate Slave Trade,* 97 (Baton Rouge: Louisiana State University Press, 2003); Richard Tansey, "Bernard Kendig and the New Orleans Slave Trade," *Louisiana History* 23 (1982), 159–178.

[53] Morris, 112.

Conclusion

The law of slavery in other parts of the United States made little resort to the civil law tradition. Mark Tushnet observes that early American decisions made almost no reference to Roman and civil law, and there was little evidence that early conceptualizations of slavery were influenced by it.[54] Richard Helmholz similarly finds that with the exception of South Carolina and to a lesser extent Virginia, there were relatively few examples of lawyers or judges referring explicitly to the Roman law on the subject.[55] Indeed any wholesale reception of the Roman law of slavery by an English colony was never expected or even feasible. Jonathan Bush points out that such a reception would have faced fatal constitutional, political and ideological difficulties, and these obstacles explain in part why colonial America never developed a systematic law of slavery. According to Bush, the reported cases were characteristically short and conclusory, almost entirely devoid of analysis or reasoning: "Nowhere in the statutes or case law is there anything remotely like a jurisprudence of slavery."[56]

In my view the slave jurisprudence of Louisiana was unique, not only in the United States, but in any other jurisdiction where slavery existed. It had the benefit of systematic sources both in the Digest of 1808 and Code of 1825 and in the Spanish-Roman *ius commune*. It will be remembered that these were the only civil codes in history to incorporate this subject within their provisions. This allowed the Supreme Court to build a coherent jurisprudence through a process of interpretation, deduction and analogy. The sheer size of the Louisiana Supreme Court's output—one thousand two hundred cases by that court alone—made it into a specialist on the subject. The method of the Digest served to expand the legal

---

[54] Mark V. Tushnet, *Slave Law in the American South*, (Lawrence: University of Kansas Press, 2003), 7.

[55] Richard Helmholz," Use of the Civil Law in Post-Revolutionary American Jurisprudence" *Tulane Law Review* 66 (1992): 1649, 1660.

[56] Jonathan Bush, "The British Constitution and the Creation of American Slavery" in P. Finkelman (ed.), *Slavery and the Law* (Lanham: Rowman & Littlefield, 1997), 385. Bush further observes that "Slave law in the English colonies was not found in a systematic text like the *Code Noir* or Las Siete Partidas. Accordingly, it lacked the breadth and analytic richness that characterize such texts." *Ibid.*, 405.

horizons and permitted the Court to pluck solutions from the vast Roman and Spanish experience. The briefs of the lawyers and the opinions of the judges in this period teemed with references and quotations to these sources. As far as I am aware, no jurisprudence of comparable richness and complexity existed in other legal systems, even in France which was progenitor of the first *Code Noir*. It is true that in 19th century France we can find, in *recueils* like Dalloz, what might be termed "slave jurisprudence." It is indexed under the heading of "Colonies." The few cases are tersely reasoned in the usual skeletal *arrêt* format employed by the *Cour de Cassation*, and of course, in keeping with tradition, no authority other than statutes and ordinances is cited. One searches in vain for any Roman law references, terminology or allusions. It is only a simplified jurisprudence of maxims and short answers,[57] with very little in common with the Louisiana experience.

---

[57] For example in the volume of Dalloz for the year 1838, we find representative statements such as" "*Le noir qui est sans maître dans l'ile est réputé libre.*" Antoine (*the case name*) I. 474: "*Est-il valable [le mariage] entre blanc et noir esclaves?*" Rodrigues (*the case name*), I. 360.

APPENDIX

The Code Noir of 1724
(in French and English)

Translation by Vernon Valentine Palmer

EDIT DU ROI

Touchant l'Etat et la Discipline des Esclaves Négres de la Loüisiane
Donné à Versailles au mois de Mars 1724[1]

Louis, par la grâce de Dieu, Roi de France et de Navarre : à tous, présents et à venir, salut. Les Directeurs de la Compagnie des Indes nous ayant présenté que la Province et Colonie de la Louisiane est considérablement établie par un grand nombre de nos sujets, lesquels se servent d'esclaves nègres pour la culture des terres, nous avons jugé qu'il étoit de notre autorité et de notre justice, pour la conservation de cette colonie, d'y établir une loi et des règles certaines, pour y maintenir la discipline de l'Église Catholique, Apostolique et Romaine, et pour ordonner de ce qui concerne l'état et la qualité des esclaves dans lesdites îles; et désirant y pourvoir et faire connaître à nos sujets qui y sont habitués et qui s'y établiront à l'avenir qu'encore qu'ils habitent des climats infiniment éloignés, nous leur sommes toujours présens par l'étendue de notre puissance et par notre application à les secourir.

À CES CAUSES et autres à ce nous mouvant, de l'avis de notre Conseil, et de notre certaine science, pleine puissance et autorité royale, nous avons dit, statué et ordonné, disons, statuons et ordonnons, voulons et nous plaît ce qui suit.

ARTICLE PREMIER. L'Edit du feu Roi Louis XIII, de glorieuse mémoire, du 23 avril 1615, sera exécuté dans notre Province et Colonie de la Louisiane: ce faisant, enjoignons aux Directeurs généreux de ladite Compagnie et à tous nos officiers de chasser dudit Pays tous les Juifs qui peuvent y avoir établi leur résidence, auxquels, comme aux ennemis déclarés du nom Chrétien, nous commandons d'en sortir dans trois mois, à compter du jour de la publication des présentes, à peine de confiscation de corps et de biens.

---

[1] Original eighteenth century spelling and punctuation have been retained in the French text.

EDICT OF THE KING

Touching upon the State and the Discipline of the Black Slaves of Louisiana Given at Versailles in the month of March 1724[2]

Louis, by the grace of God, King of France and Navarre, to all present and to come, greetings. The Directors of the Company of the Indies having represented to us that the Province and Colony of Louisiana is considerably developed by a great number of our subjects who use black slaves for the cultivation of the land, we have judged that it is within our authority and our justice, for the preservation of that colony, to establish there a law and certain rules, in order to maintain the discipline of the Catholic, Apostolic, and Roman church and in order to regulate whatever concerns the state and the quality of the slaves in these isles; and desiring to make these matters known to our subjects there who are already familiar and to those who will establish themselves there in the future, that although they live in climates infinitely distant, we are always close to them by the range of our power and our sustained efforts to assist them.

For these and other reasons which move us, by the advice of our Council, and of our own certain knowledge, full power, and royal authority, we have stated, ruled and ordered, we say, rule, order, wish, and are pleased by that which follows.

FIRST ARTICLE. The Edict of 23 April 1615 of the late King Louis XIII. of glorious memory, will be in force in our Province and Colony of Louisiana. This accomplished, we enjoin all of our officers to chase from our isles all the Jews who have established residence there. As with all declared enemies of Christianity, we command them to be gone within three months of the day of issuance of the present law, under penalty of confiscation of their persons and their goods.

---

[2] Translated by Vernon Valentine Palmer © 2012.

Article 2. Tous les esclaves qui seront dans notredite Province, seront instruits dans la Religion Catholique, Apostolique et Romaine, et baptisés. Ordonnons aux habitants, qui achèteront des nègres nouvellement arrivés de les faire instruire et baptiser dans le tems convenable, à peine d'amende arbitraire. Enjoignons aux Directeurs généraux de ladite Compagnie et à tous nos officiers d'y tenir exactement la main.

Article 3. Interdisons tous exercices d'autre Religion que de la Catholique, Apostolique et Romaine; voulons que les contrevenans soient punis comme rebelles et désobéissans à nos commandements: Défendons toutes assemblées pour cet effet, lesquelles nous déclarons conventicules, illicites et séditieuses, sujettes à la même peine, qui aura lieu même contre les maîtres qui les permettront ou souffriront à l'égard de leurs esclaves.

Article 4. Ne seront préposés aucuns commandeurs à la direction des nègres, qui ne fassent profession de la Religion Catholique, Apostolique et Romaine; à peine de confiscation desdits nègres contre les maîtres qui les auront préposés et de punition arbitraire contre les commandeurs qui auront accepté ladite direction.

Article 5. Enjoignons à tous nos sujets, de quelque qualité et condition qu'ils soient, d'observer régulièrement les jours de dimanches et de fêtes: leur défendons de travailler ni de faire travailler leurs esclaves ausdits jours, depuis l'heure de minuit jusqu'à l'autre minuit, à la culture de la terre et à tous autres ouvrages, à peine d'amende et de punition arbitraire contre les maîtres, et de confiscation des esclaves qui seront surpris par nos officiers dans le travail; pourront néanmoins envoyer leurs esclaves aux marchés.

Article II. All slaves in our Province shall be baptized and instructed in the Roman, Catholic, and Apostolic Faith. We order the inhabitants who purchase newly-arrived Negroes to have them baptized and instructed within a suitable amount of time, under penalty of an arbitrary fine. We enjoin the Directors General of the said Company and all our officers to uphold this order precisely.

Article III. We forbid the exercise of any religion other than the Roman, Catholic, and Apostolic Faith. We desire that offenders be punished as rebels disobedient to our orders. We forbid all assemblies to that end, which we declare to be secret, illegal, and seditious, and subject to the same punishment, which will apply even against the masters who allow or tolerate such gatherings on the part of their slaves.

Article IV. No commanders shall be assigned to positions of authority over Negroes who are not members of the Roman, Catholic, and Apostolic Faith, under penalty of confiscation of the blacks of the master who authorized these persons and an arbitrary punishment levied against the commanders who accepted said position of authority.

Article V. We enjoin all our subjects, of whatever quality and social status they may be, to regularly observe Sundays and the holidays; we forbid them to work or to have the slaves worked, from midnight until the following midnight in the cultivation of the land, and every other type of work, under penalty of a fine and an arbitrary punishment against the masters, and the confiscation of the slaves discovered working by our officers; nevertheless, they may send their slaves to the markets.

Article 6. Défendons à nos sujets blancs de l'un et l'autre sexe, de contracter mariage avec les Noirs, à peine de punition et d'amende arbitraire; et à tous Curés, Prêtres ou Missionnaires, séculiers ou réguliers, et même aux Aumôniers de Vaisseaux, de les marier. Défendons aussi à nos dits sujets blancs, même aux Noirs affranchis ou nés libres, de vivre en concubinage avec des esclaves. Voulons que ceux qui auront eu un ou plusieurs enfans d'une pareille conjonction, ensemble les maîtres qui les auront soufferts, soient condamnés chacun en une amende de trois cents livres. Et s'ils sont maîtres de l'esclave de laquelle ils auront eu lesdits enfans, voulons qu'outre l'amende, ils soient privés tant de l'esclave que des enfans; et qu'ils soient adjugés à l'hôpital des lieux, sans pouvoir jamais être affranchis. N'entendons toutefois le présent article avoir lieu, lorsque l'homme noir, affranchi ou libre, qui n'étoit pas marié durant son concubinage avec son esclave, épousera dans les formes prescrites par l'Église ladite esclave, qui sera affranchie par ce moyen, et les enfans rendus libres et légitimes.

Article 7. Lesdites solennités prescrites par l'ordonnance de Blois et par la Déclaration de 1639 pour les mariages, seront observées tant à l'égard des personnes libres que des esclaves, sans néanmoins que le consentement du père et de la mère de l'esclave y soit nécessaire, mais celui du maître seulement.

Article 8. Défendons très-expressement aux Curés, de procéder aux mariages des esclaves, s'ils ne font apparoir du consentement de leurs maîtres. Défendons aussi aux maîtres d'user d'aucunes contraintes sur leurs esclaves pour les marier contre leur gré.

Article 9. Les enfans qui naîtront de mariages entre esclaves seront esclaves et appartiendront aux maîtres des femmes esclaves, et non à ceux de leur mari, si les maris et les femmes ont des maîtres différens.

Article 10. Voulons, si le mari esclave a épousé une femme libre, les enfans, tant mâles que filles, suivent la condition de leur mere, et soient libres comme elle, nonobstant la servitude de leur père; et que, si le père est libre et la mère esclave, les enfans soient esclaves pareillement.

Article VI. We forbid our white subjects of either sex to contract marriage with the Blacks, under penalty of punishment and an arbitrary fine; we forbid all Curates, Priests and Missionaries, secular or regular, and even Ship Chaplins, to marry them. We also forbid our white subjects, even manumitted Blacks or those born free, to live in concubinage with the slaves. We wish that those who have had one or several children from such conjunctions, including the masters who allowed it, be each condemned to pay a fine of three hundred pounds. And, if they are the master of the slave with whom they have had these children, we wish that besides the fine, they should be deprived not only of the slave but of the children, and that they be ajudged to the hospital of the place, without ever being able to be manumitted. We do not intend the present article to apply, however, when a black man, free or enfranchised, who was not married during his concubinage with his slave, marries her under the rites prescribed by the Church, and by this means she shall be enfranchised, and the children shall be free and legitimate.

Article VII. The solemnities required by the ordinance of Blois and by the Declaration of 1639 regarding marriages, shall be observed both in the case of free persons and slaves, nevertheless the consent of the father and the mother of the slave is not necessary, only that of the master.

Article VIII. We very expressly forbid curates to marry slaves unless their masters have given their consent. We also forbid the masters to place any constraints over their slaves in order to marry them against their will.

Article IX. Children born in marriage between slaves shall be slaves and shall belong to the master of the female and not the master of the husband, if the husband and the wife have different masters.

Article X. We desire that if a slave husband has married a free woman, the children, whether male or female, will follow the condition of their mother and be free like her, notwithstanding the enslavement of the father, and that if the father is free and the mother is a slave, the children are likewise slaves.

Article 11. Les maîtres seront tenus de faire enterrer en terre sainte, dans les cimetières destinés à cet effet, leurs esclaves baptisés; et à l'égard de ceux qui mourront sans avoir reçu le baptême, ils seront enterrés la nuit, dans quelque champ voisin du lieu où ils seront décédés.

Article 12. Défendons aux esclaves de porter aucune arme offensive, ni de gros bâtons, à peine de fouet et de confiscation des armes, au profit de celui qui les en trouvera saisis; à l'exception seulement de ceux qui seront envoyés à la chasse par leurs maîtres, et qui seront porteurs de leurs billets, ou marques connues.

Article 13. Défendons pareillement aux esclaves appartenant à différens maîtres, de s'attrouper le jour, ou la nuit, sous prétexte de noces ou autrement, soit chez l'un de leurs maîtres ou ailleurs, et encore moins dans les grands chemins ou lieux écartés, à peine de punition corporelle, qui ne pourra être moins que du fouet et de la fleur de lis; et en cas de fréquentes récidives et autres circonstances aggravantes, pourront être punis de mort, ce que nous laissons à l'arbitrage des juges. Enjoignons à tous nos sujets de courre fus aux contrevenans, et de les arrêter et qu'il n'y ait contre eux aucun décret.

Article 14. Les maîtres qui seront convaincus d'avoir permis ou toléré de pareilles assemblées, composées d'autres esclaves que de ceux qui leur appartiennent, seront condamnés en leurs propres et privés noms, de réparer tout le dommage qui aura été fait à leurs voisins, à l'occasion desdites assemblées, et en trente livres d amende pour la première fois, et au double, en cas de récidive.

Article XI. Masters are obliged to have their baptized slaves buried in Holy Ground in cemeteries designated to that end; and with respect to those who died without having received baptism, they are to be buried at night in some field near the place where they died.

Article XII. We forbid slaves to carry any offensive arms, or large sticks, under penalty of being whipped and their arms confiscated in favor of those who seized them; with the sole exception of those slaves who are sent hunting by their masters, and who carry the master's letters or known marks.

Article XIII. We likewise forbid slaves belonging to different masters to gather by day or by night, under the pretext of a wedding or any other reason, whether on their master's property or elsewhere, and still less in the main roads or the out of the way places, on penalty of corporal punishment, which cannot be less than a whipping and [branding] of the *fleur de lys*; and in case of frequent repetition and other aggravating circumstances, they may be put to death, which we leave to the decision of judges. We require all our subjects to pursue the offenders, and to arrest them, even though there is no order issued against them.

Article XIV. Masters who are convicted of having permitted or tolerated such gatherings which include slaves other than those which belong to them, will be charged in their property and private name to repair all damage which was done to their neighbors by these assemblies, together with a fine of thirty pounds for the first offence, and double the amount in case of repeated offence.

Article 15. Défendons aux esclaves d'exposer en vente au marché, ni de porter dans les maisons particulières, pour vendre, aucune sorte de denrées, même des fruits, légumes, bois à brûler, herbes ou fourages, pour la nourriture des bestiaux, ni aucune espèce de grains ou autres marchandises, hardes, ou nipes, sans permission expresse de leurs maîtres par un billet ou par des marques connues, à peine de revendication des choses ainsi vendues, sans restitution de prix par les maîtres, et de six livres d'amende à leur profit contre les acheteurs par rapport aux fruits, légumes, bois à brûler, herbes. fourages et grains; Voulons que, par rapport aux marchandises, hardes ou nipes, les contrevenans acheteurs soient condamnés à quinze cens livres d'amende, aux dépens, dommages et intérêts et qu'ils soient poursuivis extraordinairement comme voleurs et receleurs.

Article 16. Voulons à cet effet que deux personnes soient préposées, par les officiers du Conseil Supérieur ou des justices inférieures, dans chaque marché pour examiner les denrées et marchandises qui y seront apportées par les esclaves, ensemble les billets et marques de leurs maîtres, dont ils seront porteurs.

Article 17. Permettons à tous nos sujets habitants du Pays, de se saisir de toutes les choses dont ils trouveront lesdits esclaves chargés, lorsqu'ils n'auront point de billets de leurs maîtres, ni de marques connues, pour être rendues incessamment à leurs maîtres, si leur habitations sont voisines du lieu où les esclaves auront été surpris en délit; sinon elles seront incessamment envoyées au magasin de la Compagnie le plus proche pour y être en dépôt jusqu'à ce que les maîtres en ayent été avertis.

Article 18. Voulons que les officiers de notre Conseil Supérieur de la Louisiane envoyent leurs avis sur la quantité de vivres et la qualité de l'habillement, qu'il convient que les maîtres fournissent à leurs esclaves; lesquels vivres doivent leur être fournis par chacune semaine et l'habillement par chacune année, pour y être statué par nous, et cependant permettons ausdits officiers de régler par provision lesdits vivres et ledit habillement: Défendons aux maîtres desdits esclaves de donner aucune sorte d eau-de-vie pour tenir lieu de ladite subsistance et habillement.

Article XV. We forbid the slaves to put goods on sale at the markets, or to carry to private homes any sort of merchandise, even fruits, vegetables, firewood, plants or animal forage, nor any type of grains or other merchandise, rags or used clothes, without express permission in writing from their master or under his known mark, under penalty of the master reclaiming from the buyer the things thus sold, without restitution of the price, and a fine of six pounds in favor of the master against the buyers of the fruits, vegetables, firewood, plants, feeds and grains: We wish that, with respect to merchandise, rags or used clothing, the offending buyers be condemned to a fine of fifteen hundred pounds, at their expense and damage, and that they be specially prosecuted as thieves and fences.

Article XVI. We wish, to this end, that two persons be placed in each market by the officers of the Superior Council or of the inferior courts, in order to examine the commodities and merchandise which is brought there by the slaves, as well as the letters and marks of their masters which they have with them.

Article XVII. We permit all our subjects inhabiting the Country to seize all things carried by slaves who have no letter or known mark of their masters, and to return the things without delay to their masters, if their plantations are neighboring to the place where the slaves were discovered in their crime; if that is not the case, they are to be sent without delay to the nearest store of the Company, in order to be deposited there until the masters have been notified.

Article XVIII. It is our wish that the officers of our Superior Council in Louisiana send their views on the quantity of nourishment and the quality of clothing that it is appropriate for the masters to furnish their slaves; said foodstuffs ought to be furnished to them each week and the clothing each year, in order to be authorized by us; and yet we permit the aforesaid officers to settle by rule the aforesaid food and clothing. We forbid the masters of the slaves to distribute any kind of alcoholic liquor to them in substitution for the said food and clothing.

Article 19. Leur défendons pareillement de se décharger de la nourriture et subsistance de leurs esclaves, en leur permettant de travailler certain jour de la semaine pour leur compte particulier.

Article 20. Les esclaves qui ne seront point nourris, vêtus et entretenus par leurs maîtres, pourront en donner avis à notre Procureur Général dudit Conseil, ou aux officiers des Justices inférieures, et mettre leurs mémoires entre leur mains, sur lesquels et même d'office, si les avis leur en viennent d'ailleurs, les maîtres seront poursuivis à la requête dudit Procureur Général, et sans frais; ce que nous voulons être observé pour les crimes et les traitements barbares et inhumains des maîtres envers leurs esclaves.

Article 21. Les esclaves infirmes par vieillesse, maladie ou autrement, soit que la maladie soit incurable ou non. seront nourris et entretenus par leurs maîtres; et en cas qu'ils les eussent abandonnés, lesdits esclaves seront adjugés à l'hôpital le plus proche, auquel les maîtres seront condamnés de payer huit sols par chacun jour, pour le nourriture et entretien de chacun esclave; pour le payement de laquelle somme ledit hôpital aura Privilège sur les habitations des maîtres, en quelques mains qu'elles passent.

Article 22. Déclarons les esclaves ne pouvoir rien avoir qui ne soit à leur maître, et tout ce qui leur vient par leur industrie, ou par la libéralité d'autres personnes, ou autrement, à quelque titre que ce soit, être acquis en pleine propriété à leurs maîtres, sans que les enfans des esclaves, leurs pères et mères, leurs parens et tous autres, libres ou esclaves, y puissent rien prétendre par succession, disposition entre-vifs, ou à cause de mort; lesquelles dispositions nous déclarons nulles, ensemble toutes les promesses et obligations qu'ils auroient faites, comme étant faites par gens incapables de disposer et contracter de leur chef.

Article XIX. We similarly forbid masters to relieve themselves of the duty to furnish food and subsistence to their slaves, by permitting them to work on a certain day of the week for their own account.

Article XX. Slaves who are not fed, clothed and maintained by their masters may notify our General Prosecutor of the said Council, or the officers of the inferior courts, and put their petitions in their hands, on the basis of which and even by authority of office, if the notification comes from elsewhere, the masters shall be prosecuted at the request of the said General Prosecutor, and without charge; this is the rule we wish observed for crimes and barbarous and inhuman treatment of slaves by their masters.

Article XXI. Slaves disabled by age, sickness or otherwise, whether because the sickness is incurable or not, are to be fed and maintained by their masters; and in case they were abandoned, the said slaves will be adjudicated to the nearest hospital, as to which the masters will be condemned to pay eight sous (sols) per day for the food and maintenance of each slave; for the payment of this sum the said hospital will have a Privilege over the plantations of the masters into whatever hands the lands pass.

Article XXII. We declare slaves can have nothing which is not their master's; and all that which comes to them through their own industry or through the liberality of other persons, or otherwise, by whatever title it may be, is acquired in full ownership by the master, without the slave's children, their father and mother, their relatives and anyone else, free or slave, pretending to rights by succession, disposition *inter vivos* or *mortis causa*; we declare such dispositions are null, as well as all promises and obligations which the slaves may make, since they are made by persons incapable of disposing or contracting in their own right.

Article 23. Voulons néanmoins que les maîtres soient tenus de ce que leurs esclaves auront fait par leur commandement, ensemble de ce qu'ils auront géré et négocié dans les boutiques, et pour lespéce particulière de commerce, à laquelle leurs maîtres les auront préposés; et en cas que leurs maîtres ne les ayent donné aucun ordre et ne les ayent point préposés, ils seront tenus seulement jusqu'à concurrence de ce qui aura tourné à leur profit; et si rien n'a tourné au profit des maîtres, le pécules desdits esclaves que leurs maîtres leur auront permis d'avoir, en sera tenu, après que leurs maîtres en auront déduit par préférence ce qui pourra leur en être dû; sinon que le pécule consistât en tout, ou partie, en marchandises dont les esclaves auroient permission de faire trafic à part, sur lesquelles leurs maîtres viendront seulement par contribution au sol la livre avec leurs autres créanciers.

Article 24. Ne pourront les esclaves être pourvus d'offices ni de commissions ayant quelques fonction publique, ni être constitués agens, par autres que par leurs maîtres, pour gérer et administrer aucun négoce, ni être arbitres, experts: ne pourront aussi être témoins, tant en matière civile que criminelle, à moins qu'ils ne soient témoins nécessaires, et seulement à défaut de blancs: mais dans aucun cas, ils ne pourront servir de témoins pour, ou contre leurs maîtres.

Article 25. Ne pourront aussi les esclaves être parties, ni être en jugement en matière civile, tant en demandant qu'en défendant, ni être parties civiles en matière criminelle; sauf à leurs maîtres d'agir et de défendre en matière civile, et de poursuivre en matière criminelle, la réparation des outrages et excès qui auront été commis contre leurs esclaves.

Article 26. Pourront les esclaves être poursuivis criminellement, sans qu'il soit besoin de rendre leur maîtres parties, si n'est en cas de complicité; et seront lesdits esclaves accusés, jugés en première instance par les juges ordinaires, s'il y en a, et par apel au Conseil, sur la même instruction et avec les mêmes formalités que les personnes libres, aux exceptions ci-après.

Article XXIII. We nevertheless wish that the masters be held accountable for what their slaves have done at their command as well as for what the slaves have managed or negotiated in the shops, and for the particular type of commerce which their masters have entrusted to them; they [the masters] shall be held accountable only for so much as they turned to their profit; and if nothing was profited by the master, the peculium of the slaves which their masters allowed them to have will be held accountable, after having deducted by preference that which may be due to the master; if not, the peculium will consist in all or in part of the merchandise which the slaves have permission to traffic in apart, as to which their masters would only come in for pro rata contribution along with their other creditors.

Article XXIV. Slaves cannot hold offices or commissions having any public function, nor can they be made agents by anyone other than their masters, in order to manage or administer any business, nor may they be arbitrators or experts; also they cannot be witnesses in civil or criminal matters, unless they are necessary witnesses, and only in the absence of whites: but in no event can they serve as witnesses for or against their masters.

Article XXV. Slaves cannot be a party litigant nor the subject of a judgment, either in civil matters, as plaintiff or defendant, nor the civil party in criminal proceedings; saving to their masters the right to initiate or defend civil proceedings, and to pursue through criminal proceedings, reparations for the outrages and excesses which have been committed against their slaves.

Article XXVI. Slaves can be criminally prosecuted without the necessity of making their master a party, provided there was no complicity between them; and the said slaves will be judged in the trial court by the ordinary judges, if there are any, and on appeal by the Council, on the same instruction and with the same formalities for free persons, with the exceptions hereafter.

Article 27. L'esclave qui aura frapé son maître, sa maîtresse, le mari de sa maîtresse ou leurs enfans, avec contusion ou effusion de sang, ou au visage, sera puni de mort.

Article 28. Et quant aux excès et voies de fait, qui seront commis par les esclaves, contre les personnes libres, voulons qu'ils soient severement punis; même de mort s'il y échoit.

Article 29. Les vols qualifiés, même ceux des chevaux, cavales, mulets, bœufs ou vaches, qui auront été faits par les esclaves, ou par les affranchis, seront punis de peine afflictive, même de mort, si le cas le requiert.

Article 30. Les vols de moutons, chèvres, cochons, volailles, grains, fourage, bois, sèves, ou autres legumes et denrées, faits par les esclaves, seront punis selon la -qualité du vol, par les juges, qui pourront s'il y échoit, les condamner d'être battus de verges par l'Exécuteur de la haute justice, et marqués d'une fleur de lis.

Article 31. Seront tenus les maîtres, en cas de vol, ou d'autre dommage causé par leurs esclaves, outre la peine corporelle des esclaves, de réparer le tort en leur nom, s'ils n'aiment mieux abandonner l'esclave à celui auquel le tort aura été fait; ce qu'ils seront tenus d'opter dans les trois jours, à compter du jour de la condamnation, autrement ils en seront déchus.

Article 32. L'esclave fugitif qui aura été en fuite pendant un mois, à compter du jour que son maître l'aura dénoncé en justice, aura les oreilles coupées et sera marqué d'une fleur de lis sur une épaule; et s'il récidive pendant une autre mois, à compter pareillement du jour de la dénonciation, il aura le jaret coupé, et il sera marqué d'une fleur de lis sur l'autre épaule; et la troisième fois, il sera puni de mort.

Article XXVII. The slave who strikes his master, his mistress, the mistress's husband or their children, and causes bruising or blood to flow, or strikes the face, will be punished by death.

XXVIII. And as to the excesses and acts of violence which slaves commit against free persons, we wish that they be severely punished, even by death if it is necessary.

Article XXIX. Thefts qualified as such, even those of horses, mares, mules, steers or cows which slaves or manumitted persons commit, will receive corporal punishment, even by death if the case requires it.

Article XXX. Thefts committed by slaves, of sheep, goats, pigs, poultry, grains, hay, wood, sap, or other vegetables and commodities, shall be punished by the judges according to the nature of the theft, and they may, if necessary, condemn the slaves to be flogged by the high executioner, and branded with the *fleur de lys*.

Article XXXI. In the case of theft or other damage caused by their slaves, masters are held responsible, beyond inflicting corporal punishment on the slaves, to redress the wrong in their own name, unless they prefer to abandon the slave to whomever the wrong was done; as to which they must choose within three days, counting from the day of the condemnation, otherwise they are deprived of this option.

Article XXXII. The runaway slave who has been a fugitive for a month, counting from the day his master denounced him in court, will have his ears cut off and will be branded with the *fleur de lys* on one shoulder, and if he runs away a second time, again counting from the day of the denunciation, his hamstring will be cut and he will be branded with the *fleur de lys* on the other shoulder; the third time he will be put to death.

Article 33. Voulons que les esclaves qui auront encouru les peines du fouet, de la fleur de lis et des oreilles coupées, soient jugés en dernier ressort par les juges ordinaires, et executés, sans qu'il soit nécessaire que tels jugements soient confirmés par le Conseil Supérieur, nonobstant le contenu en l'article 26 des présentes, qui n'aura lieu que pour les jugements portant condamnation de mort ou du jaret coupé.

Article 34. Les affranchise, ou nègres libres, qui auront donné retraite dans leurs maisons aux esclaves fugitifs, seront condamnés par corps envers le maître en une amende de trente livres par chacun jour de rétention; et les autres personnes libres qui leur auront donné pareille retraite, en dix livres d'amende, aussi par chacun jour de retention; et faute par lesdits nègres affranchis ou libres, de pouvoir payer l'amende, ils seront réduits à la condition d'esclaves et vendus; et si le prix de la vente passe l'amende, le surplus sera délivré à l'hôpital.

Article 35. Permettons à nos sujets dudit pays, qui auront des esclaves fugitifs, en quelque lieu que ce soit, d'en faire la recherche par telles personnes et à telles conditions qu'ils jugeront à propos, ou de la faire eux-mêmes, ainsi que bon leur semblera.

Article 36. L'esclave condamné à mort sur la dénonciation de son maître, lequel ne sera point complice du crime par lequel il aura été condamné, sera estimé avant l'exécution par deux des principaux habitans, qui seront nommés d'office par le juge; et le prix de l'estimation en sera payé au maître; pour à quoi satisfaire, il sera imposé par notre Conseil Supérieur, sur chaque tête de nègre, la somme portée par l'estimation, laquelle sera réglée sur chacun desdits nègres, et levée par ceux qui seront commis à cet effet.

Article 37. Défendons à tous officiers de notredit Conseil, et autres officiers de justice etablis audit pays, de prendre aucune taxe dans les procès criminels contre les esclaves, à peine de concussion.

Article XXXIII. We wish that slaves who have incurred punishments by the whip, the *fleur de lys* and the cutting of ears, be tried, and punishments carried out, by the ordinary judges sitting as court of last resort, without the necessity that such judgments be confirmed by the Superior Council, notwithstanding the contents of article XXVI of the present law, which does not apply except for judgments imposing the death penalty or the cutting of the hamstring.

Article XXXIV. Manumitted persons or free blacks who have given shelter in their homes to runaway slaves, will be condemned to pay to the master a fine of thirty pounds for each day of retention; and other free persons who likewise gave them shelter, to pay a fine of ten pounds for each day of retention. And where said blacks, manumitted or free, are unable to pay the fine, they will be reduced to the condition of slaves and sold off; and if the price of the sale exceeds the fine, the surplus will be delivered to the hospital.

Article XXXV. We permit our subjects in these lands whose slaves have run away, in whatever place they may be, to have searches conducted by such persons and in such ways they judge to be appropriate, or to conduct the search themselves, as they see fit.

Article XXXVI. The slave who receives a death sentence upon the denunciation of his master, who was not complicit in the crime for which [the slave] was condemned, shall be appraised, before the execution, by two of the principal inhabitants, who will be appointed by the judge on his own authority; and the amount of the appraisal will be paid to the master; the Superior Council shall impose a tax on the head of each black slave to satisfy the appraised amount, which sum will be discharged by a tax on all blacks, and collected by those who are invested with that authority.

Article XXXVII. We forbid all officers of our said Council, and other judicial officers established in the country, to collect any tax on the criminal proceedings against slaves, under penalty for theft in office.

Article 38. Défendons aussi à tous nos sujets desdits pays, de quelque qualité et condition qu'ils soient, de donner, ou faire donner de leur autorité privée, la question ou torture à leurs esclaves, sous quelque prétexte que ce soit, ni de leur faire ou faire faire aucune mutilation de membre, à peine de confiscation des esclaves, et d'être procédé contre eux extraordinairement: leur permettons seulement, lorsqu'ils croiront que les esclaves l'auront mérité, de les faire enchaîner et battre de verges ou de cordes.

Article 39. Enjoignons aux officiers de justice établis dans ledit pays, de procéder criminellement contre les maîtres et les commandeurs qui auront tué leurs esclaves, ou leur auront mutilé les membres, étant sous leur puissance, ou sous leur direction, et de punir le meurtre selon l'atrocité des circonstances; et en cas qu'il y ait lieu à l'absolution, leur permettons de renvoyer, tant les maîtres que les commandeurs, sans qu'ils ayent besoin d'obtenir de nous des lettres de grâce.

Article 40. Voulons que les esclaves soient réputé meubles, et comme tels, qu'ils entrent dans la communauté, qu'il n'y ait point de suite par hypothèque sur eux, qu'ils se partagent également entre les cohéritiers, sans préciput et droit d'aînesse, et qu'ils ne soient point sujets au douaire coutumier, au rétrait lignager ou féodal, aux droits féodaux et seigneuriaux, aux formalités des décrets, ni au rétranchement des quatre quints, en cas de disposition à cause de mort ou testamentaire.

Article 41. N'entendons toutefois priver nos sujets de la faculté de les stipuler propres à leurs personnes et aux leurs de leur côté et ligne, ainsi qu'il se pratique pour les sommes de deniers et autres choses mobiliaires.

Article 42. Les formalités prescrites par nos Ordonnances et par la Coutume de Paris, pour les saisies des choses mobiliaires, seront observes dans les saisies des esclaves. Voulons que les deniers en provenans, soient distribués par ordre des saisies; et, en cas de déconfiture, au sol la livre, après que les dettes privilégiées auront été payées, et généralement, que la condition des esclaves soit réglée en toutes affaires, comme celle des autres choses mobiliaires.

Article XXXVIII. We also forbid our subjects in the said country, of whatever quality and condition they may be, to torture their slaves or have them tortured, under whatever pretext there may be, nor to mutilate or have mutilated any limb of their body, under penalty of confiscation of the slaves, and extraordinary criminal proceedings: we solely permit them, when they believe their slaves merit it, to have them chained and flogged with sticks or cords.

Article XXXIX. We require the officers of justice established in the said country, to bring criminal proceedings against the masters and commanders who have killed or have mutilated slaves in their power or under their direction, and to punish murder according to the circumstances of the atrocity; and in cases of acquittal, we permit them to release the masters and the commanders, without the necessity of obtaining letters of pardon from us.

Article XL. We wish slaves to be classified as movable things, and as such, that they enter into the community [between husband and wife], that they are not subject to mortgagee's right to follow the property, that they are shared equally by coheirs, without preference or primogeniture, and that they are not subject to the *douaiare coutumier*, to the *rétrait lignager*, to feudal and noble rights, to the formalities of decrees, nor to the reduction of four-fifths, in case of a disposition by will or *mortis causa.*

Article XLI. We do not intend however to deprive our subjects of the faculty of stipulating for themselves and for those of their line and lineage, just as it is done with sums of money and other movable things.

Article XLII. The formalities prescribed by our Ordinances and by the Custom of Paris, regarding the seizure of movable things, will be observed in the seizure of slaves. We wish that the money proceeds be distributed by the order in which they were seized; and, in case of bankruptcy, once the privileged debts have been paid off, they should be distributed on a pro rata basis; and generally, the condition of slaves should be regulated in all matters like those of other movable things.

Article 43. Voulons néanmoins que le mari, sa femme et leurs enfans impubères, ne puissent être saisis et vendus séparément, s'ils sont tous sous la puissance d'un même maître: déclarons nulles les saisies et ventes séparées qui pourroient en être faites, ce que nous voulons aussi avoir lieu dans les ventes volontaires, à peine contre ceux qui feront lesdites ventes, d'être privés de celui ou de ceux qu'ils auront gardés, qui seront adjugés aux acquéreurs, sans qu'ils soient tenus de faire aucun suplément de prix.

Article 44. Voulons aussi que les esclaves âgé de quatorze ans et au-dessus, jusqu'à soixante ans, attachés à des fonds ou habitations, et y travaillant actuellement, ne puissent être saisis pour autres dettes que pour ce qui sera dû du prix de leur achat, à moins que les fonds ou habitations ne fussent saisis réellement: auquel cas nous enjoignons de les comprendre dans la saisie réelle; et défendons, à peine de nullité, de procéder par saisie réelle et adjudication par décret sur les fonds, ou habitations, sans y comprendre les esclaves de l'âge susdit y travaillant actuellement.

Article 45. Le fermier judiciaire des fonds ou habitations saisies réellement, conjointement avec les esclaves, sera tenu de payer le prix de son bail, sans qu'il puisse compter parmi les fruits qu'il perçoit, les enfans qui seront nés des esclaves pendant sondit bail.

Article 46. Voulons, nonobstant toutes conventions contraires, que nous déclarons nulles, que lesdits enfans appartiennent à la partie saisie, si les créanciers sont satisfaits d'ailleurs, ou à l'adjudicataire, s'il intervient un décret; et à cet effet il sera fait mention, dans la dernière affiche de l'interposition dudit décret, des enfans nés des esclaves depuis la saisie réelle, comme aussi des esclaves décédés depuis la saisie réelle, dans laquelle ils étoient compris.

Article 47. Pour éviter aux frais et aux longueurs des procédures, voulons que la distribution du prix entier de l'adjudication conjointe des fonds et des esclaves, et de ce qui proviendra du prix des baux judiciaires, soit faite entre les créanciers, selon l'ordre de leurs priviléges et hypothéques, sans distinguer ce qui est pour le prix des esclaves, et néanmoins les droits féodaux et seigneuriaux ne seront payés qu'à proportion des fonds.

Article XLIII. It is our wish nevertheless that the husband, his wife and their children below puberty, may not be seized and sold separately from each other, if all of them are under the power of the same master: we declare seizures and separate sales of them to be null, which is what we also wish to take place in regard to voluntary sales, under penalty that those making the said sales are to be deprived of the slave or slaves [of that same family] which he has kept rather than sold, which slaves will be adjudged to the purchasers, without requiring them to make any supplement in the price.

Article XLIV. It is also our wish that slaves aged fourteen years and above, up to the age of sixty, who are attached to the lands or plantations, and working thereupon at the time, must not be seized for debts other than those due on the price of their own purchase, unless the lands or plantations are seized: in which case we command that the slaves be included in the seizure of the land; and we forbid, on pain of nullity, to proceed with seizure of the land or plantations and adjudication by decree, without including the slaves of the previously stated age who are working there at the time.

Article XLV. The judicial assignee of lands and plantations which were seized along with the slaves, is accountable to pay the rent according to his lease, without being able to count as a profit, the children who are born to the slaves during his said lease.

Article XLVI. It is our wish, despite all contracts to the contrary and hereby declared null, that the said children belong to the seizing party, if the creditors are satisfied by other means, or to the adjudicatee, if a decree intervenes; and for that purpose the children born to slaves since the seizure will be listed on the last page of the interposed decree, as well as those slaves who died since the seizure.

Article XLVII. In order to avoid the costs and long delays of procedures, we wish that the distribution of the full price of the adjudication combining lands and slaves, as well as that which is produced by the price of judicial leases, be made between the creditors, according to the order of their privileges and mortgages, without distinguishing between what is for the price of the slaves; nevertheless feudal and seigneurial rights will not be paid except in proportion to the lands.

Article 48. Ne seront reçus les lignagers et les seigneurs féodaux, à retirer les fonds décrétés, licités ou vendus volontairement, s'ils ne retirent les esclaves vendus conjointement avec les fonds, où ils travailloient actuellement; ni l'adjudicataire, ou acquerereur, à retenir les esclaves sans les fonds.

Article 49. Enjoignons aux gardiens nobles et bourgeois, usufruitiers, amodiateurs, et autres jouissants des fonds auxquels sont attachés des esclaves qui y travaillent, de gouverner lesdits esclaves en bon pères de famille; au moyen de quoi ils ne seront pas tenu, après leur administration finie, de rendre le prix de ceux qui seront décédés, ou diminués par maladie, vieillesse, ou autrement, sans leur faute: et aussi ils ne pourront pas retenir comme fruits à leur profit, les enfans nés desdits esclaves durant leur administration, lesquels nous voulons être conservés et rendus à ceux qui en sont les maîtres et les propriétaires.

Article 50. Les maîtres âgés de vingt-cinq ans pourront affranchir leurs esclaves par tous actes entre-vifs ou à cause de mort; et cependant, comme il se peut trouver des maîtres assez mercenaires, pour mettre la liberté de leurs esclaves à prix, ce qui porte lesdits esclaves au vol et au brigandage, défendons à toutes personnes, de quelque qualité et condition qu'elles soient, d'affranchir leurs esclaves sans en avoir obtenu la permission par arrêt de notre dit Conseil Supérieur, laquelle permission sera accordée sans frais, lorsque les motifs qui auront été exposés par les maîtres paroîtront légitimes. Voulons que les affranchissemens qui seront faits à l'avenir sans ces permissions soient nuls, et que les affranchis n'en puissent jouir, ni être reconnus pour tels: Ordonnons au contraire qu'ils soient tenus, censés et réputés esclaves, que les maîtres en soient privés, et qu'ils soient confisqués au profit de la Compagnie des Indes.

Article 51. Voulons néanmoins que les esclaves qui auront été nommés par leurs maîtres, tuteurs de leurs enfans, soient tenus et réputés, comme nous les tenons et réputons pour affranchis.

Article XLVIII. It will not be accepted that lineage holders and feudal lords take the lands by decree, auction or voluntary sale, if they do not also take the slaves sold jointly with the lands on which they presently work; nor can the adjudicatee or the acquirer retain the slaves without the lands.

Article XLIX. We enjoin legal guardians, noble and bourgeois, usufructuaries, *amodiateurs*, and others enjoying lands to which slaves are attached and working there, to govern the said slaves as a good father of the family; by means of which they will not be held, once their administration has ended, to pay the price of those who died, or became incapacitated through illness, old age, or otherwise, without their fault: and also, they cannot retain as fruits to their profit, the children born of the said slaves during their administration; it is our wish that they [the children] be preserved and returned to those who are the masters and proprietors of them.

Article L. Masters aged twenty five years old may liberate their slaves by all *acts inter vivos* or *mortis causa*; and yet, since one can find some rather mercenary masters who put the liberty of their slaves up for sale, which leads the said slaves to theft and lawless acts, we forbid all persons, of whatever quality and condition they may be, to free their slaves without having obtained permission, in the form of a decree of our Superior Council, which permission will be granted without charge, when the motives which are stated by the masters seem to be legitimate. It is our wish that manumissions made in the future without such permission are null, and those manumitted cannot enjoy their freedom, nor be recognized as free: to the contrary we order that they be held, deemed and regarded as slaves, that the masters be deprived of them, and that they be confiscated to the profit of the Company of the Indies.

Article LI. We wish nevertheless that the slaves who have been named by their masters, tuteurs of their children, be held and regarded, as we hold and regard them, as free people.

Article 52. Déclarons les affranchissemens faits dans les formes ci-devant prescrites, tenir lieu de naissance dans notre dite province de la Louisiane, et les affranchis n'avoir besoin de nos lettres de naturalité, pour jouir des avantages de nos sujets naturels dans notre royaume, terres et pays de notre obéissance, encore qu'ils soient nés dans les pays étrangers; Déclarons cependant lesdits affranchis, ensemble les négres libres, incapables de recevoir des Blancs aucune donation entre-vifs, à cause de mort ou autrement. Voulons qu'en cas qu'il leur en soit fait aucune, elle demeure nulle à leur égard, et soit appliquée au profit de l'hôpital le plus prochain.

Article 53. Commandons aux affranchis de porter un respect singulier à leurs anciens maîtres, à leurs veuves et à leurs enfans; ensorte que l'injure qu'ils leur auront faite, soit punie plus grièvement, que si elle étoit faite à une autre personne, les déclarons toutefois francs et quittes envers eux de toutes autres charges, services et droits utiles que leurs anciens maîtres voudraient prétendre, tant sur les personnes que sur leurs biens et successions en qualité de patrons.

Article 54. Octroyons aux affranchis les mêmes droits, privilèges et immunités dont jouissent les personnes nées libres; voulons que le mérite d'une liberté acquise produise en eux les mêmes effets que le bonheur de la liberté naturelle cause à nos autres sujets, le tout cependant aux exceptions portées par l'article 52 des présentes.

Article 55. Déclarons les confiscations et les amendes qui n'ont point de destination particulière par ces présentes, appartenir à ladite Compagnie des Indes, pour être payées à ceux qui sont préposés à la recette de ses droits et revenus; Voulons néanmoins que distraction soit faite du tiers desdites confiscations et amendes au profit de l'hôpital le plus proche du lieu où elles auront été adjugées.

Article LII. We declare that manumissions done in the forms prescribed above, take the place of birth in our said province of Louisiana, and even though they were born in foreign lands, manumitted persons have no need of our letters of naturalization in order to enjoy the advantages of our natural subjects in the kingdom, lands and countries under our rule: We declare, however, that the said manumittees, together with free blacks, are incapable of receiving from Whites any donation *inter vivos, mortis causa* or otherwise. It is our wish that if any donation is made to them, it remains null in relation to them, and that it be applied to the profit of the nearest hospital.

Article LIII. We command manumitted persons to show a singular respect towards their former masters, to their widows and their children; in such way that insults given to them be punished more severely than if it was done to another person; we declare, however, that they [the manumitted] are free and clear of all other charges, services and useful rights that their former masters might assert as patrons, whether over their persons, their property or their successions.

Article LIV.We grant to manumitted persons the same rights, privileges and immunities which persons born free enjoy; it is our wish that the merit of an acquired liberty produce in them the same effects as the happiness which natural liberty brings to our other subjects, all of this however is subject to the exceptions laid down by article LII of the present law.

Article LV. We declare that the confiscations and fines which have no particular destination in the present law belong to the said Company of the Indies, to be paid to those who are charged with the receipt of these rights and revenues; We wish nevertheless that one-third of the said confiscations and fines be deducted in favor of the hospital nearest to the place where they have been adjuged.

SI DONNONS EN MANDEMENT à nos amés et féaux les Gens tenant notre Conseil Supérieur de la Loüisiane, que ces présentes ils ayent à faire lire, publier, registrer, et le contenu en icelles garder et observer selon leur forme et teneur, nonobstant tous edits, déclarations, arrêts, règlements et usages à ce contraires, auxquels nous avons dérogé et dérogeons par ces présentes. CAR tel est notre plaisir. Et afin que ce soit chose ferme et stable à toujours, nous y avons fait mettre notre scel. Donné à Versailles au mois de mars, l'an de grâce mil sept cent vingt-quatre, et de Notre Règne le neuvième. *Signé*, LOUIS. *Et plus bas*, par le Roi. *Signé*, PHELYPEAUX . *Visa*, FLEURIAU. *Vu au Conseil*, DODUN. Et scellé du grand sceau de cire verte en lacs de soie rouge et verte.

THUS WE GIVE THESE ORDERS to our beloved and faithful people who hold our Superior Council of Louisiana, that they have the present law read, published, registered, and the contents of it kept and observed according to its form and tenor, despite all edicts, declarations, orders, regulations and usages to the contrary, from which we have derogated and derogate by the present law. BECAUSE such is our pleasure. And in order that this be a matter firm and stable for the future, we have placed here our seal. Given at Versailles in the month of March, in the year of grace seventeen hundred and twenty four, and of Our Reign the ninth. *Signed*, LOUIS. *And further down*, by the King. *Signed*, PHELYPEAUX. *Visa*, FLEURIAU. *Seen by the Council*, DODUN. And sealed with the great seal of green wax in lakes of red and green silk.

Index

CPSIA information can be obtained
at www.ICGtesting.com
Printed in the USA
FFOW03n2256250116
20709FF